A Fool and His Eel

"*Good Luck is an eel in a bath full of fools….*"
(Hungarian proverb)

A Fool and His Eel by Mark Walsingham has a limited print run
Published in 2012 by Freebird Publishing
☎ 01293 415339 or 07941 637336
www.freebirdpublishing.co.uk
© Freebird Publishing and Mark Walsingham

All rights reserved. No part of this publication may be reproduced or transmitted in any form or by any means, electronic or mechanical, including photocopy, recording, or any information storage and retrieval system without written permission from the Publishers.

Edited & proofed by Keith Jenkins
Layout and Design by Cathy Card
Print Management by Linda Jenkins
All photography supplied by Mark Walsingham unless otherwise stated
Additional photography provided by Chris Yates and David Miller
All artwork provided by David Miller©
The views expressed in this book are entirely the personal views of the author

ISBN: 978-0-9562497-8-4

To my Mother and Father, my wife Shona
and our three fantastic children, Iain, Katrina and Alistair.

Contents

Chapter 1 – The Source 12

I have been a compulsive fisherman for most of my life and this book celebrates the joy that angling has brought me. It is a reflection on a life enriched beyond measure by rivers, lakes and streams; by fishing; and by the anglers and wildlife with which I have shared so many simple, yet deeply satisfying pleasures.

Chapter 2 – Pitt Pond 22

At the beginning of the new millennium, my wife Shona and I moved with our children into a small cottage in a secluded Somerset valley. The cottage lay a mile outside the main village along a dead-end track and the only sounds to be heard when the windows were open were the running water of the stream in our garden, birdsong and the occasional gruff bark of a roe stag in the High Wood.

Chapter 3 – Meanders 34

By the time I was in my teens I was fishing all over Somerset for a wide range of species. Access to my own car broadened my horizons still further and as soon as I had passed my driving test I bought a Renault 4, which was the perfect fishing wagon.

Chapter 4 – Golden Scale Club 48

In 1982 I was studying for my O Level exams and, according to every adult I knew, that meant it was "an important time". I'd had it drummed into me that those few, pressured weeks "could shape my future". The result was that I was bored (particularly by the maths revision) and looking for any escape from the stress and shear drudgery of it all.

Chapter 5 – The Avon Barbel 62

"But best of all I love the barbels because they roll like big brown and white cats upon golden shallows and sing in the moonlight with the joie de vivre of June. And because, so, they are all Thames to me and wild rose time and the streams running down from the weir."

Chapter 6 – Along the Ashmead Drove 74

From the back lanes of the village of Ash, an ancient cattle drove dips down to the Sedgemoor levels and runs as straight as a roman highway through the fields towards the River Yeo. The drove is one of a network of byways used by generations of local dairymen to turn out their cattle into the many small fields of the Witcombe Bottoms.

Chapter 7 – Footloose With a Fly Rod 86

I am sitting beside a roaring fire, flicking through the pages of my angling diary. A good 'West Coast' dram rests on the table nearby. Leslie MacKay poured my first West Coast dram for me, when I was working on a salmon farm in Sutherland. Leslie filled my glass to within a hair's breadth of the brim with the smoky, amber malt before asking, without a hint of irony, "And would you take anything in it?"

Chapter 8 – Lightning Does Strike Twice 100

Fishing Ashmead now must be similar to fishing Redmire in the 1950's, in terms of the number of very large carp that are present. The difference, I suppose, is that the Ashmead fish are all known, so to some extent the element of surprise, the pioneering edge, is missing.

Chapter 9 – River of Dreams..110

All anglers have a river flowing through their dreams. In their sleep, they fish in peace on a stream where the clear current reflects a perpetual summer sky. Kingfishers whistle as they dart beneath the overhanging foliage and the air is heavy with the scents of willow herb and freshly cut hay.

Chapter 10 – Silver Ghosts..120

Feel and instinct told me that the fly had passed the holding point behind the boulder and my arm moved automatically into the smooth, accelerating rhythm of the back-cast. I pictured the line uncoiling sinuously as it whispered through the air, and felt the cane flexing as the rod took the strain.

Chapter 11 – The Severn Oaks Syndicate..................................128

The Great Berwick Estate lies just upstream of Shrewsbury on the River Severn. It is a classic country estate with a large and rambling house that has been allowed to go slightly to seed because of the expense of its upkeep. It looks like somewhere that a modern day Miss Haversham might live, pining away her days.

Chapter 12 – Alchemy..142

"An early, unscientific form of chemistry that sought to change base metals into gold and discover a life-prolonging elixir"

Chapter 13 – A Fool and His Eel..154

Some years ago, my friend Steve Maynard, who owned Ashmead, told me that he needed to sell the lake for a number of reasons. He didn't want to put Ashmead on the open market but wanted instead to find someone who would respect the unique qualities and history of the pool and who had the vision and commitment to protect its future.

Chapter 14 – Crumbleholmes Demise..166

After years of searching, I have almost given up any hope of stumbling across the perfect tackle shop. I suppose this chapter might be looked upon as a crie de couer, for someone to tell me where such an establishment can be found.

Chapter 15 – The Grizzled-Wing Adams..174

Every trout angler has a favourite pattern of fly, the one to start the day with, the failsafe when the fish are uncooperative, the pattern that fooled their largest fish. Mine is the Adams, tied to the definitive prescription with a grizzled wing.

Chapter 16 – Restoration..186

When we bought Ashmead, only Goat Willow Pool at the heart of the site held any depth of water or any carp. Although the stock that had grown on naturally within the confines of that three acre pond was simply staggering, the rest of the seventeen acre site was overgrown, full of vile, black, anoxic silt and devoid of fish. Our plan was to restore the rest of the wetland and to connect Goat Willow back into it.

Chapter 17 – The Strange Case of the Attingham Salmon 202
One of the joys of my work for the National Trust is that the Trust not only owns and manages an incredible portfolio of fisheries, it also has wonderful libraries stuffed with angling books, fantastic angling artwork, collections of vintage tackle and even a Robert Adams designed fishing lodge.

Chapter 18 – Icebreaker 214
The folklore predicted last winter's arctic blast far better than the weathermen. Last autumn the trees were laden with berries and a slight frost coated the grass in our meadow one night in September.

Chapter 19 – Fishing in Nod 228
Dipping into the pages of my angling diary last night, I came across a reference to the time when I came close to catching a record carp. Looking back now, I still find it hard to believe that the fish could have escaped to join the many others that haunt the dreams of the lost.

Chapter 20 – Encounters with Pike 236
There are days in angling that stay with you forever, golden moments when everything seems to fall magically into place. For me, one such day was 17th February 2006, the day that I became a pike angler.

Chapter 21 – Salmo Salar: The Leaper 252
Before you launch into this chapter on salmon fishing, I ought to make it perfectly plain to you that I am not an expert salmon angler. I love going salmon fishing of course but I'd hate you to read any further without explaining that I don't fish for salmon often enough to have anything meaningful to say about tactics and techniques.

Chapter 22 – All That Jazz.... The Art of Stalking Carp 268
There can be few experiences in angling as intense as watching an enormous carp sidle slowly over to your bait and suck it in with a pulse of its gills, before moving off, drawing the loose line taught across the surface in its wake. Sometimes, I've been so mesmerised that I've been unable to strike before the carp realised its mistake and spat out the treacherous offering in disgust.

Chapter 23 – Move Over Laurel and Hardy 278
I've mentioned before that one of the joys of angling is that it gives us a chance to escape back into childhood. Things can get out of hand though and when reason is swept away by single-minded obsession I sometimes find myself doing things so ridiculous that my own children think I've gone mad. I'm normally a pretty rational person but angling seems to upset the equilibrium and spark moments of complete lunacy.

Chapter 24 – Simple Pleasures 290
I'm often asked what the attraction of fishing is, by people who don't understand the pastime. I gave up long ago trying to debunk the stereotype of fishing as boring and the angler as someone who sits under an umbrella in the rain for hours on end, waiting for a fish to bite.

Chapter 25 – The Leney Legacy 300

I have the stocking receipt books for the Surrey Trout Farm on loan from Chris Yates at the moment. I've always been fascinated by Donald Leney and the special carp he stocked into our lakes and rivers, but until I saw the records for the first time I had no idea how great his contribution to carp fishing in the UK had really been.

Chapter 26 – The Disposable Avocet 316

A good friend of mine called Jeremy has developed a slightly disconcerting interest in cavalry swords. He has started a collection not only of fine officers swords but also of military manuals on cavalry tactics, which go into gory detail about which stroke of the sword is most effective in killing your adversary in any given situation. The manuals have diagrams and are best avoided before meals.

Chapter 27 – Amber and Gold 328

I love Spring more than any other season. The arrival of spring transforms the atmosphere of Ashmead overnight, as the bleak harshness of winter, with its cold, grey skies, gives way to azure blue optimism.

Chapter 28 – Redmire 342

I always had a strong desire to visit Redmire, to see where so many of the greatest tales from carp angling folklore had been set and so much of carp angling's history forged. At the same time though, I'd always feared that a visit to the pool would be a profound disappointment, so clear were the images I had of how Redmire must have been during its heyday.

Chapter 29 – The Quest for Fugglestone Red 358

I'm going to take you carp fishing. I've been wondering about whether or not to take you to my favourite pool because it's such a secret place, but it has had such a deep influence over my fishing that this book would seem hollow and unfinished without a visit there.

Chapter 30 – Pitt Pond Epitaph 378

During the last twelve months, since writing the opening chapter of this book, Pitt Pond's recent history as a carp water sadly ended. The pond still hides away in the same beautiful fold in the Somerset landscape but its carp are no more.

Chapter 31 – Ashmead Dreams 386

We only really have one rule that governs the fishing at Ashmead and that is that the members must respect the environment, the fish and their fellow anglers. This ethos underpins our management of the fishery and reflects the three elements that make Ashmead so special.

Chapter 32 – Ebb Tide 404

Forty years! I don't know why it has only just struck me that I have been fishing for forty years this year. In those forty years an awful lot of water has flowed under Creedy Bridge on the River Parrett, where I first cast a line with a fishing rod.

Foreword

When Mark first told me he was about to complete the book that he'd been threatening to write for many years I was both delighted and slightly anxious. Delighted because, through his articles in the angling press and many letters to me, I knew he was a spirited and thoughtful writer and therefore the book was bound to be fascinating and entertaining; anxious because, as a member of the absurd Golden Scale Club, he might reveal certain facts that could reflect badly on certain fellow members, including me. However, having now read a proof copy of the book, I can report that while Mark does recount the story of one or two unofficial club outings from long ago, he does not dwell on any unfortunate incidents and makes no mention of the disastrous Christchurch floating piano... But what am I saying?!

This book, however, is about much more than daft fishing jaunts with like-minded friends. While there are companionable days, many of the stories revolve around solitary vigils at quiet and mostly unknown waters. In writing that is both fluent and characterful, Mark describes the experiences that have, since childhood, defined him as a very original angler.

As will soon become evident to any reader, the author of this book is obviously a gifted fisherman with a deep understanding of his quarry. Mark's success, particularly as a carp fisher, stems from his refusal to accept that any fish is impossible to catch and although he always respects the fish, he sometimes approaches them in a completely unconventional manner. Despite favouring traditional tackle – cane rods and centerpin reels – some of his methods, as described in this book, are radical, unorthodox and even crazy, although I think they are perfectly legal.

However, the book is not simply a chronicle of marvellous fishing and wonderful specimens. Mark is appreciative of and sensitive to the waterside environment. Through his professional work in fisheries management and in conservation with the National Trust, Mark has experienced first-hand the pressures that inevitably affect all rivers and stillwaters. It is his own very personal perspective developed from a lifetime at the waterside that makes Mark's bankside observations so compelling. He has fished all across the country, north and south and, as becomes evident through his vivid descriptions, he has discovered some magical places.

I have known Mark since his schooldays. With the mad enthusiasm of youth, he foolishly responded to a ridiculous Golden Scale Club application form that was published in Angling magazine in the spring of 1982. Out of almost a hundred applicants, only three were deemed suitable for membership by the club committee. Unknown to us, one of these was a 16-year old schoolboy, though his writing was more like the style of a slightly unhinged adult. He called himself Skeffington Dolrimple and he eventually came fishing with the club the following summer. We have all been good friends ever since, despite the fact that he caught the largest carp of the day. This book is therefore appearing exactly thirty years since that first meeting. We'll no doubt share many more entertaining fishing days together, but in the meantime, if the weather is too wild or the fish all seem to have vanished I can always get happily lost in these gently rippling pages.

Chris Yates *Salisbury, Spring 2012.*

Introduction and Acknowledgements

I first spoke to David Miller about collaborating on a book together about ten years ago and I am delighted that we have finally found time in our busy lives to complete this work. I find David's artwork inspirational and I'm honoured that he thinks my words will compliment his paintings and underwater photography. David's creative talent stems from his love and understanding of nature. Coupled with his technical expertise, his empathy with the natural world around him has made him one of the outstanding wildlife artists working today.

I've always enjoyed writing and even though my passion for nature led me down a scientific path through school and university, there has always been a large part of me that yearned to write creatively. My love of fishing has given me an outlet for that urge to write in recent years and I'm very grateful for the support and encouragement of the editors who thought that my articles were worthy of publication in magazines such as Waterlog, Trout and Salmon and Carpworld.

I'm particularly grateful to my friend Chris Yates for his enthusiasm for my writing and for publishing my early articles in Waterlog, produced by Jon Ward-Allen and the excellent Medlar Press. Chris is one of the people who have truly inspired me, not just in my fishing but much more broadly, and I am delighted that he has provided the Foreword to this book.

I'm equally grateful to Tim Paisley and the staff at Angling Publications for their support and for giving me space in Carpworld over the past few years to express myself through the Ashmead Diaries. Tim is someone for whom I have enormous respect and who has become a good friend in recent years. I will always be grateful for his support not only of my writing but of what we are trying to create at Ashmead. In my experience, Tim stands apart in the world of angling business and politics as someone completely genuine and who is committed to giving something back to the future of the pastime that has provided his living and pleasure.

I have been given the confidence to start this project by my friends Bernard Venables, Chris Yates, Mick Canning and Peter Wheat, who have all told me at various times that I should write a fishing book. My dearest friend, Mike Winter, has encouraged me more than anyone and this volume, like so many aspects of the life and fishing it describes, owes a great deal to him. I'm not sure what I could say here that would really reflect the depth of respect I have for Mike and how much I value our friendship, but suffice to say, that my approach to fishing and the environment owes more to this gentle man than to anyone.

One of the greatest joys of angling is the company into which it has taken me and the friendships forged through a common, slightly strange passion for catching fish. To list them all would take a book in itself but I'm grateful to the anglers of Ashmead, Severn Oaks, The Golden Scale Club and the many others I have met along the way for their friendship and for pleasures shared. I wouldn't single any out, apart from the Glorious 16th anglers, Angelus (Richard), Wigan (Darren), Burton (Bill), Demus (Mick), Prof (Mike) and Isaac (Pete) with whom I have shared sunrises and hangovers on thirty Opening Nights.

Lastly, but by no means least, this book would never have been written without the support of Keith

Jenkins and the small team at Freebird, who have done an amazing job in producing the finished book that you are holding. Keith had a natural empathy with what I wanted to create through my words and photographs and with David's amazing art. He has driven me to meet deadlines when it was all getting too difficult and yet still given me the space to let my creative writing flow and develop into something that I am proud to have produced.

I have a busy career as a senior conservation manager with the National Trust and I'm fortunate to have a job that I love. I am lucky to have the privilege of helping to look after some of the most incredible places in England, Wales and Northern Ireland, which are in the Trust's ownership and care. My passion for conservation developed directly from my early and enduring love of the simple art of fishing and of being by the waterside.

My writing has grown as an extension of that love of fishing and nature and from wanting to share these pleasures with others. This book, then, is quite a selfish creation, written for the sheer joy of writing. Like my fishing, my work for the Trust and the huge commitment I give to looking after Ashmead, writing this book has been possible only because I am lucky enough to be married to a wonderful lady who understands my passions and who supports and shares them. I have three equally wonderful children who are less patient with me but who have still given me the support and encouragement I needed to complete this work. I have written this book for Shona, Iain, Katrina and Alistair more than anyone. If reading it helps my children understand why their Dad spends so much time away at work, by the river or working down at Ashmead then I will have achieved what I set out to do. I love them all.

I hope that you find as much pleasure in reading the tales bound up within these pages as I have in living and writing them. Like slipping a brilliant, wild brown trout back into a sparkling highland burn it is time to set this book free.

The Source

I have been a compulsive fisherman for most of my life and this book celebrates the joy that angling has brought me. It is a reflection on a life enriched beyond measure by rivers, lakes and streams; by fishing; and by the anglers and wildlife with which I have shared so many simple, yet deeply satisfying pleasures.

In a time when people are more divorced from nature than ever before, fishing provides us with a direct connection to the natural world and touches something in the human spirit that is lost in the shallow, artificial maelstrom of modern life. Although angling taps into a primeval urge to hunt that lies dormant in us all, I don't go fishing just for the challenge and excitement of catching a fish. Angling provides a quiet backwater, into which I can escape and find a deeper set of experiences that enrich my soul and give me a sense of peace and fulfilment that I rarely find elsewhere. Fishing is the warp around which I have woven the various threads of my life; it has been both a constant that has fuelled my professional interest in conservation and an obsession that has filled my leisure time and many of my dreams. Angling provides the perfect antidote to the pressures of modern living.

All children share a simple delight in the mystery of water, whether it forms the fathomless depths of a still pool, the unending flow of a river or the relentless, infinite surge of the ocean. One of my earliest memories is of the rush and splash of a waterfall, tumbling onto moss covered rocks. I've no idea where that waterfall was or how old I was but I know I was very small and the sight, sound and feel of the fall are etched onto my memory, like fragmented images from a broken film.

I see glimpses of the magical excitement that being near to water still gives me reflected in the eyes of my own children. I remember our eldest child, Iain, giggling in a backpack when he was a baby, as I crouched with him next to the source of the Thames near Cirencester. His excited gurgling echoed the mesmeric flow that burst from the quiet corner of a Cotswold field, to charge our capital river. I remember Katrina crying because of the noise of the sea as it crashed onto the shifting shingle of Chesil Beach and I remember our youngest son Alistair's delight in running naked through the rain in our back garden, when he was three years old. Anglers never lose the simple sense of fun and wonder that water gives to a child. In fact, fishing gives us an excuse to hold on to some small remnant of our childhood innocence and perhaps that alone is the real reason that this simple pastime is so compelling.

Of course, I haven't always been so philosophical or interested in trying to understand and express my compulsive love of fishing through my writing. In the beginning, at the source of my passion, it all seemed far less complicated..

I have always thought myself lucky to have grown up in the countryside and throughout my childhood I lived an almost feral existence, roaming through the fields and orchards surrounding the small Somerset hamlet where we lived. I was lucky to have parents who gave me the freedom I craved and to have grown up in a time when such freedom seemed safe and acceptable. I'd disappear for entire days, to climb through the tangled laurels of the High Wood or to make dens in the dense bracken on Ham Hill. The trust my parents gave me allowed me to explore the wild places that surrounded us and develop the passionate interest in our natural environment that still forms the foundation of my adult life.

Some of the games I played with my best friends on their nearby farm would have horrified my parents, if they'd known about the risks we used to take. One of our favourite adventures was to pull a bale out from half way up the haystack in the big barn and then remove further bales, so that we could burrow into the heart of the stack, creating a warren of tunnels and vertical shafts that led to rooms big enough to house two or three children at a time. Through this labyrinth we would crawl and hide, fighting off imaginary enemies or planning escapes inspired by the television series Colditz, which was compulsory viewing at the time.

The farm sat in the well of a deep valley and the wooded hills formed a perfect amphitheatre in which we acted out our war games. We cut hazel spears and sharpened the ends to vicious points that could do serious damage at close range. We used the same hazel to cut longbows that we used to fire arrows made from dead-nettle stems, weighted with a nail at the tip and fitted with cardboard flights that made them deadly accurate. Armed with these weapons we re-enacted the battles of Crecy and Agincourt or brought to life the tales of King Arthur and of Sherwood Forest.

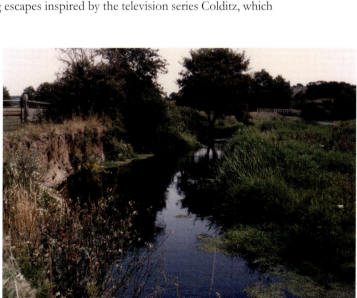

Chapter One – The Source

We had endless close scrapes but never came to any real harm and for a boy with a wild heart, it was a perfect childhood.

Of all the places where we played, the stream that flowed through my parent's garden gave us the most scope for adventure. We built complicated dams from stones and logs backed up with clay, in an attempt to stop the flow. The water would always find a way through in the end and the dam would burst, sending a flood surging downstream and over the tops of our wellies. We had races with paper boats, played "Pooh Sticks" and had water fights. The mysteries of that little brook were as boundless as our imagination.

Then, one summer's day when I was five, the stream revealed a new secret that swept away all my interest in the old games. I was wading in a deeper pool, formed by a sharp bend beneath an alder. I was looking for gnomes (I had just discovered 'BB's Little Grey Men), when an eel poked its head out from beneath a tree root and slithered off downstream like a serpent. I leapt from the water in a flurry of spray, convinced that a snake had attacked me but my friend Simon knew at once what I'd seen. Once my panic had subsided we hatched a plan to catch the beast and the following day we returned, armed with a length of thick fishing line, a hook and a big fat slug for bait. Simon lowered the slug into the monster's lair and we waited in tense anticipation for something dramatic to happen.

Five minutes passed, then ten and, as is the way with small boys, our concentration lapsed and we started to look for other distractions to occupy ourselves. Simon lashed the loose end of the line to an alder branch and we set about climbing the tree. I must have been about ten feet from the ground when I noticed the thin branch to which Simon had tied the line shake, nod and then pull down sharply towards the stream. Leaping from the tree I grabbed the line and felt a sharp tug, as something alive pulled back. I felt a squirming, writhing pulse of energy from the depths of the alder roots and then it came free suddenly and I found myself wrestling with an eel that tied itself in knots and coated the line and my hands in so much revolting slime that it made it impossible to hold.

Simon fell out of the tree and joined me, just as the eel twisted its body around into a figure of eight and used the last vestiges of its strength to dislodge the hook. The eel fell to the ground and we watched, spellbound, as our prize sensed its chance of escape and slithered quickly back down the bank towards the stream. Neither of us wanted to pick the eel up because of all the slime it was producing and before we could summon up the courage to grab it, the eel slipped back into the water and away to its home amongst the alder roots.

On that fine summer afternoon, I caught my first fish and felt for the first time the thrill of connection with another world that lay beneath the surface of that insignificant brook. What I realise now is that I was the one who had really been caught that day; the excitement of catching that eel hooked me so firmly that I have never shaken free. In that moment, when the line jagged tight, I became an angler.

Santa delivered my first proper fishing rod that Christmas. It was a six foot, grey stick of solid fibreglass with a white plastic handle and the reel that came with it was a blue tin "Tokia" centerpin that sounded like a football rattle when it revolved. Santa had also given me an assortment of floats, weights and hooks and a spool of Efgeeco line that changed through every colour of the rainbow and twisted like wire as I loaded it onto my reel.

Better yet, the foot of my Christmas stocking held a season ticket for the local angling club and this meant that I could take my new tackle and follow the stream down to its confluence with the River Parrett, to fish eight or nine miles of the main river, from Bow Mills downstream to Gawbridge Mill. It was like leaving the school football team and joining the Premier League.

Chapter One – The Source

None of my family fished, which meant I had no-one to teach me the basic skills I needed. My friend Simon had a book called 'Fishing with Uncle Bill' by W.E Davies and I soon got hold of a copy of 'Freshwater Fishing' by the same author (I still have my battered copy to this day). From these books we absorbed the little knowledge we had about the different species of fish, knots, tackle and baits but it seemed that no matter how hard we tried, all we ever seemed to catch were eels and minnows. We blamed our lack of success on the fact that we were novices but we also had no yardstick against which to judge our efforts. Looking back now, I realise that the River Parrett at Creedy Bridge, where we always went, probably held only minnows and eels and that our chances of catching anything else there were pretty slim.

Then, when I was about ten, two things happened that revolutionised our fishing. The first was that Simon suddenly took it upon himself to explore another stretch of river further downstream at Shaws Bridge and the second was that I acquired an old copy of 'Mr Crabtree Goes Fishing' by Bernard Venables.

Mr Crabtree revealed that, not only were there many other types of fish beyond the eels and minnows we were catching, but also that it was possible to set out to catch them by design. The book abounded with paintings of brilliant perch and quicksilver dace and there were pictures of rivers, marked with the initials of the different species to show you where you would catch them. Best of all, most of the book was presented in a simple, cartoon strip format that was easy to follow and which captured my imagination.

The wealth of information that Mr Crabtree gave us would have been useless though, without the move down to Shaws. Here, the Parrett thundered over two weirs and their turbulence splashed life-giving oxygen into the river. From the moment that I caught a gudgeon on my first cast into the tail of the little weir, Shaws opened up a new world where our fishing reached new heights; it was the best bit of river in the world. The weir pools not only looked like somewhere that Mr Crabtree and Peter might fish, they also held many of the species that they described. Better yet, the dace, roach and perch behaved just as Mr Crabtree said they would and we discovered that we could fish selectively for whatever we wanted to catch.

When you're young, the days pass incredibly slowly and the summer holidays seemed to last a lifetime. I have so many memories of the days I spent at Shaws, catching nets full of dace, roach and gudgeon. Winter was equally good, as the fish used to gather in huge shoals beneath the shelter of the road bridge and we enjoyed some red letter days, either trotting maggots down to them or legering upstream.

I remember one day in particular, fishing a light upstream ledger with a very long hook length of about five feet. I would run across the road (a busy dual carriage way) and drop a handful of maggots over the upstream balustrade of the bridge. Then I'd sprint back through the traffic as quickly as possible and cast my rod upstream, so that the hookbait would drift down and settle slowly to the riverbed with the loose feed. I'd caught about thirty dace and a couple of gudgeon using this technique, when I had a thumping bite and hooked something far larger. I only had two pound line on and suddenly wished I hadn't been so bold, as what was clearly a good fish bored upstream, seeking the refuge of the bridge supports. Then, quick as a flash, it turned and dashed downstream and my flimsy line proved no match for the power of the fish and current combined. I had a brief, tantalising view of a deep bodied roach, surging through the clear water before the rod pulled over and the line parted with a crack.

I can still see that fish in my mind's eye as I write this tale. It was the first of many lost fish that haunt my dreams and in that instant I knew for the first time the bittersweet joy of hooking and losing a monster. To my child's eyes that roach seemed gigantic and even now, after all these years, remembering how large it looked as it swept majestically downstream I don't think it could have weighed less than three pounds.

A memory of another lost monster has sprung into my mind, now that I've mentioned that roach. We were fishing further down the river at Parrett Works, where we had found a real hotspot for big perch. An old pollarded willow had dropped a limb into the river on an otherwise featureless straight and a shoal of large perch had taken up residence in the tangle of branches.

To catch the better fish we found we had to float fish a lobworm right in the middle of the thicket, by feeding the rod tip through the archway formed by the broken limb and the main trunk of the tree and lowering the float into the water amongst the branches. Doing this almost guaranteed a catch of ten or more good perch in a day, many of which weighed over two pounds. Such fish seemed huge to us and the fact that they were perch, with the bold tiger stripes and flaring fins of Crabtree at his best, made them all the more impressive.

In the middle of a long summer day, I remember Simon getting a classic, bobbing perch bite but on striking we quickly realised that what he had hooked was no mere two pounder. After a tussle that seemed to last for ages, a huge perch of at least Five pounds, as black as coal tar and bristling with rage, surfaced on the end of his line. Just as Simon reached for the net, the perch made one last lunge for freedom and the hook pulled. "I should have struck harder," said Simon, when we had calmed down enough to talk about the loss.

Convinced the perch would take again, despite the shock of near capture, Simon fed his float back under the willow arch at once, his hook baited with the biggest lobworm he could find. Amazingly, after just a few minutes the float bobbed, settled and then plunged under. "Strike!" I yelled and Simon did, whipping the rod back with images of record perch firing his resolve to strike as hard as he could. A tiny minnow flew out of the river on the end of his line and up into the branches of the willow where the line snagged, sending the poor fish spinning round and round a branch. It wasn't hooked at all but just had the tail of the huge worm jammed into its mouth and, after a couple of wiggles, it dropped back into the water and vanished, no doubt to be gobbled up by the monster perch we had expected.

Eventually Simon lost interest in fishing and I found that I was going out more and more by myself. Perhaps the loss of that perch hit Simon harder than I realised and he couldn't go back to catching mere two pounders after the loss of such a colossus, but in any case he suddenly discovered HiFi, Pink Floyd and girls and drifted away from the riverbank. Simon was three years older than I was and such shallow interests still seemed pointless to me when there were fish to catch and rivers to explore, so I ignored them as best I could and carried on pursuing my own dreams with a fishing rod.

Pitt Pond

At the beginning of the new millennium, my wife Shona and I moved with our children into a small cottage in a secluded Somerset valley. The cottage lay a mile outside the main village along a dead-end track and the only sounds to be heard when the windows were open were the running water of the stream in our garden, birdsong, the green woodpeckers drumming for their supper and the occasional gruff bark of a roe stag in the High Wood. It was as remote a spot as it is possible to find in the south of our crowded little island.

The cottage was on the site of an old mill, recorded in the Doomsday Book:

"St Mary's Church, Griestan (in Normandy), *holds Nortone from the count* (Robert, Earl of Mortain). *A Thain* (a pre-conquest Saxon nobleman) *held it before 1066; it paid tax for 5 hides. Land for 5 ploughs, of which 2 hides are in lordship; 1 plough there; 5 slaves; 8 villagers and 6 smallholders with 3 ploughs and 2 hides.*

2 mills which pay 20s; meadow, 25 acres; woodland 2 furlongs long and 1 furlong wide. 1 cob; 10 cattle; 40 sheep. The value was and is 100s."

The oak, ash and chestnut of the Doomsday woodland still cloaked the hills and a network of small, rough pastures covered the valley floor, little changed since the ten cattle, forty sheep and lone cob grazed there. It felt as if the tide of modern living had surged past the quiet backwater where the cottage stood, leaving it untouched.

Moving to the cottage was like coming home. I grew up just a good cast away and my foundations were set amongst the melted-honey sandstone of the hamlet. About a week after we moved in, I was walking in the fields nearby when I overheard two locals who were out rabbit shooting, discussing the cottage from the far side of a thick Somerset hedge. I couldn't help eavesdropping when I overheard a broad Somerset accent ask, "Yer! Do 'ee know who've bought Dixon's old place?"

"No," came the reply, "but Oi 'eard 'ee be local, an' grew up round 'ere."

"Well," said the first, "Oi 'eard 'ee don't speak wiv a Zumerset accent."

"Oi only said 'ee grew up near 'ere," came the swift repost. "Oi never said the bugger were born 'ere. . . " It was nice to be back.

Coming home naturally took me back along well-trodden paths to the waters where I learned to fish. The first fish I caught were eels and a multitude of minnows from the River Parrett, but by the time I had reached secondary school I had become an obsessive carp angler and most of my fishing dreams focused on a carp lake within walking distance of home. Now, nearly thirty years since I first fished the water, I rediscovered it. The intense passion of youth had gone but the beauty of the pool and its carp recaptured my heart once more and there was nowhere I would rather be.

Come with me, I'd like to take you fishing….

Pitt Pond lies hidden at the head of the lost valley where we lived. I noticed the other day that the pool lies on a fold of every map on which I have tried to find it and this good fortune means that it has been overlooked and forgotten. It used to take about twenty minutes to walk to Pitt from the cottage, if I travelled light and avoided being sidetracked by the natural distractions I met on the way. The walk was like a journey through history.

The pond lies at the foot of the largest Iron-Age hill fort in Britain and the beginning of the walk ran along an original length of road built by the Romans to service their later encampment on the summit. The cobbles of the road were polished smooth by the tramping feet of the legionaries and two thousand years of other traffic. The path to the pond branched off the Roman road through a gate and into steeply sloping fields, still hatched with the strip lynchets of primitive cultivation. Here, centred on a spring in the floor of the valley, lies the site of a medieval village that was wiped out by the Black Death. As I passed, I almost expected to hear the murmur of long-dead voices and the clink of plough harnesses carried on the breeze.

The route then followed King John's ride, a broad sweep of meadow beneath an oak wood. I don't know if King John ever rode this way or hunted these fields but the oldest oaks in the wood would remember his passing. The grassland is managed without the use of agricultural chemicals and is home for a wide range of insects, including some increasingly rare species such as the glow worms that shimmer in the grass like a thousand glowing emeralds on a summer's night. Across the valley, the ground rises to form two distinctive, rounded hillocks that create a decidedly feminine landscape.

Few people visit this remote spot and it provides a haven for wildlife. It is common to see badgers snuff-scuff-shuffling their way across the grassland in feet a size too big, and one summer evening I walked right up to a family of foxes, before they reluctantly abandoned their game of rough and tumble and melted away into the wood. Buzzards often wheel by overhead in a spiralling dance on the thermals, their mewling cries lingering on the dense summer air.

At the end of the ride, the sandstone obelisks that held the gate of the original Elizabethan estate survive and beyond them is the wood that hides the pool. Pitt lies in the heart of the wood, nestling below a steep slope that is covered in a blanket of primroses every spring. The pond is enclosed behind a tall fence and dense hedge; so that only tantalising glimpses of water can be seen until you push open the huge gate that secures the privacy within. Through the gate, you walk out of the woodland and into a sunlit glade, filled with an oasis of clear water.

One of my favourite writers, Llewelyn Powys, wrote about Pitt Pond in his Somerset Essays and his connection with the water has been well researched by a local man, John Batten, on behalf of the Powys society. Llewelyn Powys' account provides a fascinating insight into the pond's history. The stream that feeds the pool was first dammed during the eighteenth century, to create a feature in the estate landscape of Montacute House and to provide ice in the winter for the icehouse of the mansion. Powys tells of skating on the smooth, dark surface of the frozen pond in the depths of winter, the ice creaking, cracking and booming beneath his blades. Perhaps it is a sign of our warming climate that I've only seen the pond frozen once in all the years I have known of its existence. It's definitely a sign of our risk-adverse society that I wouldn't dream of taking to the ice in such a remote spot, even if it had been.

The pond is less than three acres in size and has the classic estate lake shape. Two shallow arms of water merge to form the body of the pool, held back by the clean line of the dam at the far end. In contrast to the natural disorder of the woodland, the surroundings of the pool are cultivated but not manicured. The pink and white flowers of the extensive lily beds and the dense green of the surrounding trees are mirrored in the surface of the water.

Three striking monkey-puzzle trees, each of which must be more than forty feet tall, dominate the far bank. Two of the trees are female and one male and their progeny can be found springing up all around the pond. The male and female trees can be told apart by running your hand along the branches towards the tip, grasping the spiked leaves tightly as you do so. The male has soft leaves that collapse harmlessly under your grip, whilst those of the female are more rigid, with spines that can cut your palm. I can never remember which tree is which and I scratched myself repeatedly finding out.

Once you can pull your eyes away from the monkey-puzzles, you realise that the other trees and shrubs surrounding the pond are a mixture of natural grandees, including some lovely old oak and ash, and the more formal plants of an eighteenth century landscape garden, including Portugal laurels, camellia and azalea. To these, the current owner has added other exotic species such as fox-glove trees, weeping birch and corkscrew willow. The overall effect is quite beautiful and within their mantle the pond is magical and full of promise.

The existence of Pitt Pond today is tribute to the imagination and determination of two men, Jack who owns the pond and John, with whom I had the lease of the fishing rights. Powys wrote of the collapse of the original dam in the early 1900's, following the break-up of the old estate. When Jack's family bought the land in the 1960's, nothing of the pond survived except for the vague outline of the margins and some of the formal trees (including the monkey-puzzles). The remainder was a thicket of alder and willow carr, rooted in the silt of the forgotten pool.

Jack found the pond in an old photograph whilst pursuing his interest in the history of the estate and, inspired by Powys' writing, he set about restoring the water as a labour of love. He started work on Good Friday in 1963, armed with just a spade and wheelbarrow to attack the decades of accumulated silt. In his youthful mind's eye, he held a vision of the pool, surrounded by the plants of this lost garden. It was this vision that sustained him throughout the eleven years until the pond was flooded again in 1974. Jack carried out much of the restoration work manually, through dogged determination, sweat and years of hard labour.

John became involved when his search for some peaceful fishing led him to the swamp, where Jack had started work on repairing the dam. As the years passed and the scale of their undertaking became clear, they eventually brought in a huge dragline to dredge the pool and remove the trees from its basin. The pool today is a fitting tribute to the remarkable character of the two men, whose toil over three decades reclaimed this jewel in the Somerset countryside. If Llewelyn Powys visited today, he would think he had seen a spectral landscape from his childhood, so perfectly is Pitt Pond restored to its former glory.

If you look across the water now, it is easy to picture times long past when, as Powys described, *"The pleasure boats would be brought out of their dark house into the sunshine and the estate owner, after the manner of a highly endowed benevolent mandarin, would pleasure himself with the guileless occupation of rowing silently absorbed children over his fish-filled water."*

Powys goes on to tell of how *"It was at Pitt Pond that I learned first to fish. Though in later years I have sometimes felt uneasy about the moral propriety of this diversion, in those thoughtless days such misgivings were far from my mind. I exulted in every one of the processes that had to do with the treacherous pastime. I marvelled at the fact that a few minutes after mustard-water had been poured between its stone slabs the backyard would be alive with worms ready to be picked up and placed in an empty cocoa tin as bait. The ingenious method of mixing dough with cotton wool, that it might hold to the hook the better, excited my admiration; as also did the look of the dainty hooks themselves, so deftly barbed; and the hair thread, with its tiny weights of slit shot, almost invisible at the end of a rod elongated to a surprising length by its neatly fitting sections. What an intensity of suspended excitement used to take possession of me, as I sat at the deep-end near the sluice, watching the brightly painted float, till at last, after a few tentative bobs, it would suddenly disappear. I would jump to my feet and in a moment a red-finned roach would be flicking its taut electric body to and fro in the tangled grass. With fingers smelling of water-mint and fish scales I would remove the merciless steel from the creature's throat, leaving it with its detached staring eyes and spasmodic leaps to gasp away its life in its basket bed of earth fragrant moss."*

One of the original "pleasure boats", a graceful Edwardian punt, has been restored lovingly and the "treacherous pastime" is once again practiced here, although only a privileged few are fortunate enough to be allowed to fish. There are no roach these days but the pond holds a good head of tench and some lovely carp. The fishing is as relaxed as it was in Powys' time and my greatest pleasure was to wander up from the cottage on a summer evening after work, to spend an hour or two stalking carp and shed the stresses of the day.

If I bait up a swim near the dam with corn and hemp, we can wander off with some floaters to try and find a carp, while the tench settle in to feed. On the southern shore is one of the best places to intercept the pond's wary carp. The great trunk of an oak tree sweeps out over a strip of water that forms a channel between some lilies and the marginal reeds. The carp often patrol along the channel and from above it is possible to drop a bait into the path of a fish without it ever sensing your presence. I'll have to scramble up the trunk and take up a slightly precarious perch on that branch, about ten feet above the water. I'll leave the net at the bottom and just take the rod and some floaters.

There! The broad, bronze shoulders of a common, pushing stealthily through the pads directly underneath us. If I drop some floaters in amongst the pads, one at a time, their arrival will sound as innocuous as the falling of an acorn. From above we can see every movement of the carp; the pulse of the operculae, each flick of a fin, and its eyes swivelling slowly in their sockets. I thought it was going to come up and take that biscuit just then but it passed underneath. No, wait! The pectorals are fanning rapidly in reverse, the head tilting up and…. Yes! With a slow, relaxed gurgle the floater has been sucked in. The carp is more animated now, on the look out for other tasty morsels.

Time to lower in the hook bait, just off the edge of the lilies in open water, where the carp can find it easily. That's it, no line on the surface to give the game away. My hands are shaking with the tension but if I flick the line over that twig, it will stop the bait trembling in the surface film. Another free offering has gone and now a third. Suddenly, the shadow looms up under the bait and a confident slurp is followed by a lunge on the rod as the carp takes in the bait and is hooked. Hold on! I can't give an inch or all will be lost in the pads. The carp thrashes the surface and the rod kicks and writhes in my grip. Side strain and pressure from above only just turned it in time. There was a horrible, rubbery grating sensation of line on lily, before the fish turned suddenly and the line cut leftwards, into open water. Finally it is over and the dazed common carp hangs in the water below, waiting for me to shimmy down the tree trunk and use the net.

It is a superb fish, fully scaled and just short of Twenty Three pounds. There is a full curtain of skin inside its mouth and no other hook marks, so this may be the first time it's ever been caught. Evening sunlight dazzles on golden flanks as I carry the carp down to the water's edge and cradle it in the margins until, in a flurry of spray, I'm left with a smile and a memory.

I first fished here when I was fourteen, after I discovered the pond with my father on one of the long summer walks we used to share. A few tantalising glimpses of water through the blackthorn hedge were enough to convince me that I would have to fish the pond one day. I probably shouldn't confess (especially as Jack and John will inevitably read this) but I eventually plucked up enough courage to return with a rod, to scramble under the wire and spend a furtive afternoon catching small carp on float-fished worms. As I left, I pinned a note addressed to "the owner" to the gate, begging to be allowed to fish legitimately. Jack called at my parents' house a few days later and, after a severe telling off and some careful questioning, he granted me the permission I sought.

I lost count of the many days I spent at Pitt as a teenager, catching tench, carp and eels on my simple float tackle, and grass snakes, frogs and slowworms with my hands. It was an idyllic place in which to pass a childhood full of natural wonder and adventure. My experiences of Pitt Pond, and the other wild places to which my father introduced me, forged the passion for nature conservation that has shaped my later life.

I have so many memories, but one visit to the pond in particular stands out in my mind. I was fishing

the swim we have just baited near the sluice, on a muggy summer evening just like this one. A mass of black cloud, that had been building all afternoon, swept in from the west and blocked out the setting sun, bringing the premature onset of a night as dark as any I have experienced. The pool was silent and still as I crouched under my umbrella and waited for the storm to arrive. When it came, it crashed onto the stage with a roar of thunder and a flash of lightning that lit up a wall of rain, sweeping in a straight line across the pond towards me. In front of the approaching line the water was mirror calm but behind it was a seething maelstrom. As it struck, the squall tore my shelter from the ground and sent it spiralling off into the black sky and at that very moment, just as the thunder and lightning crashed about me again, the unearthly scream of a vixen in the woods behind me rent the night. It was as if all the powers of Hades had been unleashed and I fled terrified, not stopping for breath until I reached the sanctuary of home.

I returned the following morning to recover my sodden tackle, although I never saw my umbrella again. Apparently, in Powys' time, a resident of the nearby village committed suicide by drowning himself in that very spot. Had I known of this at the time, I would have been convinced that the pond was haunted and would never have returned after my ordeal.

The powerful atmosphere of Pitt Pond certainly affected both Llewelyn and his brother, John Cowper Powys, much as it affects me today. Llewelyn's Somerset Essays compared the pond to *"one of the dark tarns of Edgar Allan Poe's lurid imagination."* John Batten's research indicates that John Cowper Powys used Pitt Pond as his model for 'Auber Lake' (the title of one of Poe's poems), in his book 'Wood and Stone'. The novel tells of the insane young woman, who would escape at night from the keeper's cottage in the woods to run around the pond, dressed in white and screaming out in her madness.

I have copies of two photographs from the late 1890's, one of which shows the keeper's cottage beside the pool and the second the keeper himself (I think his name was Mr. Lane) feeding ducks from the dam. The cottage still existed as a ruin at the turn of the last century and in its time was quite a stylish building, with a pillared veranda overlooking the eastern end of the pond. When I look at these two old and faded photographs, it feels like I'm looking at the ghosts of the pool. In time, perhaps my own faded image will join their company; some small part of my soul trapped by the timeless atmosphere of the place.

Let's take the punt out and float fish our baited swim for the last few hours until sunset. Gliding silently on a surface like silk, the boat skims across the pool to rest against the lilies near the dam. From here it just takes an underarm flick to send the float out to where diamond bubbles pepper the surface, betraying the presence of fish feeding on the hemp and corn below. The orange tip of the quill stands out proudly against the dark water. Every now and again it flickers and bobs, as a carp or tench brushes against the line. Then it raises, waves, drifts sideways and vanishes and the strike meets a vibrant resistance, deep within the heart of the pond. It is the first emerald tench of the evening and there should be more to follow.

We can fish like this until the day fades and the scene takes on the sepia tints of a Victorian sunset. Time stands still and then flows backwards like an ebb tide as the spirits of times long past draw breath. Then the moment has passed and the first Daubenton's bat of the evening starts its dance across the water. Our journey home will be lit by glow worms and the mercurial wash of a new moon.

Meanders

By the time I was in my teens I was fishing all over Somerset for a wide range of species. Access to my own car broadened my horizons still further and as soon as I had passed my driving test I bought a Renault 4, which was the perfect fishing wagon, being both cheap to run and spacious.

The fishing on the Stoke sub Hamdon club ticket on the River Parrett still provided the main outlet for my enthusiasm but I had also discovered the great winter pike fishing on the River Brue, and the tench and bream fishing on the same river in the summer months. I'd also found the superb Holemore fishery run by Andy Carpenter on Chard Reservoir+, and Prof and I had taken to exploring the lovely fishing on the River Isle together.

The Stoke waters seemed less exciting than the new places I had found, yet when I look back the Parrett was where most of the significant stepping stones in the development of my fishing life were laid.

It was on the Parrett, for example, that I caught my first big roach, trotting casters on a deep, slow bend below Parrett Works. It was a rather ugly fish because the disease columnaris had struck the river and the roach was scarred with lumps and lesions, but it still weighed nearly Two and a half pounds and its size alone was impressive.

It was also on the Parrett that I caught my first carp. The river had suffered a pollution and hundreds of fish of all species had died in the aftermath, so the Stoke Club undertook a restocking of the river, which included a large number of carp of between one and three pounds. I didn't know about the stocking, so when something snaffled my float fished flake as I trotted it through a classic glide, I thought I'd hooked a new best chub. I was taken aback slightly when a chubby little mirror of about Two and a half pounds came to the surface instead. I went on to catch four more carp that day and whilst none of them was big, they all fought well on the light tackle and impressed me enough to inspire me to try and find some carp fishing for bigger specimens in the area. These fish eventually led me to Ashmead and I'll take you there with me later in this book.

Through my early association with The Golden Scale Club, I met Mike Winter, or The Professor as he is known in the Club. Mike will always be "Prof" to me and over the last thirty years we have shared many adventures and he has been my closest fishing friend. When Prof was learning to fish he met Dick Walker and, as Prof puts it, he was "taken under the wing" of Walker and his "Happy Crew". In a similar way, Prof took me under his own wing and he enjoyed taking me carp fishing on some of his secret Devonshire waters.

Prof is a true traditionalist and a man of huge honesty and integrity. He fishes with the MKIV carp rods he made himself in the 1960's and uses a huge cane landing net he constructed from components made for him by Dick Walker. Prof has never used a hair rig and never will because he considers it unethical. He is far from the serious man this description may paint him to be, however, and his love of good beer, laughter and the sheer fun of fishing make him the best of companions on a day's fishing.

Prof formed the Devon Carp Catchers Club with Larrie Beck in 1958 and they were joined by Pete Thomas when he moved to Devon in 1960. Prof used to fish with Walker and the Taylor brothers at Walker's fishing hut on the Ouse, where they sought out the enormous chub that inhabited that river. The way Prof describes the fishery is so exciting and vivid that I can picture it perfectly, even though I've never been. The shadows of chub lurked in the deep bends below the willows and they fished for them with simple tackle and baits ranging from crust and worms to slugs and frogs. On warm summer evenings they fished the shallows with the fly or floating crust, taking chub to over Five pounds. It sounded like glorious, exciting and adventurous fishing, matched by the fun and camaraderie of the evenings in the hut at the end of each day.

I took Prof to the little River Isle for the first time in 1982 and he immediately fell in love with the fishery because it reminded him so much of the fishing on the Ouse. The chub were much smaller and the average Isle specimens were only half the size of their Ouse counterparts but that didn't matter one jot to Prof because the fun of fishing for them was just as great. We used to pass the day walking the river, flicking a freelined slug under the willows or ledgering lobworms in the pools, but my favourite form of fishing was to float a line of crusts across the shallows and follow them through with the hook bait when the chub started to bow wave after the free offerings. On light tackle it was tremendous fun and we always had plenty of tales to swap over a pint in The Barn Owl at the end of the day.

Photo courtesy of David Miller

If the conditions were suitable we also used to fish for the amazing roach at Holemore. These days anglers know Chard Reservoir as a carp fishery but in the mid-eighties Andy Carpenter, who ran the fishery, had only just introduced the carp and Holemore, as it was known, was probably the best big roach water in the country. Float fishing the deep water off the dam in the winter months could be especially productive and it was common to catch bags of thirty or more roach in a day, of which many would be bigger than the magical Two pounds. Prof and I only found Holemore at the tail end of its prime roach fishing, before the carp took over and the cormorants moved in, but the fishing was so good that I've never really fished for roach since because I've never found anywhere to match Holemore's quality.

For my birthday one year my parents arranged for me to go on a fly-fishing course on the River Exe on Exmoor. The course was run by the owner of a garden centre in Exbridge, who had the river flowing through his property. In fact, the "course" as such just consisted of half an hour in the back garden of the chap's house casting a piece of red wool into a washing up bowl, after which I was given a rod and box of flies for the day and abandoned to my own devices on the river. I loved it! I'm sure I could have learned far more if my tutor had given me some indication of which fly to use and shown me how to keep my Greenwell's Glory afloat, but actually it was the best introduction to fly fishing for trout that I could have had.

In the end I caught two lovely little wild brown trout. I returned one alive to the river but the owner saw me catch the second one and he insisted that I knocked it on the head and took it home for supper, even though I thought it was too small and pretty to kill. I think he wanted to show my parents that he hadn't ripped them off and that the fee for the day had been value for money.

Whilst the quality of the tuition left much to be desired, however, that day set me adrift on a current of fly fishing that has carried me from the Exe and the Barle to some of the finest salmonid rivers in England, Scotland and Wales. That same current eddied into my professional life and stirred my passion for the management of salmon and trout fisheries. If I am proud of anything I've achieved during my

career in conservation, it is through my work to help restore and protect our salmonid rivers where I think I have done the most good. In the widest sense, then, that day on the Exe proved to be one of the most valuable presents that anyone has ever given me.

I think it best if I gloss over the years I spent at University in Liverpool studying Marine Biology. Suffice to say that girls and sex and rock and roll caught up with me at last (I've always been high on life and I avoided all of the drugs apart from alcohol). Liverpool came as a massive culture shock after my rural upbringing, especially because I was there through the height of the Toxteth riots. If I'm honest, I loved the buzz and excitement of the city but my time in Liverpool really served to confirm that I'm a country boy at heart.

The highlight of the course was my Honours year, spent studying Marine Biology at the University field station at Port Erin on the Isle of Man. The marine students lived a parallel life to our friends in Liverpool and we exchanged the social maelstrom of student pub crawls for a year spent drift diving with the seals in the Calf Sound. In the gin clear waters of the Gulf Stream, we flew through underwater canyons on the tidal currents, shadowed by the island's grey seals and lost in a forest of kelp. Sometimes we would let the current push us up against one of the many rock outcrops and the inquisitive seals would come close enough to touch, sometimes tugging on our fins or clipping us playfully with their flippers. I dived most days after lectures, making friends with the conger eels that lived in the crevices under the breakwater in Port Erin Bay. They used to come out and greet me if I brought them the remains of the day's scientific experiments for food.

Somehow I managed to get enough work done amongst these distractions to scrape a good Honours degree but when the education system spat me out into the world I really didn't have any idea about what I wanted to do for a living. Many of my friends from university went into "proper" jobs but I was determined to use my degree to get a job as a marine biologist.

Then fate took a hand and for want of something better to do I applied to go on Operation Raleigh. Raleigh was a five-year programme of expeditions that took young people all around the world to work on social projects, scientific research and to enjoy an adventure. The selection process was pretty intensive and designed to push the candidates to their physical limits and then test how they worked in a team under this duress. I remember spending a particularly cold night on a snowy Welsh hillside, gutting a rabbit for dinner whilst soaked to the skin and chilled to the bone, wondering if it was all worthwhile. It was, of course, and I soon found myself joining Expedition 11F to the Torres Strait Islands, which lie along the northern extension of the Great Barrier Reef between Queensland and Papua New Guinea.

Even the journey out to the islands was exciting. We travelled out via Bali, where we enjoyed the white sand beaches, and Darwin, where we explored the Kakadu National Park and saw our first saltwater crocodile. The croc was a thirty-foot terror that had been captured when it started taking dogs from a local beach. I was genuinely frightened by its speed and power and I listened with fascination when a Ranger fed it some chicken carcasses and explained about the crocodile's ecology. The Torres Strait has one of the largest populations of saltwater crocodiles in the world.

From Darwin we took an ancient Douglas DC3 out to the islands. The DC3 was a battered twin-engine propeller plane dating back to the Second World War and it didn't look like it had been serviced very often since it retired from active service. We had been flying over mile after mile of featureless outback for about two hours when one of the two propellers stuttered and died. Boffs, a Unionist skinhead from Belfast who turned out to be as nice a guy as you would ever want to meet, pointed out the stationary propeller to the stewardess. "Oh shit!" she said, in a broad Aussie accent, as she headed off to let the pilot know.

The pilot's loud drawl came over the intercom soon afterwards. "Say, this is great! We've lost one of the bloody props and we're gonna have to turn back for Darwin. I've never done a crash landing before but they sounded bloody great in training, so it looks like I'm gonna have some fun! Say, if we don't make it and I have to put down in the rough stuff we're probably for it but I guess we'll see how it goes." In a perverse, terrifying way his dry humour was quite reassuring. We made it back and when we'd disembarked from the DC3 the pilot insisted on having his photograph taken with everyone next to the broken propeller.

The Torres Strait has over 270 islands of which only three are inhabited. I don't know if you remember the Oliver Reed film Castaway, which was based on the book by Lucy Irvine, but the Torres Strait is where the events portrayed in the film took place. The islands themselves are a string of coral atolls and rocky outcrops with white sand beaches, spread across the reef. They are beautiful and rich in wildlife and local culture. The Islanders are a proud race from a Melanesian and Polynesian origin and it is rare for the Island Council to allow visitors into the area.

The Island culture had been all but destroyed by the clumsy interference of the Australian Government in their attempts to support the aboriginal people. The government had provided the islanders with cheap, prefabricated housing and over a relatively short period of time they had lost their traditional house building skills, even though the prefab alternatives weren't sturdy enough to withstand the island climate. I spent a month of the expedition working on a project led by an inspirational young Australian architect called Paul Haar, who was teaching the islanders how to build modern houses with traditional materials and techniques, using mangrove timbers and mud brick construction.

Even more sadly, the Islanders were heavily subsidised with grants, even though they could earn a fortune during the crayfish season. The result was that their work ethic had all but been destroyed and the islanders had adopted an astonishing "throw away" culture, to the extent that if a spark plug failed on an outboard they would throw the whole motor away and simply buy a new one. The populated islands looked like a scrap heap. Modern island culture revolved around the monthly arrival of a supply boat that carried essential supplies of alcohol to the remote island communities. When the "Booze Boat" arrived, an orgy of drinking ensued that went on until the supplies ran dry, at which point there might be only a week or so to wait before the next delivery. It was a tragic example of how well-intentioned interference can cause real cultural damage. Without the government "help" the islanders would probably have continued quite happily making a good living from selling their crayfish, whilst retaining their cultural identity and values.

In addition to the time working on Paul Haar's project, I also led an expedition to the largest uninhabited island in the chain called Prince Edward Island, to help with a survey of the island's wild horses, boar and other wildlife. We were there in the dry season and all of the major rivers on the island were just dry tracks across the arid landscape. There were a number of large waterfalls which ran as raging torrents

when the rains came but that, during "The Dry", formed spectacular cliff faces that towered above deep, enclosed pools of clean water. These plunge pools were the only source of fresh water on the island and they acted as a magnet for the island wildlife. We hiked between the pools, camping at each one and recording the birds and animals that visited to drink. Of course, we needed fresh water to drink ourselves and there were times when our supplies nearly ran out only for the pool we had spent more than a day hiking toward, in the ninety degree heat, not to exist or turned out to be poisoned.

Photo courtesy of Keith Jenkins

The most intimidating pool was at the foot of a dry fall which formed a vertical chimney through the sandstone that was one hundred feet or more high. The walls of this cave shimmered with silver gossamer and closer inspection showed that the rock was woven with the webs of thousands of Black Widow spiders. Any bite in that remote spot would have probably proven fatal and we retreated to find a safer drinking supply. On another occasion a six foot long King Brown, one of the most poisonous snakes in the world, struck at one of the expedition members but fortunately it only sank its fangs into the wide brim of his hat.

In truth, the dangers were minimal and insignificant in the presence of the natural beauty that surrounded us. We watched fish eagles hunting, we saw the wild boar and the majestic wild horses, we watched the Green and Leatherback Turtles struggle up the beaches to lay their eggs and we watched the young turtles hatch and scramble down to the sea, avoiding the predatory birds and fish as best they could. Above all, we discovered a love of true wilderness for the first time in our lives and with it the realisation that anything is possible, that life is short and that we owe it to ourselves to make the most of every moment.

The largest pool on the island was at a spot called Dugong Storey. It was over a hundred yards in circumference and must have been about sixty feet deep. Three of us found it as an advance party for the main group and we stripped off our boots and socks to soak our tired feet in the cool water before heading back to find the others. We were immediately surrounded by hundreds of tiny fish that nibbled at the skin of our soles and we relaxed to enjoy a natural pedicure. I believe the same service is now a popular luxury in beauty salons throughout Britain.

When we set up camp, I trapped some of these tiny fish and hooked six or seven onto a handline as bait. On the first cast into the pool I landed a freshwater eel of about Ten pounds that fed the entire camp. On the second cast I hooked another eel that felt simply enormous in the brief moments before it won our tug o' war and smashed the sixty pound line around a rock in some fathomless crevice in the depths. The eels looked identical to our European species and I'd love to go back with a proper rod and line one day to see what I could catch, but I don't suppose I ever will.

I also spent a month on a pure adventure, canoeing around the uninhabited islands to explore them and discover their secrets. This phase of the expedition was led by a local white islander called Greg Malone, who was a real character. Greg and I hit it off when he told me about his search for a supply of fresh water on an island called Kulbai Kulbai that he had heard of in local folklore. The reef around Kulbai Kulbai had some of the best fishing in the area and Greg said that if he could only find the freshwater spring he would be able to camp there and make the best of this natural larder. What was unusual about the spring was that it was supposed to lie on a rocky beach on the north of the island, below the high tide mark. Rumour had it that at low tide, a fissure in the rock allowed fresh water to flush into a rock pool, so that for an hour each day it ran clean and fresh. No one had found the spring in decades and after many attempts to find it, Greg had decided it existed only in local myth.

On our first day on the island, an Italian girl called Monique and I set out to explore our surroundings by completing a circuit of the island's perimeter beaches. It was a fantastic day in which we swam with black tipped reef sharks and crunched across coral sand beaches that no-one had walked on in years. We reached the northern beach at low tide and just as we headed back I noticed a flock of doves clustered around one of the rock pools. It was the fresh water spring that Greg had been seeking. I think my "Pommy Bastard Bushcraft" impressed Greg and it sealed a strong friendship based on a mutual respect for each other and the nature around us.

I'd been sleeping on the beach on Kulbai Kulbai for the two nights prior to my discovery of the spring, but that evening Greg strolled down from the camp to pass some time with me. As he left he said "You know the saltwater crocs love these beaches. They look for patterns of behaviour, like an animal coming down to the beach regularly of an evening. If they see it once they pay no attention but if they see the same animal two or three times they lie up in wait and grab it for food. One took a bloke off the beach on TI [Thursday Island] last month and I saw a twenty-five footer in this bay just yesterday. Bloody great thing it was!" I packed my kit up quickly and followed him back to camp and the safety of higher ground.

The next day we went out fishing in Greg's little ten foot "Tinny". He knew a spectacular drop-off where the shallow water on the edge of the barrier reef plunged into the indigo depths of the ocean. There were two great stacks of coral just out from the main reef that provided a sanctuary for the reef fish and an attraction for their predators. We trolled big silver spoons on thick handlines off the back of the boat, catching the usual array of Spanish mackerel and small barracuda. Then I hooked an enormous fish that almost stopped the little boat in its tracks. We played it carefully, using the boat's outboard to follow the fish whilst keeping the line under tension to tire it out. Eventually a massive barracuda broke surface and thrashed to the side of the boat where three of us manhandled it aboard. I have no idea of its weight but it fed thirty people and I have a photograph of three of us holding it up for the camera, with me holding its head, someone else holding its body and a third person holding its tail.

Even that wasn't the biggest fish we hooked that day. A guy called Martin who was with us hooked a fish that Greg followed for over an hour before it began to tire. Eventually a tiger shark rose up to the surface alongside Greg's boat, with Martin's line disappearing into its cavernous, tooth lined mouth. Tigers are man eaters and this one was a good foot longer than the boat. "The hell with that," said Greg when he saw the shark and he cut the line quickly. The shark cruised alongside us for three or four beats of its great tail and then, realising it was free, it sounded into the inky depths.

On another occasion I went out snorkelling on the reef on my own to try and take some underwater photographs of the coral. I found a secret cove, where the coral reached up to the surface but a gap in the reef just wide enough for me to pass through led to a natural, circular amphitheatre with a floor of smooth white shell sand. Dropping down onto this sand, I took out my camera and started to take some pictures.

A movement in the sand caught my attention and I glanced down and spotted two bulging eyes looking back at me. The sand suddenly seemed to come alive, shimmering and rippling as a huge stingray pushed itself out of its camouflaged bed and swam towards me. I had nowhere to go but nor did the ray and as it began to circle around the confines of our cell I turned with it, clicking away with the camera. The ray must have been five feet across from wingtip to wingtip and it had a long whiplash tail armed with two vicious poisoned spines. Just as I thought I would run out of breath the ray found the exit and it banked steeply and glided away into the heart of the reef. I surfaced and checked my bearings before swimming quickly back to shore, buzzing with adrenaline from the encounter.

Photo courtesy of Keith Jenkins

Most of my photographs from Raleigh were stolen a long time ago and I don't have many images to remind me of my time on the expedition. I do, however, have a lasting reminder of that fantastic time in my life that is better than any picture. On the expedition I met a lovely girl from Aberdeen who I knew only as "the girl with the big brown eyes and stripey shorts." I met her again at an Operation Raleigh reunion, held at The Royal Albert Hall in London to mark the end of the five-year programme of projects. Out of the hundreds of young people who were there that evening we got talking to each other. We were still talking at six o'clock the following morning when we ended up in a China Town restaurant together, with a group of friends from our Torres Strait expedition.

It transpired that she was from Aberdeen and had returned there to live at the end of the expedition. I had also moved to Aberdeen at the end of Raleigh, to take a job as a fisheries scientist, and by that time I'd been living there for nearly two years. We arranged to meet up when we got home and before long we were seeing quite a lot of each other. I fell very deeply in love as a result and within a year we were engaged to be married.

Shona and I were married at Kings College Chapel in Old Aberdeen on the longest day of the summer of 1991 and we've been happy together ever since. Perhaps part of the secret of our lasting relationship is that we share the experience of Raleigh and all that it taught us about taking our chances and living life to the full. All I know is that I love Shona more now, after twenty years of marriage, than I did when we walked out of the Kings College Chapel together, into the torrential rain of an Aberdeen summers day.

*I*n 1982 I was studying for my O Level exams and, according to every adult I knew, that meant it was "an important time". I'd had it drummed into me that those few, pressured weeks "could shape my future". The result was that I was bored (particularly by the maths revision) and looking for any escape from the stress and shear drudgery of it all. Respite came on the 1st April, when my regular copy of Coarse Fishing Monthly dropped through the letter box, which meant I could leave the mysteries of the binomial equation behind for a few hours and let my imagination go fishing with the likes of Jim Tyree, Dave Plummer, Mike Winter and Chris Yates. Little did I realise that the magazine would do more to "shape my future" than the final grades from the Board of Examiners ever did.

Club H.Q.
Vale Cottage
Whitmore Vale
Hindhead
Surrey
4th April '82.

Dear Skeffington,

Contrary to the chairman's belief that there was no-one left in the Terrible Wilderness who had the qualities, potential or lunacy to make a New Member of this club, it has now been shown that there are indeed a few stalwarts left in the world. And it would appear that you are one of them.

The committee met in a shady public house recently to discuss the wisdom of the recent publication of our Application form. Though there was a certain amount of dissent, kicking & gaffing to begin with (from the members who hadn't been informed about the publication) I soon calmed the situation by producing the best of the first batch of applicants.

'This man is an imbecile — but a very proper imbecile,' said the president, after reading your entry — he particularly liked your explanation of the great Tweed mystery.

But before you book a flight for S. America, or take to the hills in terror, let me quickly add that you are what we term a 'qualifier'. There are, so far, only four qualifiers & the rest of the applicants, though interesting, were mundane by comparison to the few favourites. P'raps there will be no more than a dozen 'correct' applications by the month's end. At the AGM, in May, these will be put into the chairman's hat & the gaff will be used to pick the two new members. (No doubt you are already regretting your rash decision.) Whatever happens, thankyou for a first class & utterly

PTO

> insane application. May your ale always be strong, may your rods never get woodworm, may your gaff-point be kept sharp & may your net be blessed with many a fine Golden Scaled beauty. Also, we would like you to remember our Sixth Golden Rule. 'Only fall in when there is someone else there to appreciate it.'
>
> Splintering Cane,
>
> Ferneyhough
>
> Hon. Sec.
>
> P.S. We have just revised our Fifth Golden Rule. 'Tolerance is a virtue. However, if you discover someone using electric-bite indicators, forget tolerance — & gaff the bounder.'

In the back of the magazine was an application form for The Golden Scale Club. Even though the editor had clearly included the form as an April Fool spoof, I found my physics revision so tedious one afternoon that I filled it in as a way of cheering myself up and posted it off to the magazine. A few weeks later, a brown envelope arrived, addressed to me in a spidery hand with black fountain pen and with a sketch of a long, lean common carp beneath the address; a letter from Ferneyhough had arrived.

"Dear Skeffington," read the letter, "Contrary to the Chairman's belief that there was no-one left in the Terrible Wilderness who had the qualities, potential or lunacy to make a New Member of this club, it has now been shown that there are indeed a few stalwarts left in the world. And it would appear that you are one of them.

"The committee met in a shady public house recently to discuss the wisdom of the recent publication of our Application form. Though there was a certain amount of dissent, kicking and gaffing to begin with (from the members who hadn't been informed about the publication) I soon calmed the situation by producing the best of the first batch of applicants.

"'This man is an imbecile – but a very proper imbecile,' said the President, after reading your entry – he particularly liked your explanation of the great T'weed mystery."

The letter was signed "Splintering cane, Ferneyhough. Hon. Sec."

I wrote back eventually and so my association with The Golden Scale Club began, with a flurry of insane correspondence with Ferneyhough. On midsummer day he wrote again to let me know that the Club had met and that they had decided to offer me "Associate Membership" for a year and that "Full Membership, the ultimate accolade, will be poured all over you if you are deemed worthy after that time…" I was on a slippery slope and there was no way back, even if I had wanted one. By the end of the summer, Ferney had described the Club's latest wildie fishery to me and we had set a date to meet there for a day's fishing.

As an impressionable young teenager, the prospect of meeting and possibly even fishing with The Golden Scale Club thrilled me. After all, hadn't both the Golden Scale Club's new President, Water Rail, and the Secretary, Ferneyhough caught record carp from Redmire Pool? I knew all about the club from Ferneyhough's writings in Angling Magazine and its successor, Coarse Fishing Monthly. The quirky, irreverent humour in his articles about the club appealed to me and I loved the sound of the timeless carp pools to which the club seemed to have access. I remember one article in particular about an Opening Night meeting of the club. The article started with a tale of disaster when the Club found the lake where they planned to start the season over run with modern carp anglers, but finished with the Secretary and Birtwhistle finding a traditional, unspoilt lake, where Ferneyhough landed an Eight pound wildie in the dawn. The photograph of Ferney returning that carp was incredibly atmospheric and the article seemed to capture the very essence of the escapism I sought in my own carp fishing.

Now I was going to meet and fish with Golden Scale Club myself. Actually, the idea that I was going to fish with anglers of such skill and experience was pretty daunting, as at that time I had only ever caught a few small carp from the River Parrett near my Somerset home. Surely the members of the Golden Scale Club would just laugh when a sixteen year old boy turned up and they saw my feeble attempts to catch a fish? I felt quite nervous when my dad, who had driven me all the way over from Somerset, left me on the doorstep of Ferneyhough's cottage.

Photo courtesy of Mike Canning

The Secretary's old wooden cottage lay hidden in a steep little valley below a Surrey oak wood. The cottage was timber framed with clapboard walls and it swayed and creaked in the October breeze, in sympathy with the trees that surrounded it. With the exception of an old adder skeleton that was pinned to the front doorpost, the whole cottage seemed to be alive. Ferneyhough met me at the door and in the study he introduced me to Jasper and Trottingshawe, who were just tucking into some plum cake. We were due to meet another "new" member, called Parker, at the train station in Haslemere and then amble over to the Club's wildie lake, called Rivertree, for the crack of lunchtime.

I needn't have worried. Not only were the members I met friendly and welcoming, some of them also turned out to be nearly as cack-handed as I was with a rod and line. It dawned on me very quickly that this wasn't a club of expert anglers but rather a gathering of like-minded friends, who shared an appreciation of the simple pleasures of just being by the waterside. Technical skill was surplus to requirements, to the extent that it was almost an anathema, something that got in the way of the simple enjoyment of going fishing.

As carp fishing days go, it was far from ideal. Rivertree looked brooding, cold and lifeless under a lowering grey sky and soon after we arrived it started to drizzle. Within an hour it was raining heavily and the prospects of catching a carp seemed bleak. Not that I cared; with the pressure of exams finally released I was enjoying myself so much that I hardly noticed the rain. I smiled as I remembered the journey to the lake through the narrow Surrey lanes. There had been a running blowpipe battle, as Ferneyhough and I took the lead in his old white Renault van and tried to delay Jasper, who was in hot pursuit, with a bombardment of dog biscuits and sweetcorn, fired through the open back door.

More than anything, though, I remembered my first sight of Rivertree and I couldn't imagine a more lovely water for my first day out with the Club. We approached the lake along a driveway with some rambling old farm buildings on the left hand side. There was no sight of the lake until the drive swept around beyond the house and onto the dam. Rivertree lay before us, a long grey ribbon of water curving away into the distance, with the farm now revealed as the converted remains of an old, moated monastery that backed onto the water. Lines of alders shrouded the pool and the occasional majestic oak gave the lake a sense of timeless mystery but Rivertree was large enough to prevent the encroaching trees from making the water look gloomy, even on that grey autumn day.

We parked on the far end of the dam wall and elected to fish from some rickety old landing stages that jutted out like Victorian piers from the dam itself. These landing stages gave a wonderful view up the lake and access to some deeper water, where we hoped the carp would have gathered to shelter from the wintry chill. Jasper and I fished the corner boards and Ferney and Parker shared the next set along, near the centre of the dam. I was particularly impressed by the fact that Ferney had taken along the Windsor armchair from his study to fish from, and he looked rather regal on this throne, despite his soggy hat.

All the way over to the lake, Ferney had fired my enthusiasm with tales of previous visits, when the sun shone and the carp had fed like minnows, bubbling freely over his offerings of corn. He had described vividly the way his quill ducked and danced before it finally sailed away to the bite of one of the lake's wild carp.

I tackled up with a three piece Allcock's cane rod and my old 1920's Aerial (which is still my favourite reel for stalking carp) and set a red tipped porcupine quill on the line. I spread a small scattering of corn just a rod length off the dam and followed it up with a cast holding three grains on the hook, just as the Club Secretary had described. I was slightly horrified when Jasper set up next to me with leger tackle and simply whacked a hook baited with corn as far out into the lake as his rusty old Mitchell 300 would allow. I was even more alarmed when he immediately hooked a lovely wildie of about Three pounds which thrashed the water next to my float to foam as he brought it to the net.

I considered making an official complaint to the Secretary when Jasper hooked a second wildie within minutes of recasting his line, with even less finesse than before. Then a miracle happened. A solitary bubble rose next to the tip of my quill, a second bubble joined it a moment later and then a little fizz that could only have been caused by a carp rooting for the free offerings below. Without any of the prevarication described by Ferney, my quill simply slid away and a gentle strike set the hook into a dancing, darting resistance in the depths. The line blurred from the reel and the ratchet rasped as the fish made for the supports of the landing stage but I checked it in time and it turned for open water. "Skeff's hooked one!" I heard Parker exclaim and I instantly forgave Jasper his earlier crass behaviour, as he handled the net expertly, enmeshing the glowing fish at the first attempt.

The scales of the wildie flowed like liquid bronze across its body and its fins were suffused with coral pink and deepest orange. The carp bristled with indignation, tensing its muscle and flicking its fins as Ferneyhough took its portrait, and when I bent to return it to the lake it flipped from my hands and shot off like a golden bullet. I would have been thrilled and relieved to have caught anything in such company but to have caught a wonderful wildie like this one, on my first day with the Golden Scale Club, left me glowing with pleasure and pride. I suppose it might have weighed Three pounds. I've caught many much larger carp over the thirty years that have passed since I landed that first Rivertree wildie but few that meant more or that gave me greater satisfaction. The two further wildies that I landed later in the day were equally memorable and I must have bored my dad to tears on the long drive home to Somewhereset.

Parker and I were both welcomed (or should that be condemned?) to full membership a year later.

In the early days, the Club had two carp pools of our own that we used to fish; Rivertree which I have just described and Sheepwash, a small secluded Leney water that lay hidden away in the Sussex countryside. Living so far from these lakes meant that I only visited them occasionally but I really enjoyed those stolen days when I could travel up from Somerset to fish. The traditional Opening Night gatherings were especially good. We met in a pub in the evening for the AGM, which was usually a fairly riotous affair, before setting off for the chosen Opening Night venue in time for midnight.

Perhaps the most memorable Opening Night was held at Rivertree. I travelled up from Yeovil and Ferneyhough met me at Haslemere station to chauffeur me to the lake. The train left just two hours after the end of my last "A" level exams and I remember rushing through the Maths paper to make sure I didn't miss it.

A lethal game of cricket was underway on the Rivertree wicket when we arrived. The wicket was a ploughed field by the lake and the unpredictable bounce made Jasper's vicious bowling all the more deadly. I survived just three balls before retiring to nurse my injuries, and after little more than half an hour the Secretary had to call a truce on the whole game to prevent the Club's first Opening Night fatality. Jasper was the only member to escape unscathed, after a bowling display that made the infamous "bodyline" Ashes series look like a polite game of French cricket.

The AGM in the nearby Lickfold Inn was unusually chaotic. The Chairman, Dandy, resigned (as usual) and was dishonourably expelled from the Club and then (as usual), immediately re-elected to his post. This time, Trottingshawe insisted that his term should last "beyond life and beyond death" in order to relieve us all of a tedious repeat performance the following year. The Chairman emigrated to America soon afterwards and the Club has run far more smoothly as a result because although he still holds office, we've hardly seen him since.

The usual Club awards were also discussed and presented. I think that was the year the Golden Scale Award for the season's most noteworthy endeavour was presented to Jasper who had hooked an Intercity 125 train whilst fishing (by mistake) from a railway bridge. Unfortunately he lost the beast when it smashed him up in a tunnel. "You should have seen the way it stripped the line from my Mitchell 300..." I seem to recall the Black Gaff going to one of the Water Authorities for a pollution incident, and that the Titanic Cup (for the season's greatest disaster) went to the Secretary who had smashed the tip of his Walker-built MKIV Avon whilst playing a Twelve pound mirror at Sheepwash. This was the rod on which he had landed the British record just a couple of seasons before and so the loss was even more poignant.

The evening ended with Ferneyhough and Parker recounting the astonishing events that had occurred at Winchester Cathedral, when several of the members had met on the 299th anniversary of Isaac Walton's death. They had invited Isaac to join the Pantheon, a spiritual membership of the Club that included many of the greatest ghosts in angling history. In a simple ceremony, they deposited a golden hook in a crack in Walton's tomb before making the request to Isaac that he grace the Club with his presence. Everyone agreed that several omens seen since that time were sure signs of Isaac's acceptance.

We returned to the lake in time to settle into our pitches before the witching hour of midnight. I had laced the margin of my chosen swim with a tin of sweetcorn before we had set off for the pub, so when the Secretary marked the start of the season with a note on his hunting horn, all I had to do was flick out my hookbait and settle back to savour another Opening. I didn't get much time to relax, though, because the line drew tight in my fingers before I'd even wrapped the silver foil bite indicator around it. A reflex strike set the hook and had the rod bouncing and within five minutes of the season's start I scooped my net under a thrashing wildie of about Three pounds.

This had to be some sort of Club record and I carried the carp around to Ferneyhough's swim in the landing net to show him my prize, only to find him unhooking a carp of

his own. "I think that makes me first man," he said lifting up his carp to show me. "I think second," I replied, holding up my own fish. We slipped them back together and I returned to my swim to cast again.

I landed two other carp within the hour but then the night turned chill under the clear sky, with its crescent moon and myriad stars. The carp stopped feeding and I reeled in and tried to sleep but the ground was hard and cold, so I ended up going for a run across the field behind me to warm up instead. Dawn eventually brought relief as the welcome warmth of the sun's first rays brought an end to my shivering, and in the next swim to my right Anglepen's chattering teeth fell silent.

At a second blast from the brass horn, we met on the dam to count our catch, before going over to the farmhouse for breakfast. The count took some time because between us we had landed sixty-three carp! We have never had another opening like it and we took the miracle as further confirmation that Isaac had been fishing alongside us and had been guiding our casts.

A final highlight of a wonderful day for me came in the afternoon, when the Secretary let me have a cast with Excaliber, the MKIV carp rod with which our President, Water Rail, had landed Clarissa from Redmire Pool. I landed a glorious wildie that weighed one twelfth of Clarissa's weight before handing the rod back to its caretaker.

The Golden Scale Club has changed over the years that I've been a member but its essence has remained the same. We no longer have our own carp waters, although we have access to a lovely perch and roach fishery on the Dorset Stour. I do miss the GSC carp pools, though, and the traditional Opening Nights when the Club met on a lake to greet the new season, rather than meeting on the river to say farewell to the old one on the Last Day.

There have been brief times when the soul of the Club seemed under threat from incomers who tried to impose an elitist and pretentious persona on the Club that is completely at odds with its true ethos, but they never succeeded. At the Club's heart, despite the silly Club names, anachronistic humour and love of old cane rods, the members of the GSC are nothing more than a group of friends who enjoy each other's company and who like to fish quiet and unspoilt waters, where angling can still be enjoyed as a gentle art.

When I said at the start of this chapter that my application to join the Golden Scale Club shaped my future I really meant it. Through the Club I've met some truly inspirational people who gave me the confidence to follow my interests in nature conservation and to pursue it as my career.

Ian "AH" Carstairs, in particular, probably had no idea how great his influence on my future would be when we sat and talked on a Rivertree platform about his conservation work. Ian's efforts to save Yorkshire's River Derwent from pollution and commercial exploitation for navigation were inspirational and his work was honoured with an MBE in 1995. Ian encouraged me to follow my heart away from a better paid, corporate career and towards work of a far less lucrative but ultimately more satisfying nature. Without Ian's influence, I might never have followed my career in fisheries management and conservation, through to my current senior conservation role with the National Trust. Ian's work continues to inspire me and I was delighted when he was given the OBE in 2007 in recognition of his continued commitment to conservation.

Of course, membership of the Club also influenced my angling profoundly. Fishing the Golden Scale Club waters with the man who had just landed the largest carp ever caught in Britain was bound to have an impact on my own angling. Ferneyhough is a living testament to the fact that you don't need to follow the latest trends, use the latest gear or even be very technically competent to be a successful angler. His connection with the waters where we fished, his watercraft and his almost mystical empathy with the natural world, were more than a substitute for the lack of modern equipment and tactics. Indeed, it seemed to me that the nature of his simple tackle and uncluttered approach made it possible for him to forge a connection with his surroundings which made catching large fish seem simple. When Ferneyhough is in tune with a water, his instincts seem to lead him unerringly to the largest fish of the day. I also realised very quickly that using the natural hunting instincts to seek out fish (especially carp) was far more satisfying and exciting than the modernist "trapping" approach. Whilst I will sit in a swim for a day on the river or fish a session behind a set of carp rods when conditions dictate that it's necessary, I much prefer to adopt a more active and intuitive approach for most of my fishing.

Meeting and fishing with Bernard Venables was truly inspirational. Bernard, perhaps more than any other angler I've known, really understood the esoteric side of fishing

Photo courtesy of Mike Canning

Chapter Four – The Golden Scale Club

and its expression as a gentle art. For Bernard, fishing was all about the experience as a whole and catching the quarry was always secondary to the joy of simply being there at the waterside. Like me, he found the egotistical posturing so prevalent in the modern angling press quite baffling. "It just misses the point of fishing completely," he would say, shaking his head. Above all, Bernard was an all-round angler and meeting him re-enforced the love and respect for all facets of our sport instilled in me by his creation, Mr. Crabtree. This all-round approach flew in the face of the modern trend to develop a single-minded obsession with a particular branch of angling. It was Bernard who saved me from a lifetime restricted to fishing for just carp, to the exclusion of any other species of fish, and I will always be grateful for that rescue.

At one of the GSC meetings I struck up a conversation with Bernard about trout fishing on the Aberdeenshire Don. "One of my favourite rivers," Bernard said, his eyes gleaming. "I used to fish the Alford Arms water." "But that's where I'm fishing!" I exclaimed. "Really?" Bernard asked. "When I fished there, if you went downstream through the first bends you used to come to a stile where a boulder on the near bank created a lovely eddy that always held a good trout." "I know it!" I said. "I fished it just a few weeks ago. The cast is almost impossible because the drag of the eddy always tugs on the fly just as it reaches the holding spot..." "That's right," said Bernard. He paused "I was last there in the spring of 1968..." In 1968 I was just three years old, yet Bernard's memory was as fresh as my own recollections of just a few months before.

Bernard and I once had a long conversation about the fact that there are so many anglers these days writing about how to fish and yet so few that tried to explore the far more interesting questions about why we fish.

"It's because writing about knots, rigs and bait is so easy, whilst capturing the essence of our pastime is so difficult to achieve," he said.

"Not only that, writing technical articles sells tackle and bait and so much writing is wrapped up in corporate sponsorship these days that it's the tackle companies that dictate what the magazines publish," I said.

"Ah!" Bernard replied, "But any good editor will still publish a well written article, even if it isn't tied to advertising revenue. It just needs someone willing to write more atmospheric and evocative articles instead of the tedious technical material."

Now I wasn't about to argue about editorial freedom with the founding editor of Creel and the Angling Times but I had my doubts...

"You can write quite well," Bernard said. "You should write some articles, instead of just complaining about things."

I rose to the challenge of Bernard's skilfully cast fly and I've been writing occasional pieces for magazines such as Waterlog, Trout and Salmon and Carpworld ever since. This book is a direct result of Bernard's gentle encouragement and in many ways it is my tribute to him. I miss him a great deal.

Bernard was honoured with his MBE in 1995. This was the same year that AH received his first honour and the GSC met to celebrate with them both at the Club AGM at the Mayfly, beside the Test. It was a record turnout for an AGM, which was testimony to the respect of the other members for these two Golden Scalers. The meal was relaxed and enjoyable, the Ringwood ale outstanding and we passed an enjoyable hour feeding marshmallows to the roach and trout that lurked in the clear waters of the Test, which flowed past the beer garden. Ferneyhough noted that the bigger fish definitely seemed to prefer the pink marshmallows over the white ones.

We never thought for a moment that we would end the meeting with us all being thrown out of the pub and barred. The trouble started when one of the members produced a few fireworks and suggested we should set off a rocket to honour Bernard and AH and their achievements. It seemed like a great idea and Dunkeld duly took down one of the garden parasols, so that he could use the pole as a launch tube. Just as he lit the blue touch paper and retired to a safe distance, the landlord came running out of the bar.

"You can't do that!" he exclaimed. "I'm afraid you're all going to have to leave."

Bernard tried to calm him by explaining that it was a special occasion, but to no avail. "I would have thought you of all people would have known better," he said to Bernard. "You might hit a swallow!" And with that the meeting came to a surreal close, as the two Honoured members, accompanied by the rest of the Club shuffled out of the car park like a bunch of guilty schoolboys.

The Avon Barbel

Patrick Reginald Chalmers was an Irish writer who wrote for the Field and Punch magazines. As is the way with the best Irish writers he had the gift of language and could craft poetry from the simplest description. My favourite work by Chalmers is "At the Tail of the Weir", in which he wrote;

"But best of all I love the barbels because they roll like big brown and white cats upon golden shallows and sing in the moonlight with the joie de vivre of June. And because, so, they are all Thames to me and wild rose time and the streams running down from the weir."

Lovely! In those few lines he captured the essence of barbel; their graceful beauty, the surge and movement of their environment and their carefree nature. Unlike the pursuit of carp or wild trout, I can never take barbel fishing too seriously and I love it dearly because it represents the perfect balance between the challenge of catching a big, powerful fish and the simple, uncomplicated fun of just going fishing.

Somerset is not blessed with barbel rivers and so I was into my twenties before I ever sought them out. It was Chris Yates who took me barbel fishing for the first time on the Hampshire Avon, upstream of Ringwood. Chris discovered barbel at a time when he had become rather disillusioned with carp fishing and he fell so deeply in love with their pursuit that he ended up moving house to be nearer the Hampshire Avon.

My first couple of trips to the Avon at Breamore and Burgate were unsuccessful and I felt horribly out of my depth fishing such a clear, deep and powerful river after the sluggish waterways of Somerset.

The first barbel I ever caught came from the Ugly Weir on the Hampshire Avon at Ringwood. Several Golden Scale Club friends had gathered at the Ugly Weir to fish from the day ticket bank on the right hand side as you looked downstream from the lasher. Despite the slightly industrial feeling of the weir pool, and the constant traffic noise from the busy main road, I quite liked the fishery. In fact, I liked the river upstream of the weir very much indeed and there were some glorious looking glides up there between the waving ranunculus beds, but it was the weir pool itself that was the hotspot for barbel.

I fished intently, just at the tail of the weir, searching for Chalmers' "big brown and white cats" with a feeder full of maggots. Although I didn't even get a bite I enjoyed the fishing and I remember someone (possibly Biffo?) catching a good chub on meat from the last swim below the weir. It was a momentous day, though, because late in the afternoon I saw my first barbel in the flesh. The Colonel was fishing directly opposite me on the "Club Bank" of the weir and I saw his MKIV Avon thump over when he hooked the fish. It bored deeply across the pool towards me, getting dangerously close to the concrete of the weir sill, but The Colonel turned it before it could use the stonework to grate through his line. Once turned, the fish simply plodded around beneath the Colonel's rod tip until he brought it up and used the current of the back eddy to sweep it into his net. We all gathered to admire a barbel of just less than Nine pounds that looked just like the barbel that had been swimming through my imagination all day.

I remember feeling just a little bit jealous but also wonderfully inspired by The Colonel's success, and now that I had seen a barbel I knew I would have to persevere until I caught one myself. Just a fortnight later we returned to the Ugly Weir and this time Chris and I opted to pay the premium ticket price required to fish the "Club" water. It was a hot summer day and no-one expected any chances until last knockings, when we hoped to emulate The Colonel's success. Just after lunch I wandered downstream to explore a swim that rejoiced in the romantic name of "The Big Concrete" because of the gabion platform that jutted out from the riverbank. The actual swim may not have been my idea of a classic barbel spot but the glide downstream to which the "Concrete" gave access definitely was. Two dense beds of Ranunculus bordered the swim; one ran through the central line of the riverbed and another ran in parallel along the near bank, the two of them sweeping together to merge at the tail of the pool. Between them lay a clean bed of golden gravel that glowed with promise under the high summer sun.

Chris joined me and we started trotting maggots down the swim beneath a big chub float, taking it in turns to feed the head of the glide with a handful of grubs, whilst the other cast and followed the loose feed through with their float. I don't think Chris' heart was in the fishing and after half a dozen casts he left me and wandered back up towards the weir. His lack of confidence rubbed off on me and I was just about to go and join the others as well when a little bell rang in my mind. For no particular reason I had a sudden urge to swap the size twelve hook for a size six and to run a lump of meat down through the swim, instead of the maggots.

Never one to ignore an impulse I made the change and cast again, with a lump of meat about the size of a big grape impaled on the larger hook. I'd bunched four swanshot onto the line about a foot above the hook and set the tackle well over depth, so that the bait trundled along the riverbed downstream of the feathered float. I felt slightly ridiculous fishing like this but on my third cast the float dived under as it neared the tail of the glide, just where the weedbeds joined to form a canopy above the gravel. A long, sweeping strike set the hook and I was suddenly playing my first barbel.

The fish held at the tail of the glide, thumping impressively on the rod tip and sweeping across the river towards the thickest weedbed, where it gave one last pull and then went horribly solid. I shouted for help and Chris appeared. Quickly taking stock of my predicament, he rolled up his trousers and jumped into the margin of the river, shouting "Follow me, Skeff!" as he splashed downstream towards the fish. I rolled up my jeans and followed him, trying to keep the rod under tension as I slipped and splashed through the shallows until we were level with the fish. "Steady now..." Chris said, "It'll come out in a moment..." We watched the curve in the locked cane and both breathed a sigh of relief when it suddenly came alive once more, kicking and bucking as I bullied the barbel back across the river and into the waiting net.

The barbel was less than half the size of The Colonel's fish but that didn't matter to me at all. It was my first barbel and I grinned from ear to ear as I held it up proudly for a photograph. Two things struck me when I looked out the photograph of the barbel for this book; the first is how much smaller the barbel looks than I remember (although it is just as beautiful, dark and sleek as my memory of it) and the second is how incredibly young I look, yet it seems like only yesterday that I watched that barbel glide away into the clear Avon current when I returned it.

Someone asked if I'd had the barbel on maggots and when I showed them my setup and told them I'd caught the barbel on luncheon meat they were incredulous. Apparently it was common knowledge that barbel in the stretch never took meat before dusk. The advantage of being a complete novice of course was that I had no idea of this piece of barbel law and I can only assume my first barbel was similarly naive.

"I'll catch another one for you," I said and cast again, holding back hard as the float reached the hotspot. It dived under, just like before, and my strike once again connected with a pulse of life that surged through the heart of the river, setting my own pulse racing. Chris set off downstream again with the net but this time I was more confident and assertive, so I landed my second barbel with none of the drama and tension of the first, even though it was a pound heavier.

I returned the barbel to polite applause from the gallery of Golden Scalers that had gathered to witness events.

"Go on, Skeff," said Parker. "I bet you can't do it again!" So I did and landed my third barbel on the next trot through. Three barbel in three casts! Three! After all the blank days that had led to that moment it seemed incredible and in the evening I took the others to the The Fish Inn to celebrate my success and commiserate (gloat?) over their straight rods, because no-one else had a bite all day...

I thought I'd cracked it but in truth I still don't understand the Hampshire Avon and its barbel, nearly thirty years after that red letter day. I've caught Avon barbel, of course, including one or two really big fish by my standards, but seldom by design.

Take Bisterne for example. I've fished odd days on the Bisterne fishery almost every year for about twenty years and in total I suppose I must have enjoyed thirty days or more on this wonderful looking piece of river. In all that time, I've only ever caught one Bisterne barbel and that came on a winter's day, so unlikely to produce a bite that we spent most of it enjoying a three-hour lunch in the nearby pub. When you walk the banks of Bisterne it looks to an untutored eye like one long barbel swim, but the fish seem to hold up in just one or two areas and in my experience much of the river is devoid of fish. The barbel that are present are very finicky and the only realistic chance of a bite seems to be in the last hour or so before the fishery closes at dusk. No, I've found that fishing Bisterne is a profoundly frustrating pastime that's likely to drive any barbel angler to hang up their rods and take up match fishing.

I've enjoyed my greatest Hampshire Avon success on the Royalty, where members of The Golden Scale Club used to gather for a day or two each winter. Where the steady flow from the Parlour Pool converges with the flow from the big weir in The Rushes swim was the place to fish, because barbel from all over the river gathered in the lovely slack beneath the alders when the river was running high and cold. The exact hotspot varied, though, from day to day and it was always a game of chance to see who would be the lucky man to pick the gap between the alders where the barbel wanted to feed.

Sometimes three or four of us would fish in a row with our wicker creels and cane rods, looking for all the world like some fishing match from the nineteen forties, where they had forgotten to blow the final whistle. On these busy GSC sorties it was often the case that one of us would catch two or three barbel whilst the others would blank. Of course, it was accepted practice that everyone would converge on the prime swim and fish together, accepted that is by everyone apart from the original occupant, who would defend their pitch to the bitter end from all comers. The rough and tumble that ensued was great for warming up on a cold day, when an easterly wind was cutting across the frosty expanse of the field opposite.

Just downstream from the Rushes is the famous Pipe Swim and when the water levels dropped from their winter peak, this was my favourite pool on the fishery. I liked the far bank best, simply because fishing it gave me the excuse I needed to spend all day climbing backwards and forwards over the pipe itself, like an overgrown schoolboy. One autumn, my friend Dunkeld came down from Aberdeen to stay and we arranged to fish the Royalty with Chris, Demus, Jeff and Max for two days, so that Dunkeld could try and catch his first barbel. The river was low and clear so three of us chose to fish the Pipe, with Demus fishing the slack water from the near bank, whilst I swung over the pipe to fish the far bank with Dunkeld.

Dunkeld is an expert salmon angler and it took him a few casts to get used to the feel of the coarse rod but the basis of touch-legering is similar to that of working a salmon fly and he soon got the hang of casting upstream to the head of the slack water and feeling a lump of meat down through the swim.

Demus on the other hand is a true expert in two fields; he is certainly the best barbel angler since Wallis and he is also an accomplished pipe smoker. The essence of pure contentment is to see Demus standing beside his beloved Avon, with his Wallis Wizard in one hand and his other hand cupped around the bowl of his favourite pipe. Demus fished the tail of the slack water opposite me and at about midday I saw him strike into a barbel. He took a moment or two to assess the size of the fish and then

Photo courtesy of Chris Yates

Chapter Five – The Avon Barbel

reached into his jacket pocket for his tobacco pouch with his spare hand. Loading his pipe and tamping down the tobacco, he struck a match one-handed, with practised ease, setting the tobacco alight. With a gentle sigh, he sent a billow of rich Whisky pipe smoke adrift across the river and then finally applied himself to the task of landing his barbel. I could read his mind; "The barbel are feeding, the tobacco is mellow and all is right with the world!" If angling is truly the contemplative mans recreation, then I know of no better angler.

I took my camera and climbed across the Pipe to photograph his Five-pounder. I was on my way back when Dunkeld looked up at me and shouted "Skeff, I'm hooked up in the weed. Can you see where I'm snagged from up there?" Of course there was no weed in the swim and I just had time to shout "It's a fish!" before his rod thumped round into its full curve and the barbel swept away downstream. I nearly fell in as I swung down to help but I needn't have rushed because Dunkeld quickly had the fish under control. Like a veteran barbel angler he ran downstream of his fish, using the current to tire it out ready for the net. By the time I reached him it was all over and he was smiling down at a stunning Eight pound barbel that had shoulders like a bull. Not only was it the finest "first barbel" anyone has ever caught, it was also two pounds heavier than my own best barbel, and I vowed to return the next day to see if I could catch one as big.

When we returned, I elected to fish the head of the Pipe slack from the opposite bank to where I had been the day before. A bright winter sun cast shadows across a cold and frosted landscape from an azure blue sky, and although it was a lovely day to be out in the fresh air, conditions couldn't have been worse for catching a barbel. I spent the first hour filling a feeder with maggots and casting to the head of the slack but I didn't even have a dace-tap on the rod tip to arouse my interest. Everyone else, apart from Dunkeld, had gone up to the big weir for a game of Frisbee, but Dunkeld wanted to fish on, fired by his success, and I was happy to keep him company.

Just for something to do, I cast again, but this time instead of letting the feeder settle I flicked the rod to keep it bouncing down through the swim. Half way through the slack I felt a slight tap, a strange vibration through the rod, and then a firmer knock which I struck. It was definitely a fish but although it held out in the flow it didn't feel very big and the bite had been very finicky, so I thought I'd hooked either a small barbel or a slightly better chub. I wanted some photographs of me playing a fish on my newly acquired Allcock's Super Wizard so I called Dunkeld over to help. I held the fish lightly on a gently curved rod while I explained to Dunkeld how to work my camera and described the sort of photograph I wanted to get.

"Ok," I said. "I'm going to land it just down below the Pipe, so get ready to take some shots of it as I use the net." With that I bent into the fish, expecting it to come in easily but instead the rod just bent through to the butt and the clutch on my Hardy Altex only just gave line in time to prevent a disaster. "Bloody hell!" I exclaimed, "It's bigger than I thought…" I played what was clearly a barbel quite firmly for the next few minutes and although it didn't do anything too dramatic my estimate of its

size kept growing. It had tucked itself under some dense weed in the middle of the river and every time I moved below the fish and applied some pressure to get it moving, it would turn and surge back across the flow and into the safety of this haven. I was unable to stop these ponderous, powerful runs and on just six-pound line I had to let it go where it wanted. All the time, Dunkeld was clicking away with my camera, oblivious to the tension I was now feeling. At one point he even asked me to turn my head slightly to improve the framing of the shot.

Eventually, the barbel showed its first sign of weakness. I teased it out from cover again but this time, instead of sweeping back to the same lie, it turned with the current and ran downstream into another weedbed. I repeated the process of slowly increasing the pressure from downstream and then holding

the rod bent, with the line singing at breaking point, and again the barbel turned and ran but with less power this time and more panic. Whilst its early runs had been purposeful and determined thrusts in a specific direction, now it just ran blindly, looking for any possible sanctuary. For the first time I stopped it short of the weed and turned it back under my own bank. I found I could draw it up off the riverbed now and Dunkeld readied the net, then swept it under the fish as it rolled at the surface. I panicked, thinking he might miss and snap the line, but Dunkeld is an expert at netting salmon and he never misses a fish.

The barbel was not much longer than Dunkeld's fish of the previous day but where his barbel had muscular shoulders, mine was solid throughout its length and its girth was enormous. At Ten pounds Four ounces, it was my first double and although I've landed bigger, I still count it as my favourite barbel. Better still, Dunkeld had captured the whole fight in a series of photographs that still make me smile to this day.

Dunkeld and I shared a dram from my hip flask to celebrate before he went up to the weir to look for the others and tell them the good news. I went back to the swim and decided to have another cast before I got the kettle going for some tea. This time the feeder didn't even settle and I felt it rattling across the gravel as a fish dropped downstream with the bait. I struck into another big barbel and when Dunkeld arrived with the others it was just in time to see me slip a Seven and a half pounder back into the shallow water below the Pipe.

My most memorable encounter with an Avon barbel was at Ibsley, fishing a deep, slow bend well downstream of Ibsley Weir. Chris was with me and we were heading for a lovely barbel glide he knew that lay a few fields below the weir pool. To get there we had to pass the Slumber Pool, as Chris knew it, and I fell in love with this intimate piece of water as soon as I saw it. I told Chris I wanted to stay and have a cast or two there and so he headed off upstream by himself, leaving me to tackle-up amongst the thicket of willow carr beside the bend.

I'd discovered The Severn Oaks water on the River Severn by this time and I set up my tackle to fish a big piece of freelined meat, using the tactics that had proven to be so successful for the Severn barbel. The Severn Oaks water deserves a chapter of its own, so you can read about it elsewhere in this book, but suffice to say that your average Avon angler would consider the tactics that I used there to be laughably crude and simple. Even though I thought the tactics would work equally as well on the Avon as they did on the Severn, I was quite glad that I could hide behind the willow as I tied a size 1/0 Aberdeen Long Shank hook to the end of my six pound line and loaded it with a quarter of a tin of bacon grill for bait. I didn't want any serious Avon barbel experts spotting my set up because I knew I'd suffer no end of ribbing if one did…

I swung the baited hook out gently into the head of the slow, deep pool. I cast right into the thickest of the ranunculus beds above the bend and eased the bait down through the fronds of weed, keeping in touch on a moderately tight line as the bait bounced down the gravel bed of the river towards me. On that first cast I felt the knock of a fish as it attacked the bait. It was typical of the bites I'd grown to expect on the Severn, a few sharp, well-spaced knocks followed by a long slow pull as the barbel grabbed the meat and ran for shelter.

I'd never hooked a barbel of such power before I struck into that fish and I've never played one as powerful since. For ten minutes or more the barbel simply did as it pleased. Sometimes it plodded slowly and purposefully around the pool, sometimes it ran upstream against the full force of the current and fully bent rod, and sometimes it just sulked immovably in the depths. I never felt in control and I knew instinctively that the fish could smash my inadequate tackle whenever it wanted.

I'm not going to draw out the description of the fight because the memory is too painful even now, but I only caught a glimpse of the barbel once, as it turned deeply in a shaft of sunlight at the head of the bend. Eventually, it embedded itself solidly in a weedbed and none of my tricks could get it moving again. In the end I moved downstream of the fish and bent into it as hard as I could to try and get it to move. It suddenly thumped the rod tip down unexpectedly, just as I applied the maximum pressure that the tackle could take, and the line parted with a sharp crack before the loose end knotted itself around the tip of my straight, lifeless rod.

How big? I've seen the cased specimen of the barbel foul hooked by Mr C Cassey on 6th March 1960, when he was spinning for salmon in the pool below Ibsley Bridge, and I think my own Ibsley barbel was much larger. Mr Cassey's fish (pictured in a famous photograph being held by Colonel Crow) weighed Sixteen pounds One ounce and its cased remains are a lasting testimony to its existence. My big barbel is a weightless, ephemeral memory of a golden flash in the depths of an Avon pool.

Along the Ashmead Drove

From the back lanes of the village of Ash, an ancient cattle drove dips down to the Sedgemoor levels and runs as straight as a roman highway through the fields towards the River Yeo. The drove is one of a network of byways used by generations of local dairymen to turn out their cattle into the many small fields of the Witcombe Bottoms.

Llewellyn Powys described the landscape through which the drove slices as "timeless" in his Somerset Essays, published in 1930. The unchanged patchwork of rich meadows and thick Somerset hedges is testament to the accuracy of his description and Powys would still recognise the countryside today. Powys wrote that *"Izaak Walton would have found these fields to his liking. In such water-meadows he would have felt himself no stranger, listening to the dairymaid's song as he came along Cows-Lease-Drove, his creel on shoulder, full of 'leather-mouthed' chub lying on moss."*

Powys described how the farming and sporting practices of the time marked the march of the seasons. At that time, the River Yeo was still the strongest natural influence in the landscape it had created and the seasonal moods of the river also shaped the rural traditions. These days, the river has been canalised and tamed, to a degree, by the draining of the levels and the installation of the vast pumping station at Long Load. But its presence remains a vital force, despite man's best efforts to dominate its power.

When Powys wrote his essay on 'The Sporting Dairymen of Sedgemoor', the annual auction of the Kingsmoor leases marked the start of the farming year. When the winter floods subsided and the land had dried sufficiently to be used by livestock, the local farmers gathered in an area called 'the Island' to bid competitively for the grazing rights. It is likely that their forefathers had followed the same practice since mediaeval times. Grazing secured for the year, the fields of Witcombe were stocked with colts, cattle and sheep from the small, mixed farms of Witcombe and Ash. For a while, the droves would be busy with jostling animals, eager to reach the lush pastures where they remained until the autumn floods returned the meadows to the dominion of the river.

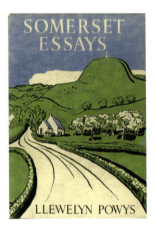

Late spring brought the first flush of elvers in from the sea. Elvers are still a highly prized and valuable catch and on any early summer night when the tide is favourable, the rhynes of the Somerset levels are marked out with twinkling lights, as the elver men ply their nets. Competition is fierce and serious fights have been known to break out over access to the prime netting stations.

When I worked as a fisheries scientist in the North West, I used to monitor the elver catch on the Wyre in Lancashire. The sight of millions of tiny, thread-like elvers flooding in on the tide and then wriggling upstream along the margins of the river is a natural wonder I feel privileged to have seen. There was a weir that formed a barrier that the migrating elvers were only just able to pass. At the peak of the tidal flood, the sill became a black mass of writhing elvers that glistened in the moonlight, so that it seemed as if the stonework itself had melted and come to life.

In Powys' time, May and early June brought out the eel-baiters with their primitive but deadly tackle, to crop the adult eels. Almost every villager from Ash and Martock gathered on the levels to harvest the annual bounty.

I've never tried "bobbing" for eels but it sounds like great fun. Lobworms are threaded onto a strand of coarse wool, which is rolled into a ball and dangled into the river on the end of a long pole. The eel's teeth become entwined in the wool when they grab the worms and the "bobber" can simply lift them out and shake them off into a tub. I must give it a go one day.

I heard recently about an extreme, modern version of bobbing that takes the approach to a whole new level. Apparently the trick is to bury three or four chicken carcases in a weighted bale of straw and then lower it into the river. It is then left for a week to allow the eels to burrow into the bale after the chicken meat, at which point the bale is pulled out with a tractor, complete with literally hundreds of eels of all sizes. I must say I prefer the sound of the more traditional approach!

On their downstream migration to the Bristol Channel and across the Atlantic, the adult eels pass the incoming generation of elvers that has drifted as plankton on the whim of the Atlantic currents, from the breeding grounds in the Sargasso Sea. No one understands the means by which the adult eels navigate, let alone how a life-cycle dependent upon the vagaries of the oceanic gyres evolved. I have always found the life cycle and migration of the eel to be more fascinating and mysterious even than that of the salmon. Nature's miracles should command our respect and it always annoys me when I see an angler abusing a bootlace eel that has snaffled his maggots and tangled his line.

Ashmead is a wildfowl shoot of some note, although it has always been managed as a low-key affair enjoyed by the local farmers, rather than as a money making venture. Flights of mallard, teal and widgeon whistle in from the moor each winter, accompanied by an occasional skein of geese. On a clear winter evening, the flights are outlined against the dying sun and starlit skies, providing difficult, fast moving targets, mere shadows for the guns. The wildfowling is superb, not only because of the quality of the environment but also because Ashmead is so remote and the duck are hardly ever disturbed. In winter, the only disturbance is from the fox hunt, which traditionally visits the Witcombe Meadows each season. According to Powys, there was a particular covert where *"the Blackmore Vale foxhounds never drew a blank."* These days the hunting ban restricts traditional hunting but members of the Seavington Hunt still gather to pursue this rural pastime each winter, within the constraints that the law now imposes.

It is in the winter months, too, that the long-eared owls arrive, taking shelter amongst the thick hedges and on the branches of the crack-willows during the daytime, then haunting the meadows at night. These owls are huge, yet very difficult to spot because they perch motionless in the fork of the willow branches where there plumage blends perfectly with the mottled grey bark. Often you sense their large yellow eyes following you, long before you see them. Steve Maynard once counted fourteen of these owls at the pool at once, which must be some sort of a record parliament.

The activities of the farmers, eel-men, wildfowlers and huntsmen are still bound by traditions as strong and as ancient as the hedgerows of the mediaeval field system. Indeed, their culture shaped the very countryside itself and was in turn determined by the natural history of the levels and the annual cycle of the seasons. In recent times, industrial agriculture, the decline of the rural communities and even the recent hunting ban have all threatened this landscape and its pastoral way of life, yet somehow it has survived. As you wander down Ashmead Drove on a still summer evening, with the rooks cawing in the crack-willows and the chiff chaffs scolding from the blackthorn hedges on either side, it feels as if it always will.

The scene is set; I walked into it to take my minor role upon the Ashmead stage nearly thirty years ago, when I had just discovered carp, and hunting waters that held them was an obsession. Ashmead was the first pool I fished that held a substantial number of double-figure carp (the fish of my dreams) and I was to learn most of my carp fishing skills stalking the banks of this lovely Somerset wetland.

The carp were introduced to Ashmead in the early 1970's "from a Surrey trout farm" and I suspect that they may be some of the last carp produced by Donald Leney before his retirement. I have the Leney stocking records on loan from Chris Yates and I am hunting for any reference to the pool, so far without success. The Ashmead carp may be pure 'Galiceans' but they are more likely to be a derivative strain, bred at the Haslemere farm from the original imports from Holland. On the other hand, the carp may not be Leney's at all and may have come from another source altogether.

One day I will find out but, either way, many of the Ashmead carp certainly have the look of the Leney strain and are exhibiting the classic Leney longevity and growth.

Their growth has in fact been quite phenomenal. In the mid 1990's Steve Maynard, who owned Ashmead, dug a separate, three-acre lake called Goat Willow Pool in the heart of the seventeen acres of wetland. He stocked about fifty double-figure fish from the main wetland area into the new pond and it is these carp that now form the backbone of the Ashmead stock.

The rich environment of Goat Willow, combined with the low stock density, allowed the carp to grow to their true potential: genetics and the environment coming together with spectacular results. The only carp weighing less than twenty pounds in the pool nowadays are offspring of the original fish. Most of the original stock is now approaching thirty pounds in weight, with many commons and mirrors of thirty pounds, upwards to over fifty pounds.

I am jumping ahead of myself. Let me take you back to the beginning and the first time I followed Ashmead Drove across the Witcombe Bottoms.

Every visit to a new carp pool is special and my memories of that first day at Ashmead are still as clear as if it were yesterday. It was late summer and the hedges smelled of dog rose and honeysuckle. I thought I was lost as I bumped along the rutted drove on my bike and only when I reached the secluded gateway and caught the first scent of water did I know that I had arrived. It was BB who said that all the best carp lakes were to be found down narrow, winding lanes.

There is something special about a gated pool. Heavy gates block the entrances to both Ashmead and Pitt Pond (two of my favourite waters) and the act of heaving them open on groaning, rusted hinges, is like a rite of passage. The gates mark out the confines of these pools as special, private places to which only a privileged few have access. There is also something about the first glimpse of the pool, through the restricted iris of the gated entrance, which adds to an air of mystery and intimacy.

At Ashmead, the original gate leads to a rickety bridge across a dyke and then to a few crumbling steps that take you onto the bank of Tom's Pond, one of the three main areas of open water that are linked by a maze of serpentine channels that writhe through the sedge.

That first view encapsulates everything that makes Ashmead special. The heavily weeded water is overhung by two weeping willows at the eastern end and opposite, from each of the western corners of the roughly square pool, two channels lead off into large beds of reedmace. The channels are each about the width of a small canal and they lead the eye and imagination into the heart of the fishery. You are faced immediately with conflicting urges to stop and fish the open water in front of you or to follow the channels deeper into the whispering sedge, to discover the mysteries they conceal. Ashmead is a paradise for anglers who love stalking carp and adopt a mobile approach.

I caught two carp on that first day, both mirrors of about Ten to Twelve pounds, which I tempted on floating baits. I explored the whole fishery, creeping around the channels and throwing a few floaters out here and there into the weedbeds. By the time I had completed the first circuit, several carp had discovered the new food source and the weed in some of the baited pitches bulged and swayed as fish sought out the individual mixers. I was fascinated by how methodical and precise the carp were, carefully locating and testing each bait with their lips before sipping it down gently.

It looked as if it would be easy to catch one but appearances can be deceptive and the carp were far wiser than they first seemed. Several times I found myself watching a bow wave disappear along the channel ahead, when my approach towards a moving fish was too clumsy. Casting the bait too close to a feeding carp caused them to melt away, yet casting beyond the fish and trying to draw the bait back into its path usually caused the hook to catch in the hornwort stems, with the same frustrating result. Any abnormal resistance of line or hook snagging the weed as the carp tried to take a bait led to its instant rejection and at times the carp seemed to show a mystic ability to differentiate between the free offerings and the hookbait.

I hooked four carp, which all fought insanely hard, making searing runs along the channels as soon as the hook struck home. I had to jump in and follow the fleeing fish, unpicking the line from the dense weed as I went. The channels varied in depth from two to ten feet and the bed was often thick with accumulated silt. By the end of the day I was filthy, soaking wet and smelling like an old compost heap but I was very, very happy and had enjoyed the best day's carp fishing I'd ever experienced. Two fish shed the hook in the dense weed but the two that I netted successfully were stunning specimens and as large as any carp I'd ever caught. It had been a challenging and thrilling day and I had learned more about carp behaviour in one afternoon than in all the preceding seasons. My long-lasting love affair with Ashmead had begun.

That first visit set the pattern for the next few seasons. The Ashmead carp were a challenging quarry but it was usually possible to catch two or three fish on each visit if I was careful and the gods smiled. As I honed my fishing skills through experience, the carp too became more attuned to my careful approach and the fishing was a constant test of initiative and my ability to stay one step ahead of the fish. Only by stalking their quarry at close quarters can an angler really engage in this intimate game of strategy. The constantly evolving set of challenges presented by the stalking approach is why I love this form of fishing so much.

I also love the direct contact with the carp, getting close enough to see the way the carp behaves, to see every fin-flick and eye movement. I love the thrill of watching the fish you have selected approach and take the bait and the explosive energy of the fight when the hook is set at close range. Stalking is endlessly fascinating and can leave you shaken with the adrenalin rush caused by a confrontation with a big fish.

The pleasure of Ashmead reached far beyond the challenge presented by the carp. The wetland was a haven for wildlife and I know of few places that are more alive. I've seen every species of dragonfly and damsel fly that is indigenous to the South West skimming the surface of the pool. The butterflies can be spectacular, and green veined whites can be found in numbers amongst the sallows each summer. Summer and winter migrants refresh the resident bird life, so the mix of species is constantly changing. I saw my first hobbies at Ashmead, hunting large hawker dragonflies between the reedbeds. I also saw my first egret here and one spring a migrating osprey dropped in for a brief respite from its journey north after a winter in Africa. There are the owls of course (long-eared, tawny and barn owls all haunt the pool) and in summer, the reedbeds and sallows sing with the fluted, tumbling cascade of notes of the willow, sedge and reed warblers.

The most spectacular animal reportedly sighted at the pool is a Siberian lynx, a large white cat that has been seen by several anglers over the years. I'm a little sceptical but if there is anywhere that an escaped big cat could survive undisturbed and find enough rabbits and other prey for food, the dense undergrowth around Ashmead is that place.

I continued to fish Ashmead at least once a year even when I had moved out of the area to go to university, find a job and eventually get married. I also continued to help the owner, Steve Maynard, with the development of the fishery and helped advise him on the creation and stocking of Goat Willow Pool in 1995.

When I moved back to Somerset with Shona and the children in 2002, I was delighted when Steve invited me back to fish. Steve told me that little had changed at the lake, except that the carp had grown. Steve always was a master of understatement. I joined the syndicate in 2003 and realised just how *much* the carp had grown when I hooked the first carp of the year, and after a dour fight brought a graceful linear mirror of just less than Thirty pounds to the net. At the time it was the largest carp I'd caught.

Close observation of the movements of the carp allowed me to catch my first Thirty-pounder a few weeks later, by lightly baiting a small clear patch in the weed that I'd seen a large carp visit on several occasions to feed. Then, in September, I hooked a carp in the margin of one of the small bays that led me a merry dance all over the lake. When I finally drew the near leather carp over the drawstring of my large landing net, I realised immediately that I'd caught a personal best for the third time within the course of a single season. The carp was tremendously long and broad across the shoulders and it shone like polished marble in the dawn light. The members had named the carp Moonscale after the large scale on its shoulder and it weighed Thirty One pounds Ten ounces.

Moonscale remains the largest fish I've caught on a centerpin reel. I used a sturdy stalking reel called the Cob which has ball-bearings rather than a true pin and a finger break, which helps when struggling to net a large fish; the brake 'gives' just enough when applied to dampen the last, panicky plunges of a fish when it sees the mesh. Every carp angler should experience the direct feeling of playing a big carp on the pin, rather than through the gears and clutch of a fixed spool, before they hang up their rods and retire.

The best was still to come. A week later I returned to the lake for a short evening session. I crept around the margins and found a huge common cruising through the weedbeds at the back of a small island. One at a time I flicked out a few mixers, being careful to avoid spooking the carp. I left the area in peace but when I returned half an hour later I thought the carp had gone. Then I noticed a mixer, just a few feet from the bank, begin to spin in the surface film before sinking into a small whirlpool. Other than the movement of the floater, the surface was completely undisturbed and for a second I thought I'd been hallucinating. Then a second mixer a few inches away vanished in the same manner and I realised that a carp must be lying just out of sight below the surface, sucking the bait down like some large sub-aquatic vacuum cleaner.

I replaced the last mixer with the hookbait by simply lowering the bait onto the surface from the rod tip. A few seconds later, it disappeared and the line drew taught, so that all I had to do was to raise the rod to set the hook. For a fraction of a second nothing happened as the carp gathered itself, but then the rod slammed over as it tore off along the margin in a blind panic. I like to backwind when playing a carp on my old Mitchell but this time I had to follow the carp along the bank to ease the pressure and keep up with the speed of that first run. The carp led me fifty yards or so along the bank under sustained pressure before it turned and sped back the way it had come. A series of plunging, determined runs followed that had me praying that the hook hold was a good one. The area was fairly open and free of weed and snags, however, I felt confident that I would win, provided that the hook held.

It was nearly ten minutes before I scooped the mesh of my landing net around the frame of a magnificent common of Thirty Three pounds Eight ounces. I've always found commons to be more attractive than mirrors and at the time this carp was by far the biggest common I'd ever landed. It was simply stunning and set the seal on my best season in more than twenty years of carp fishing. Ashmead had welcomed me back in spectacular style.

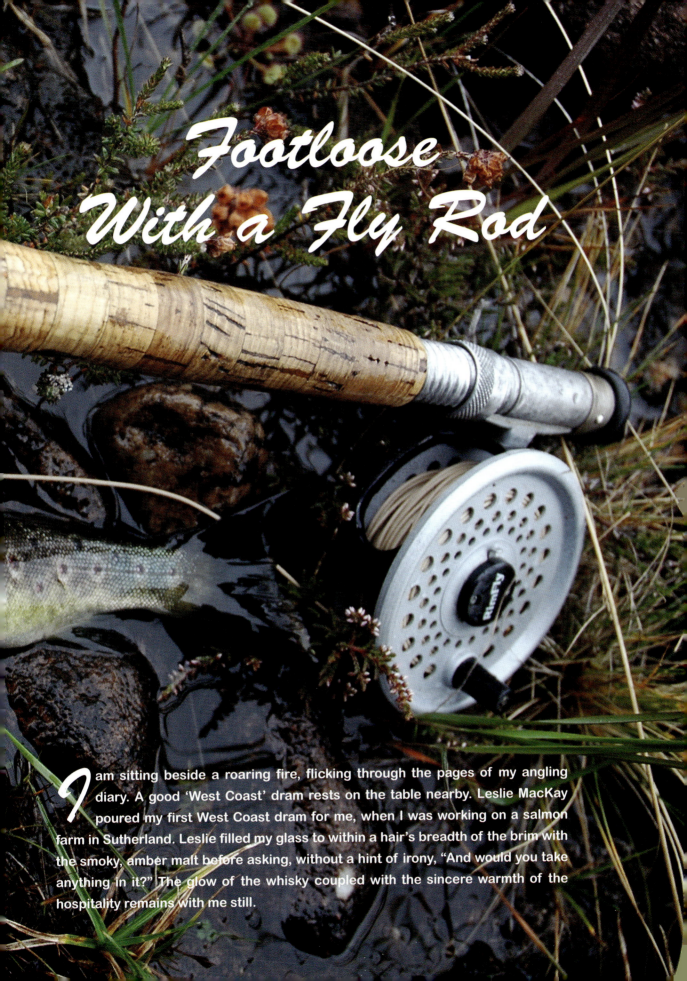

Footloose With a Fly Rod

I am sitting beside a roaring fire, flicking through the pages of my angling diary. A good 'West Coast' dram rests on the table nearby. Leslie MacKay poured my first West Coast dram for me, when I was working on a salmon farm in Sutherland. Leslie filled my glass to within a hair's breadth of the brim with the smoky, amber malt before asking, without a hint of irony, "And would you take anything in it?" The glow of the whisky coupled with the sincere warmth of the hospitality remains with me still.

A piercing wind is rattling the windows of our cottage and it feels cold enough for snow. Winter has always been a low ebb in the year for me. The short days and eternal nights depress my spirit and the damp cold of southern England seeps into my bones, sapping my energy. My mind wanders north, to sharp winter days enjoyed climbing in the Cairngorms, when the sky was bright and the ground snow-crisp under foot. On days like this one could see forever and life was icily clear. Here in the south such days are rare and there are no mountains upon which to savour them. In their absence, winter is that bit more depressing and spiteful.

As an angler, I like this season even less. The trout season has drawn to a close and it feels too cold for the late season barbel. This is a time for fires, whisky, old diaries and good angling books, for reminiscing and planning the summer ahead.

This evening my mind has been drawn six hundred miles north, by the fiery taste of the malt and a hurried scribble discovered in my diary. It says simply "August. Sutherland. Ten miles. Three lochs and four good trout (returned)." It is surprising how few words are needed to evoke vivid memories of a day's fishing. Just a few stilted phrases on the page and I am back amongst the Sutherland heather.

Of all the areas of the British Isles where I have fished, Sutherland and Torridon stand out when I think of trout and salmon. Nowhere else is the sense of natural grandeur, of remote beauty, of wilderness so overwhelming, as amongst the barren moors around Ullapool. In the Sutherland landscape, man's influence pales into insignificance when confronted by the mountains that dominate the scenery. The mountains stand alone and remote, lesser in height than their Cairngorm counterparts but far greater in stature. A list of their names reads like a stanza of Viking poetry - Quinnag, Suilven, Ben Mor Coigach and Foinhaven; names that stir the soul or freeze the blood; dragons had names such as these.

On a bright sunny day the mountains appear benign and the moors below their peaks sparkle with the reflections from a hundred lochs. These lochs are the jewels of the landscape and the Ordnance Survey maps are speckled with sapphire promises. They vary in size from pools that are little more than a peat bog to vast inland seas, where the far shore is just a shadow across the water.

My work with the fish farming industry first brought me to the area when I was in my early twenties. Fresh-faced and bursting with enthusiasm, I had come back from my three months in the Torres Straight to face the reality that the world only needed one Jacques Cousteau and that the job was taken.

After several months driving delivery vans, working in the local builder's merchants and serving in a pub, I finally found an advertisement for a vacancy in Aberdeen. The interview went well and I secured a job, working in conjunction with the government marine laboratory to research the commercial triploidisation of Atlantic salmon. I didn't have a clue what that meant but if I would be working with salmon, in quite a well paid scientific job, that was good enough for me!

In fact, triploidisation is a means of making salmon sterile through tampering with their genetic make-up. The process is potentially of huge benefit to the fish farming industry because salmon stop growing when they mature and their flesh quality deteriorates rapidly. In any population of salmon, sometimes more than thirty percent of the stock will mature as grilse after just one year spent growing in the sea and the fish farmer must sell these small fish within a short marketing window. The grilse need to be sorted from the salmon that are still growing, which is labour intensive and can damage the more valuable fish that the farmer is going to keep. All of this means that grilse are a nuisance. If sterile fish can be produced on a commercial scale, it would mean that the salmon farmer could have a predictable stock that requires minimal handling and that would maintain its quality, so that it could be marketed throughout the year.

To achieve this you first need to generate a stock of all female fish, because only female triploids maintain their flesh quality (male triploids can still go through the physical changes associated with maturation). Treating a population of newly hatched salmon that are just starting to feed with the male sex hormone means that the females will develop physically as males, even though they retain the female genetic blueprint. As these fish mature, it is possible to select the fish that are genetically female but have male reproductive organs that produce viable sperm. If the sperm from these 'sex reversed' females are crossed with the eggs of a normal female, the resulting young will be an entirely female population of fish.

If the eggs of these salmon are then triploidised, the population of all female triploids that is produced will be sterile. It's as simple as that...

The triploidisation process involved treating the eggs in batches of 2 litres at a time in a large, water charged pressure vessel at a set time after they have been fertilised. The pressure vessel takes the eggs up to pressures of 9,500 pounds per square inch, which hampers the normal developmental processes, causing the eggs to develop with three sets of chromosomes instead of the normal two. Using hydrostatic pressure we could ensure that all of the fry that hatched would be triploid and that survival rates would be very similar to those of untreated eggs.

It all sounds like a bit of a Frankenstein process and in truth I had real qualms about getting involved in the research and commercialisation of the techniques. The major benefit that justified the research from my perspective, though, wasn't to do with improving the commercial efficiency of salmon production, it was that I believed that the production of sterile salmon on farms was an essential tool to protect the diminishing stocks of wild Scottish salmon. The possible escape of salmon from fish farms threatens the wild stocks because of the risk that they will enter the rivers and breed with the wild salmon, undoing thousands of years of genetic selection in the blink of an eye or the flick of a fin. The production of sterile triploids removed that risk and from my point of view this alone made commercialisation of the complicated science worthwhile.

Unfortunately, the industry shared the same qualms about the effect such genetic manipulation would have on the wholesome, pedigree image of their farmed Scottish salmon as I did and the work wasn't a commercial success. In a sense, I think that was the right decision for the industry from a marketing perspective but sadly it meant that the wild stocks are still threatened every time a farm cage sinks or a net splits in a storm.

Quite aside from any concerns I might have had about the genetic manipulation of the fish farmed salmon stocks, the job was a joy because of the opportunity it gave me to explore the rugged landscape of western Scotland. I would leave Aberdeen at five in the morning and drive the back routes to Ullapool and beyond. The road led through Donside and across the cold shoulder of the Lecht, before it dropped into the comparative homeliness of the Spey valley at Grantown. From here I would head west to Inverness, across the Moray Firth with its dolphins and on to Ullapool. After a brief wander along Ullapool's bustling quay, I would turn northwards into the Sutherland wilderness.

Work would start immediately on arrival at the salmon farm and I spent long summer days sorting fish and taking samples for the experimental studies I was managing. Then, from about six in the evening, my time was my own and during the endless days of mid-summer there might be five or six hours of daylight and dusk remaining. These were precious hours in which I would set off across the moors with backpack and fly rod or scramble up the precarious slopes of one of the Highland peaks. Sometimes work would keep me in the area for a week or more but often I would travel back to Aberdeen the same night and collapse exhausted into bed.

I came to love the west coast, its scenery and its people. Good people, like Leslie Mackay, who took their time in getting to know you, took longer to accept you and whose friendship meant so much more

because of that. I'd worked with Leslie for nearly two years before he poured me that dram; hard days on the fish farm and long winter nights staying at his family croft, from which his wife Amanda provided bed and breakfast. The dry humour with which he filled my glass reflected the generous spirit with which the west coast locals took you to their hearts, once they had decided that you were alright.

When I didn't stay with the MacKays, I'd stop with a lovely elderly couple called Ruraidh and Moragh. They were both in their eighties and both still worked from dawn to dusk, as they had without a break for holiday or illness throughout their lives. Ruraidh was an ox of a man and he could still heave in a net full of salmon on the fish farm cages faster than many men half his age. Ruraidh and Moragh were 'Wee Free's', staunch Presbyterians who would do nothing on the Sabbath other than pray, read the bible and go to church. Moragh wouldn't cook on a Sunday but she would leave cold cuts of beef out from the Saturday meal and if I was heathen enough to make myself a sandwich she didn't object.

I remember working with Ruraidh one winter day on a little freshwater loch cage, weighing and measuring the two thousand young salmon parr it held. The sleet and snow were horizontal and incessant and by the time we finished I was soaked to the skin, despite my oilskins, and freezing cold. In fact, I was so cold that my hand had nearly frozen where I had been dipping in and out of the freshwater to catch the small salmon; and there was a thin glaze of ice across the back of my hand. "It's a hell of a day," I said to Ruraidh at one point. He was wearing his usual work shirt and no waterproofs at all. "Aye," he said, looking up briefly from his work. "It's a wee bit misty." He was as hard as nails.

Ruraidh was the "watcher" on the salmon farm, ensuring that the salmon stayed put in the cages and didn't disappear under the cover of darkness. He was also the bailiff on a river which has one of the best salmon runs on the west coast. After a keen salmon fishing friend and colleague of mine had known Ruraidh for a couple of years, Ruraidh invited him to fish the river on his next visit. He duly timed his work carefully to coincide with the prime grilse run and arrived in September to stay with the couple, taking his fishing tackle with him.

After work Ruraidh and my colleague headed up to the local pub for a beer and a dram. There was quite a crowd in the bar that night and one drink led to several more and it seemed that Ruraidh had forgotten about the fishing tip. Then, just when it was almost dark outside, Ruraidh sobered up suddenly in the way that only a west coaster can after half a bottle of malt and said "Come on then, let's go and catch some salmon."

They headed up to the river but by the time they got there it was well after dark. Ruraidh parked near the bridge and my friend went to get his rod from the boot of the car. "You won't be needing that..." said Ruraidh and nimble as a stag he leapt over the fence and was off into the darkness, where the river roared in its autumnal spate. A short length of wire appeared in his hand and he went down on his hands and knees next to the first pool, feeling in the water below some tree roots with his other hand. In short order he had a large grilse out on the bank beside him and with a swift tap on the head with his priest, he dispatched his catch and headed back to the car. "Ruraidh," my friend asked in hushed tones, "isn't this a bit illegal?" "Och, it's just for the pot," he replied, with the oldest and easiest justification of the poacher. "Anyway, I'm on duty tonight and I'll no be turning myself in!"

My favourite tale of illicit goings on though was published in the Glasgow Evening Herald. Apparently, one Christmas the residents of a local housing estate awoke to find a parcel of salmon on their doorstep, with a card saying "Merry Christmas! From your local poacher." One concerned lady rang the police immediately and asked what she should do with the fish. "Well madam," the local bobby advised "if it was me, I'd poach it lightly with some parsley butter and serve it with some steamed vegetables..."

I digress! I could enthuse for pages about the work, people, mountains and wildlife of the west coast but this is a fishing book and I should come to the topic in hand. Let me take you back then, to that August day and those "Ten miles. Three lochs and four good trout."

The tactics employed on these fishing expeditions were based upon a simple, uncluttered approach. I found that the location of feeding areas was always more important than any choice of fly or finesse in presentation. Indeed, the enjoyment of the fishing lay partly in the simplicity of the style employed. The angling was about immersion into the landscape and its natural rhythms, rather than technical intricacies that detracted from these more esoteric pleasures.

The key to success was in timing my arrival on the loch shore to coincide with one of the feeding periods of its residents. That might sound simple but in reality it entailed careful planning, local knowledge and an understanding of contours. Each loch was unique and size and depth often varied considerably between lochs less than a mile apart. The trick was to plan a circular yomp across the heather that took in two or three lochs and time the journey so that one arrived at the prime feeding time for each water.

The larger, shallow lochs were usually productive environments, with plenty of weed and insect life upon which the trout thrived. These lochs also provided ideal spawning habitat and were often crowded with small fish. Amongst these, one occasionally encountered a larger individual that had benefited from the rich and varied diet. Such shallow lochs warmed and cooled quickly. They usually fished well in the early morning and early evening but were a waste of time during the heat of the day or after-dusk chill.

The deeper lochs were hostile environments for both trout and angler alike. They often contained fish stunted through lack of food and any small wet fly would be snatched immediately by a starving four-inch brownie. The pleasure of catching such easy prey was limited but they were amongst the prettiest trout I've seen. They invariably had a mixture of large blood-red and jet-black spots, overlaying scales of the same peaty gold as the loch water. These lochs sometimes contained a population of large and voracious ferox trout that had adopted a predatory lifestyle and waxed fat upon their lesser brethren. The deep water took a long time to warm up but these lochs would produce fish from late morning onwards and well into the evening.

Best of all were the lochs that lay between these two extremes and had both deep bays and weeded shallows. On a good day, the edge of the deeper water could produce a succession of fish of all sizes from dawn until dark.

The ideal rod for these excursions was my five-weight Scottie, which fitted easily into the ice axe straps of my rucksack. This rod had enough backbone to cover most of the lochs adequately from the shore. It was responsive enough to make the playing of lesser fish entertaining but retained sufficient power to counteract the runs of a bigger trout, should I be fortunate enough to hook one.

The first of the three lochs visited on that August day was four miles from the road. I followed a gurgling burn down through a tight little glen and arrived at mid-morning beside a large shallow bay at the loch's western end. The loch was a lovely place to make my first cast of the day. It nestled in a gentle bowl of heather moorland with the Sutherland peaks as a backdrop. Someone had tipped a pot of purple heather over the hillside and it flowed down the slope and into the burn where it was diluted in reflection and washed away into the expanse of shimmering water.

The first of the three lochs visited on that August day was four miles from the road. I arrived at mid-morning beside a large shallow bay at the loch's western end. Choice of fly was simple, Pheasant Tail nymph on the top dropper and size 10 Pennel on the point, fished on an intermediate line. The day was bright and a warm, blustery wind rattled the dry heather.

The wind was very welcome, partly because it would blow insects into the lochs and encourage the trout to feed but mainly because it would deter that curse of the West Coast, the midge. It's hard to believe a creature so small is capable of causing such intense discomfort and irritation. It is great sport to sit in one's car on Ullapool quay and watch the flailing tourists trying to enjoy the view from amongst a shroud of these venomous insects. Incidentally, the only effective midge deterrent I have found is an Avon bath oil called Skin So Soft, applied neat to exposed areas. Apparently it is so effective that the US Marines

used it to protect against sand flies during the Gulf War. Imagine the Iraqis, confronted by America's fighting elite, armed to the teeth and smelling of Evening Primrose!

I circled the loch until I reached the windward shore before starting to fish. My casting range would be restricted but I knew there was deep water close in and that the trout would have followed the drifting food down-wind. The very first cast confirmed the assumption, with a quick snatch that I failed to hook. Three more casts of no more than ten yards and there was a more positive take. I tightened into a fish that dashed towards the shore faster than I could strip line. When I regained contact, I simply raised the rod and plucked a surprised five-incher from the water beneath my feet!

Four casts produced two identical fish. Then I struck a slow draw on the tail fly and found myself attached to something of a different calibre altogether. The trout hung deep in the water and cruised away parallel to the bank, taking line against the full pressure of the rod. Despite applying as much strain as I dared to the three pound leader, I couldn't turn the fish and was forced to follow it a short way along the shore. Then it sounded and made a series of deep, diving runs before the pressure told. It shone like amber as it came to the net. He was a male of just under Two pounds with an aggressive kype; not the monster I expected but an encouraging start to the day. I had to nurse the trout in the margin for nearly ten minutes before he flicked his tail and disappeared back into the depths.

It was mid-day and I found a sheltered heather bed upon which to enjoy lunch before walking the two miles to the next loch. Leslie MacKay's sandwiches were as generous as his drams and I must have dozed for nearly an hour in the warm sunshine. I heard a lark, mimicking the burble of a burn that entered the loch nearby, and when I raised my head I was startled to see a red deer stag no more than a hundred yards away, up wind. The stag was even more surprised and burst into a graceful run, seeming to float across the heather. It paused to glance back at me, looking just like a Landseer painting, before its silhouette disappeared over the horizon.

The second loch was tiny, a blue pinpoint on the map that I could have walked around in less than half an hour. Appearance is deceptive and I knew some very good trout cruised within its depths. It was sheltered and no one area seemed more likely to hold fish than any other. I began casting at once, working my way clockwise around the water. Then, to my left, there was a boil on the surface, as a fish turned. The slow, silent distortion of the mirror indicated a good trout and I covered the general area at once. Fortunately, my casting did not let me down and on the first, slow figure of eight the line ripped from my fingers and the water bulged a second time as the trout took the dropper. The fight was dour and unspectacular, a series of long, slow runs that never tested my reflexes or threatened the line. The trout on the other hand was magnificent and looked all of Three pounds. The fish was very dark, almost black, and the scarlet markings stood out dramatically. I released the Pheasant Tail from the crook of its jaw without removing it from the water.

Further around the shoreline I found a grassy knoll marked with a fresh otter spraint. I often used to see otters scouring the rock pools along the seashore at low tide, as dusk fell. I think they used the isolated lochs as nursery areas in which to teach their cubs to fish.

I thought the loch might give up a brace of trout but I completed its circumference without another chance. I shouldered my rucksack, checked the map and set out for the final water, a large loch I hadn't visited before. The loch was exposed and the surface was fractured by wavelets cast up by the strengthening breeze. Dusk was approaching and the dying sun made the landscape glow like a fire; rock outcrops crouching like coals amongst the embers. Flat spots in the ripples marked trout that were harvesting a crop of craneflies, swept from the shoreline. The trout were feeding close to the shore, intercepting the craneflies as they hit the surface. This was an opportunity to enjoy my favourite form of fishing and it took moments to strip down the leader and replace the intermediate line with a floating one, armed with a big daddy on a size eight.

A high, floating cast sent the imitation dancing across the waves, almost as if I was dapping. Seconds later a large bow wave converged with the fly and I felt a solid thump as a trout hooked itself. The trout was an acrobat and it threw itself from the water in a string of somersaults that left me breathless. Each time it crashed back into the water I thought leader or hook-hold would fail. I was never in control and it was more by good luck than good management that I landed my third pound plus fish of the day. I removed a couple of scales before releasing the fish. It is always interesting to look at trout ages and growth rates on a 'new' water. Sometimes this information will identify a loch with the potential to produce a true monster.

The rise continued and I hooked and lost two more good fish before landing the next one. This was the prettiest of the day and as I returned her I knew it was time to leave. The sun had dipped below the horizon and I had a two-mile trek back to the car ahead of me. The trout glowed pink in the reflected sunset as I slipped her back. Suddenly, the breeze died completely, as if a switch had been thrown, and I was left with a lasting memory of the rose-pink sheen of a glassy loch, shining in the dark and shadowy landscape.

There is something almost exotic about brown trout. I still remember the wonder of seeing my first 'brownie' — a six inch, fin perfect fish from the River Tame, Saddleworth.

Lightning Does Strike Twice

Fishing Ashmead now must be similar to fishing Redmire in the 1950's, in terms of the number of very large carp that are present. The difference, I suppose, is that the Ashmead fish are all known, so to some extent the element of surprise, the pioneering edge, is missing. An exciting compensation for the relative lack of mystery, though, is the thought that the carp are still young and growing fish, so from one season to another we don't really know how much larger the carp might have become. The first indication that Ashmead might be a very special carp water indeed came at the start of the 2006 season, when it seemed possible that the anglers fishing the pool might see the capture of a fifty pounder.

Three short visits early in 2006 were unproductive but I saw signs of fish in the same area of the lake on each occasion and thought I had found where the carp were feeding. It was with huge anticipation that I made my way down to the lake again at the beginning of May. When I arrived at the water, I made my customary tour of the banks looking for signs, before getting the rods out of the car. I found an area of disturbed silt in the margin of one of the small bays, in exactly the same area where I had seen carp earlier in the year. No fish were evident but it was clear that at least one carp had been feeding there.

I baited the area with a mixture of particles (hemp, corn and partiblend) and some pellets, which a friend of mine had suggested I try. I left the spot in peace and didn't fish it immediately, because the carp are very shy of tackle and disturbance. I wanted the carp to settle in on the bait and gain their confidence before confronting them with lines and hooks. A few hours later I returned with a rod to find a fish feeding hard over the bait, sending up plumes of silt, like the ash clouds of an erupting volcano. I gently lowered the bait onto the spot, just two feet out from the bank and in two feet of water.

Even though I'd been as quiet as possible, the activity ceased as soon as I introduced the hookbait and I thought I'd missed my chance. I needn't have worried, though, because after ten minutes or so a lovely bloom of silt appeared and the water surface curled beautifully as a carp unfurled its tail below. They were back and they were feeding. I sat as still as possible, trying to ignore the cramp building in my legs: I knew that at close quarters, the carp would melt away at the slightest movement or vibration. My nerves stretched unbearably as billowing silt clouded the water and at one point the very tip of an orange tail broke surface, not three feet from me. This is what carp fishing is all about to me; tension so intense that you want to scream.

In the Science Museum in South Kensington, I remember being mesmerised as a child by a vast Van Der Graaf generator that produced artificial lightning. The device hummed and crackled as the electrical energy built to a peak and then, with a massive crack of thunder it discharged the current in a flash of purest light, stunning the audience and causing shrieks of excitement and fear, even though they had anticipated the bolt. A haunting silence followed, the air tainted with ozone.

The tension generated by watching those carp feeding over my bait was every bit as great and the charge built for nearly an hour before the lightning struck. One moment rod and reel were still, the next the water erupted, the rod tip was dragged down to the surface and the reel span wildly as a hooked fish bored away across the pool.

The fight that followed was dogged and determined rather than spectacular. The carp swam slowly, almost ponderously but with tremendous power and substance, heading for the far bank reedbed. Chris Yates' description of playing a forty-pound common as feeling like being attached to a garden roller going down a slope sprang into my mind. I knew that I was attached to a carp far larger than any I'd ever hooked before.

I was using one of a pair of new cane rods of my own design that I'd had made for me. I've always found the classic MKIV carp rod to be a little shorter than I would like and without the power in the butt section that is needed for some of today's modern tactics or for stopping a really big carp in its tracks. The new rod felt superb but I'd rather have christened it with a smaller, less testing adversary, building up to a battle with a leviathan only when I'd had a chance to get to know its capabilities a little better.

I hesitated for a second but knew that I must turn the fish before it made the reeds, or all would be lost. I tucked the rod butt into my stomach and clamped down, half expecting the rod and reel to explode but instead the curve in the cane simply increased and then locked up wonderfully, as the full power of the rod came to bear. For a fraction of a second time stood still, with everything poised at breaking point; the singing line; the straining cane; the carp's resolve; my pounding heart. Then, with a bow wave that flattened the reedmace, the carp swung off course and back out into the open water of the bay. I thanked Barry the rod-maker under my breath for his craftsmanship.

The carp made several more, long, powerful runs but it didn't make many really dramatic moves. I felt like a child being taken for a walk by a Saint Bernard, there was the illusion of control but I knew that at

any moment I might be towed off over the horizon. Then the carp applied a tactic I'd never come across before. Ploughing into the deepest part of the bay, it upended and sounded like a harpooned whale. Great clouds of silt rose from the lakebed, and vortices from the carp's tail appeared on the surface and merged into a flat spot the size of a snooker table. A terrible pounding sensation transmitted down the rod and I realised that the carp was driving its head into the silt in an effort to shed the hook. It felt like an eternity before I managed to get it moving again by running down the bank to change the angle of the pressure.

Skippy, one of the other syndicate members, joined me and took the net. The carp seemed to be slowing and the runs were less determined yet I didn't think it was tired, just sulking whilst it worked out its next move. The carp was near the surface now and we both caught sight of a pale flank as it turned. "That's a good twenty," said Skippy. "Then it's foul hooked," I replied. "It feels like a monster!"

The fish circled around the bay, just below the surface and, as it came past for the third time, Skippy simply scooped the net under the bulk of the carp, enmeshing it and heaving it up onto the bank in one swift movement. It was an impressive piece of netmanship, as calm and accurate as an experienced ghillie landing a salmon. We didn't realise how big the fish was until we unfolded the mesh on the unhooking mat and saw the shear bulk of the carp. There, in the middle of its coral pink flank, was a mirror scale as large and golden as an Olympic medal. "Single Scale!" breathed Skippy. We both knew this fish had weighed over forty pounds when last caught and, lying in the early morning light, it looked simply enormous.

We weighed the carp twice and we agreed on a weight of Fifty pounds and Four ounces, well over the Somerset record. As Skippy took some photographs, I took time to admire the carp. It was a very long, lean fish, with all of its tremendous weight in the broad shoulders. Most impressive was the huge orange tail, the wrist thicker and more powerful than my arm and sprinkled with constellations of tiny golden scales. The carp was immaculate. An unbroken line of gilded scales ran along its back, either side of the long dorsal. Its sides were a pale blue-grey above the lateral line and pastel pink below, fading to ivory on the belly. Its beaten bronze head shone in the reflected sunlight.

I cradled the carp in the margins when I returned it, waiting as it recovered its strength. I held on for an age, wanting to imprint every detail on my mind, not wanting the moment to end. Eventually, the carp had had enough and with a slap of its tail it left me, soaked and happy, standing in the margins of the lake.

Later, looking through my old photographs, I realised that the carp was one that had been introduced to Goat Willow in the original stocking from the wider wetland. Then the carp weighed just ten pounds and it was wonderful to capture a fish that had grown with me to become the highlight of my carp fishing; we had come full circle together.

Throughout the summer months, work commitments stopped me from carp fishing. I didn't fish Ashmead again until early September, when I slipped down to the lake for a brief overnight session.

According to the diary, the lake had been little fished since my capture of Single Scale and there was a peaceful, yet expectant atmosphere. The hornwort was up and the pool looked almost unfishable because of the thickness of the surface weed. Beneath the cloak of green however, I knew there would be plenty of clear spots and channels that marked the highways used by the carp to move between their feeding areas.

I was pleased to see the signs of neglect as I crept quietly around the lake; lush grass in the popular pitches, the dense weed, and carp cruising confidently wherever I looked.

The weed was most dense on the south bank but I also found two small clear spots here, which marked places where the carp had been browsing, disturbing the silt and exposing patches of hard clay in which the hornwort couldn't take root. In three acres of water, these two insignificant patches drew my attention hypnotically. Every sense told me that this was the place to fish.

I crouched for a while in the gathering darkness, looking for signs but none materialised. Night was falling with an autumnal swiftness and I knew I had to follow my instincts and get the rods out before I lost the light completely. By the time I was ready to cast, the clear patches were discernable only as salvers of reflected moonlight, settled amongst the black mass of the weed. I fed two pouches of hemp and about a pound of pellets into each silver dish, followed by a PVA bag of pellets, containing the hook bait - a boilie flavoured with Madagascar Clove and steeped in a mixture of corn liquor and Marmite.

A warm southerly wind chased clouds across the night sky, so that the stars appeared and vanished behind their scudding shadows. From time to time, the clouds merged and a stronger squall of wind brought in a brief shower of rain. I was glad of my brolly and felt as cosy as a dormouse beneath its thin shelter, as the raindrops drummed out a staccato jazz beat on the fabric. I've always loved camping in the rain.

A carp rolled, as smoothly as a breaching porpoise and without any sound. Had I not been watching the nearest of the baited spots I would have missed the fish but I caught the shadow of its dorsal as it cleaved the surface and the ripples of silver, where the water rocked gently and then settled in the wake of its passing.

The take came just as the church clock a mile away struck the first note of eleven. Even though I was ready and grabbed the rod in the blink of an eye, the first run still took about twenty yards of line before the carp buried itself in the weed. In truth, the run had been so fast that I hesitated for a fraction of a second too long before really putting any pressure on the fish.

Impasse; I knew the fish was well hooked because every now and then I felt a pulse of power down the rod as it pushed further forward into the weed but it couldn't move far and I certainly couldn't recover any line. I put the rod back into the rest and slipped on my chest waders. If the fish wouldn't come to me, I had no option other than to go in after the fish. As I suspected, the hornwort formed a thin, dense surface layer, with little of substance beneath. The fronds parted like cotton as I slowly made my way deeper into the pool, following the line out towards the stranded carp. Even so, it wasn't easy to push through the weed, holding both rod and net and taking care that the line didn't tangle.

Eventually, I felt the leader knot and released the line, bringing up the rod just as the carp pushed free. The carp rolled, showing a broad flank, and its tail slapped the surface as it powered down to the lakebed and away, the line pulling clumps of loose weed in its wake. The rod absorbed the pressure beautifully and I was beginning to enjoy the fight with what was clearly a very big fish. I clamped down and the carp rolled again, almost under control.

Soon it was boring and plunging beneath the rod tip on a short line and I readied the net. Then, just as I raised the mesh around the flank of the fish, the rod sprang straight. The carp had slipped the hook and I was suddenly alone, standing chest deep in the cold grip of the lake.

The loss of a big fish is one of the most intense experiences in fishing. The transition from euphoria to despair happens so quickly that it makes your stomach lurch, like the plunge of a roller coaster. The loss of a carp as large as this one (I'm sure it was well over thirty pounds) is simply devastating. I stood, head back, staring at the starry skies for an age, before plodding disconsolately back to the bank, where I flung my rod into the hedge and crawled into my sleeping bag.

On the following Saturday I returned to Ashmead with my two eldest children Iain (who was 7) and Katrina (who was 5), who joined me for a night's "camping fishing". To be honest, I didn't think I had much hope of catching one of Ashmead's wary carp with the two of them dancing around but the lost carp of the previous week haunted my dreams and I felt compelled to be at the lake.

We set up their tent and enjoyed some fish and chips before I got them settled for the night and read them their bedtime stories over a steaming mug of hot chocolate. Dusk was falling when I finally cast out, positioning the baits on the same two small clear areas of clay as before.

I decided to try out some new "seamless" hooks developed by my friend John Walsh. They looked great; needle-sharp and I particularly liked the fact that the sealed eye removed any risk of the hook knot chafing if a large fish rolled on a tight line. I like attention to detail and lost carp were preying on my mind.

It was a clear but unusually warm September night and Orion hunted brightly on the western skyline, until an autumn mist rose across the Somerset levels and smothered the landscape. Twice during the night a large fish crashed out but the fog deadened the noise and made it impossible to pinpoint the splash. At least they were moving.

Nothing came in the night and I was just thinking about taking the little ones home for breakfast when I had a fast run on the left hand rod. As soon as I bent into the fish, I knew it was another good one. It ran hard and straight for just a few seconds before everything went solid with the weight of weed, but even in that short time I could sense the solidity of the carp through the fibres of the rod. I had a horrible sense of deja vue as Iain and Katrina helped me struggle into my waders and I followed the fish into the lake, carefully disentangling the weed from the line as I went. As I got close, the carp surged away again and I was very grateful for the controlled, yielding power in the cane, as another twenty yards of line was taken before the fish once again became encased in the hornwort.

The fight carried on like this for forty minutes or so, the fish charging from one bed of weed to another with me in pursuit, arms aching from the pressure on the rod and cold water seeping over the top of my waders. Each time I had to unpick it from a weedbed, the carp had plenty of time to recover its strength and I was beginning to wonder which of us would give up first. If I'm honest, I was also less assertive with the fish than usual. I don't normally mess around when playing a fish and like to bring them to the net as quickly as possible but I really didn't want to lose this one and the lost fish of the previous week had knocked my confidence.

Finally, the strength of the fish began to ebb away and the runs became shorter and controlled more easily. All through the fight I had been aware of the solid weight of the carp and when a huge pale flank rolled beneath the rod top, I thought I might have hooked Single Scale again. Eventually, I eased the fish over the drawstring of the net and floundered back to the bank where the kids were whooping and cheering in excitement. I recognised the carp as Moonscale, one which I had caught four years earlier at a weight of just under Thirty-Two pounds. It had grown considerably but still retained the long, lean, muscular physique I remembered. This time it weighed Forty One pounds Eight ounces; just a pound less than my son Iain. Sometimes lightning does strike twice.

Ten minutes later, after a quick phone call, my wife Shona appeared with our youngest son Alistair, who was three. It was lovely to see how enthralled the children were at the direct contact with the fish, how scared and excited they were when I suggested that they might like to touch it and how gentle they were when they finally plucked up the courage to do so. All of us were simply stunned by the grandeur of the carp. Well, nearly all of us…

"Catch another one Daddy," Alistair demanded, as I slipped her back after a few photographs. "Catch another one, Now!" Some people are so hard to please…

River of Dreams

All anglers have a river flowing through their dreams. In their sleep, they fish in peace on a stream where the clear current reflects a perpetual summer sky. Kingfishers whistle as they dart beneath the overhanging foliage and the air is heavy with the scents of willow herb and freshly cut hay. The river meanders; shallow riffles race into sleek glides and mysterious pools, and a bed of golden gravel is revealed between the waving fronds of ranunculus.

Of course, there are fish. Shoals of dace and grayling shimmer in the riffle, flashing at flies and chasing their shadows over the gravel. In the slacks and eddies, sleek roach drift slowly beneath the shelter of the lilies and fleets of tiger-striped perch hunt their prey like pirates. Gangs of bullyboy chub fight for drowning slugs and stealthy pike hang motionless in tense anticipation of a careless meal.

Whilst many anglers only see such a river through closed eyelids, there are some of us fortunate enough to have fished a place where our dreams could merge with reality.

As I have been writing, images of a piece of river that I haven't fished in nearly twenty years have been flowing through my mind. In 1992, Brian Moreland invited me to join his syndicate on the River Ure near Ripon. The river flowed through an old estate and was wild and untamed in comparison to the cultivated southern waters to which I was accustomed. It changed dramatically in nature and mood over the length of the fishery and offered something for every angler.

The top two miles of slow, deep water were home to specimen roach, perch and pike. Occasionally, an angler hooked one of the large and solitary barbel which roamed this area. These fish were extremely difficult to locate, even harder to tempt into taking a bait and almost impossible to bring to the net. They had a degree of subtlety and power that was humbling.

Downstream, the river became shallower and increased in pace, flowing over flood banks of shifting gravel. Trees abandoned in the fields, a hundred yards from the normal riverbed, bore testimony to the awesome power of the winter spates. This area was the playground of the dace, grayling and wild trout. The latter were far beyond the limitations of my fly-fishing skills but the dace and grayling often filled an enjoyable hour. I sought them out with a tiny built-cane brook rod made by Allcocks & Sons, which can place a dry fly with a watchmaker's precision and make a six-ounce dace feel like a tarpon.

The last few miles were a mixture of pool and glide that ran through completely wild surroundings. I knew this area as 'The Jungle', and an angler had to crawl and limbo through willow thickets and waist high butterbur to reach the swims. There was a great sense of adventure in fishing here and another angler's footprint was a rare intrusion.

On my first visit to the river in late June, I left my tackle at home, with a view to exploring as much of the fishery as I could walk in a day. What a day it was! I started at the top boundary and worked my way downstream, fighting through nettles to reach the river, peering into pools, scrambling up trees and wading the shallows in bare feet and rolled up trousers. It was a Boys Own adventure, straight out of my childhood and the best day out I'd enjoyed in years.

The exercise also proved fruitful in deciding where to concentrate my early efforts to catch a barbel. I found a small gap in the dense riverside undergrowth that led down to a comfortable stance at the head of a steady glide. Beneath a willow-shrouded undercut, the flow ran smoothly over a bed of clean, amber gravel. Just downstream a fallen tree formed a perfect refuge and upstream an extensive area of shallows provided an ideal foraging area for any barbel present. It was to this swim that I made my way the following weekend.

It was dusk when I made my first cast. Flicking the bait out into the flow, I felt a gentle plucking on the line across my finger, as it tripped across the bottom before coming to rest beneath the trailing mass of willow fronds.

I always touch leger at night, partly because I find that staring at an isotope is a strain but mainly because I find the sense of touch to be the most sensitive way of detecting bites. Done well, the angler can map the contours of the riverbed in the same way that a blind person can read a face. The path of the lead can be traced as it bounces towards its resting place and every dip and rise in the gravel noted. Equally, the slightest change in this progress, which might indicate the attentions of a fish, is sensed immediately. The smallest of bites are detected at once and, because the rod is held, the strike becomes an instinctive reflex. Strangely, it seems to me that you can almost always tell the size of the fish present by the feel of the bite. Even though it might be the smallest of plucks on the line, the bite of a larger fish can often be detected through an indefinable sense of "substance" that always raises the hair on the back of my neck.

As the sun sank the river came to life. A good trout began to rise regularly under the alders on the far bank, chub and dace slashed at the evening hatch of sedge and a smear of iridescent blue marked the path of a kingfisher returning to its roost. Suddenly, a bar of purest gold split the surface at my feet and rolled back into the flow with a splash. Everything paused, mesmerised by the spreading rings that marked the spot where I had just seen my first Yorkshire barbel.

Almost at once there was a quivering vibration along the line, as if a violinist was drawing an un-rosined bow across the nylon. A moment later, a couple of small taps on the rod top were followed by a strong pull and the cane of my Avon Perfection swept round as a hooked fish ran for the safety of the snag. By the time I finally managed to gain some control the fish was well downstream and the line ran through a tangle of willow branches, which shuddered and grated with each shake of the barbel's head. Surely the line must fray and break?

I clambered precariously out onto one of the lower limbs of the tree in an attempt to change the angle of pull. At first there was no result but eventually the fish started to move again. There were a few anxious seconds as the willow twigs stabbed at the line, but then it was free and the line cut the surface as the fish moved towards the far bank and began to accelerate upstream. I had to wind in furiously to keep in touch but the odds were now in my favour for the first time. Eventually, the steady strain of the rod took its toll and I felt the strength of the fish ebbing away. Soon she was circling slowly beneath the rod top and not long afterwards a Six-pound barbel glided into the folds of my net.

After gently removing the hook, I took a moment to admire the fish. The layer of mucous covering the scales split the evening light like a prism, so that each scale was shot through with a spectrum of colours that coalesced to give the fish her beaten-gold colouring. Delta-winged pectorals and a tail that seemed incredibly large in relation to her size, accentuated her grace of line. The setting sun provided just enough light for a photograph, before I released her.

That barbel was the first of many. These were not stocked fish, unlike their counterparts of the southern and western rivers such as the Hampshire Avon and Severn; they thrived in the environment where they had evolved over the millennia since the retreat of the continental ice sheets. Ure barbel are tremendously long and sleek fish, with broad and powerful shoulders. An eight-pounder may be a large fish for the river but a fish of this calibre has the length of a twelve or thirteen-pound barbel from the Hampshire Avon or Stour and twice the speed and power. As a consequence of carrying less weight, the fight of a big Ure barbel is faster, more dynamic and far more exhilarating than the plodding doggedness of a southern fish of the same length.

The barbel also benefited from the very light pressure to which they were subjected by anglers and demonstrated patterns of behaviour I haven't come across on other rivers. They rarely took fright when observed, even if they were aware of an angler's presence, and on several occasions I watched a shoal of a dozen or more fish feeding over a gravel bed, picking up stones as big as a child's fist and spinning them around in their mouths to dislodge any invertebrate food, before spitting them out again.

On one notable afternoon I spent over an hour watching a shoal of twenty barbel cruising at the surface of a deep pool, enjoying the warmth of the sun on their backs like basking carp. On another occasion, one early July dawn, I waded out amongst a group of large barbel that were feeding on chub fry in the shallows. Seven or eight barbel could be seen, the tips of their tails and dorsal fins breaking through the surface like those of cruising sharks. They converged on the fry shoals, herding them against the riverbank in a pincer movement and sending them scattering through the surface in panic. I could imagine the less fortunate prey being gulped down as the barbel withdrew to regroup and make another attack.

As I grew to know the river I learned more of their haunts and habits but that first barbel swim remained my favourite. That summer I treated the swim like a base camp, roaming the river in search of barbel and chub during the day and returning there in the evening for a last cast. During early August I decided to spend a weekend on the river. I took plenty of provisions and set up camp at the "home" swim.

Catching chub on floating crust is one of the most exhilarating experiences to be had whilst coarse fishing and the shallow runs of the Ure were ideal for this favourite pastime. I spent the first day fishing my way downstream and caught several good chub to just over Four pounds using this approach. Several lumps of bread were set adrift at the head of each riffle and I followed their passage downstream, wearing waders. When the first crust was taken, a free lined lump containing the hook was introduced and allowed to float down to where the fish lay. The dark shapes of the chub bow-waved across the shallows to intercept the crusts and when the hook bait was taken the fight would be short but explosive, with spray flying and the light rod kicking.

The riverbanks were as alive as the flow they contained. In the lazy heat of the summer afternoon I relaxed and enjoyed the natural beauty that surrounded me. A sparrow hawk hunted the willows on the opposite bank, sending the warblers scattering in panic. A pair of hares tried to hide behind the isolated clumps of nettles in a field. They burst from cover as I approached their twitching ear tips and sprinted away in an ungainly but deceptively fast lope.

Later, I found a long, shallow glide, where the shadows of fish could be seen ghosting over the gravel. A few handfuls of maggots soon produced the familiar golden flashes of a shoal of feeding barbel; their flanks reflecting the sunlight as they turned to chase the loose feed downstream. I cast a light float carrying a bunch of grubs on a size ten, shotted so that the bait would trip lightly across the shingle and flutter enticingly at the slightest check in its passage.

I missed the first three bites but then the float slid under decisively and the strike met with a solid resistance. The surface heaved as the hooked fish rocketed across the river. Playing a small barbel on light trotting tackle in fast, shallow water is every bit as exciting and challenging as defeating a big fish on more substantial gear. The tactics are also similar and I waded quickly out below the fish to bring the force of the current to bear in conjunction with that of the rod. The fish was a fin perfect Four-pounder. Lying in the mesh it looked bewildered by the way a simple meal could result in such a strange experience. It had probably never been caught before and I returned it, chastened and wiser.

Dusk arrived and I headed back upstream towards camp. As I made my way across the meadow I spied something metallic that was catching the evening sunlight. I got closer and realised that it was an empty meat tin, apparently cast aside after use. I was furious: not only was someone abusing the estate by dropping litter but also they were obviously an angler. Worse still, they had to be poaching, as I was sure that none of the members would be so thoughtless. A little further on I found an empty bread bag and further on still, the litterlout had discarded a half eaten packet of crisps.

Suddenly, a suspicion crept into my mind that all might not be as it seemed. It dawned on me that the crisps were my favourite flavour and that the empty tin had once contained my failsafe brand of barbel meat. By now I was almost back at my barbel swim and it became clear that the litter formed a trail across the field to my tackle.

As I approached the steep bank above the swim a weasel appeared, dragging a second loaf of bread that was easily three times its own size. Engrossed in this Herculean task, it didn't notice me and I watched it drag its prize off into the centre of the field, where it proceeded to savage it. The weasel danced about the loaf as if it was a rabbit, darting in to attack it repeatedly with a shrill cry of anger. Once satisfied that the loaf was dead, the wraith skipped back towards me, intent on yet another raid on my tackle bag. Just short of its goal, the weasel spotted me and reared up on its short hind legs, its body moving sinuously like a cobra. Then it spat out a mustelid expletive, darted into the cover of the nearest hedge and I saw it no more.

The wild brown trout were by far the most elusive species and provided the most challenging fishing. In the four years in which I fished the syndicate, I only caught three trout intentionally but these remain my most memorable fish from the river. The largest weighed almost Three pounds and was caught on one of my last visits to the fishery, just before a new job took me away from the syndicate.

I caught the trout late one summer evening. I remember the close atmosphere, the thick scent of dog rose and a flight of swallows scything through the clouds of midges that cloaked the stream. It was one of those evenings when the threatened thunderstorm would have provided a welcome relief to the tension, the heavy rain diluting the air and allowing the world to breathe.

I had my favourite Allcock's "Halcyon" three-weight with me and I was travelling light to cover as much water as possible. All the tackle I had, apart from the rod and a small net, was some leader material, floatant and my small fly box, crammed into the pockets of my tatty old Barbour. I love this sort of fishing; the freedom of simply going for a relaxed walk with a rod, looking for signs or likely trout lies and hoping that something might turn up.

I found a pool where the flow tumbled and bubbled into a deep, slow eddy beneath the bankside alders. Peering through water the colour of weak Bovril I couldn't make out any trout at first and I turned to leave and wend my way on downstream. Just as I turned I spotted a slow, graceful roll at the head of the pool, just where the broken water merged with the calmer surface. I stopped and watched and three or four minutes passed before there was another disturbance in the same spot. I focused on the gravel of the riverbed and spotted the long, living shadow of the trout even though its camouflage rendered the fish itself invisible.

I tried a couple of speculative casts well below the trout's lie, to work out the best approach and then extended my next cast to cover the fish. It ignored the Adams at the first time of asking but then a second, lucky cast threw the fly deep into the shadow of the trees. There was a boil and then the line shot tight as the trout hooked itself against the flow of the eddy on the line. The trout turned and surged off down the pool and I had to thrust the rod tip under water to avoid the alder branches and then draw the line slowly but surely with my left hand to turn the fish before it made it down to the next piece of faster water. The Halcyon took the strain beautifully and cushioned the last few lunges from the fish before it gave up the ghost and let me draw it over the net.

It was a classic brown trout, all bristling fins and blazing crimson spots. I remember cradling her briefly in the cold, clear water before letting go and watching as her golden outline dissolved into the dream that was her home.

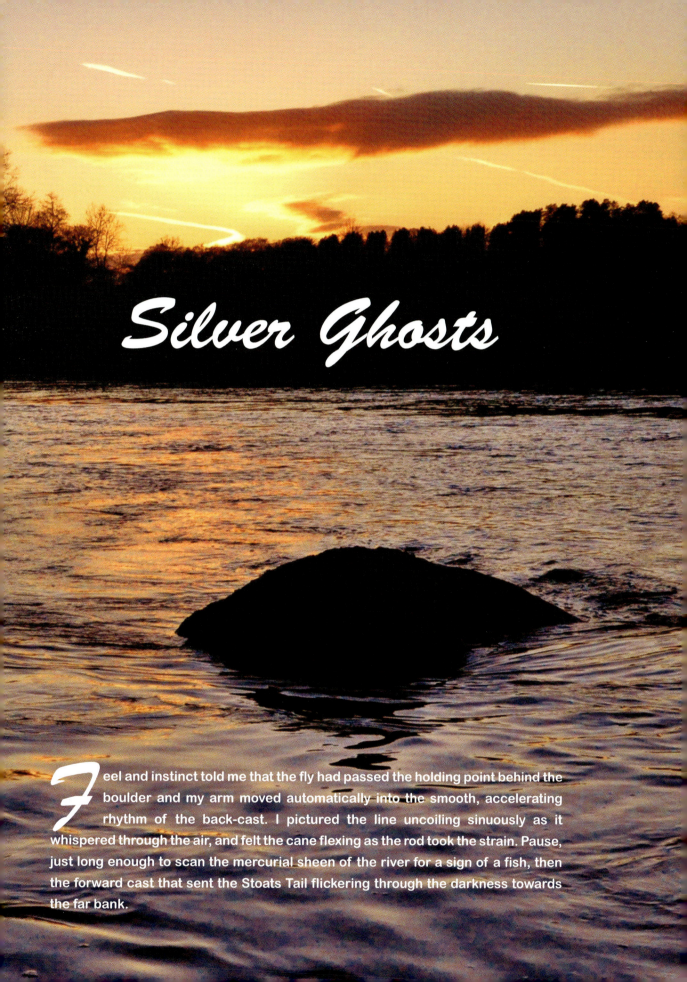

Silver Ghosts

Feel and instinct told me that the fly had passed the holding point behind the boulder and my arm moved automatically into the smooth, accelerating rhythm of the back-cast. I pictured the line uncoiling sinuously as it whispered through the air, and felt the cane flexing as the rod took the strain. Pause, just long enough to scan the mercurial sheen of the river for a sign of a fish, then the forward cast that sent the Stoats Tail flickering through the darkness towards the far bank.

Night fishing for sea trout requires an absorbing concentration of the senses of touch, sight and hearing. There are few nights when the darkness is so complete as to render the power of sight redundant. Nevertheless, dependence upon the other senses undoubtedly increases after darkness falls. The senses of hearing and smell that are secondary to visual stimuli during the day become focused and enhanced at night. The sense of touch becomes so acute that slight changes in the air currents can define the contours of one's surroundings. In a world of vague shadows and shapes without substance, no one sense is dominant. Only at night are all the senses so finely tuned.

I believe that this heightening of the senses also enhances the power of other dormant natural instincts. In the unfamiliar and slightly hostile environment of darkness, I become aware of a link with my surroundings that reaches beyond that of normal sensory awareness. There are moments when my usually inadequate casting instinctively sends the fly to precisely the right spot and a take is immediately forthcoming. I am often drawn to a particular pool or riffle that looked innocuous and uninviting during the day. Often, too, I am aware that a series of casts to a particularly tight, tree-lined mark would have ended in tangled disaster if their accuracy depended upon my usual senses and skill alone.

The sensory overload of darkness strings every nerve at breaking point and a fear of the dark adds a very distinctive edge to fishing for sea trout. There is a definite adrenaline buzz and sense of mystery and excitement that is missing from most of my other fishing. The tension can be addictive and it draws me out time after time, even when there might be no more than the slimmest chance of making contact with a fish.

The most exhilarating and enjoyable sea trout fishing I have ever experienced involved fishing forays during which contact with my quarry would have been little short of miraculous. I was living in Lancashire at the time and working for the National Rivers Authority, as the technical officer in charge of fisheries research and stock assessment in the Ribble and Lune catchments. The fishing to which I refer originated from a fish trapping study carried out early one June on the Ribble, near Clitheroe, as part of the migratory salmonid stock assessment programme…

"Salmon, fork length 85cm, weight 6.35kg, good condition, silver with sea-lice." Darryl handed the fish to me and I carefully plucked a couple of scales from just above the lateral line, slightly behind the dorsal fin, with a pair of forceps. I made a note of the details on a cellophane wallet and dropped the scale sample inside, to be read later. The salmon was then held immersed in the cold push of water in the main trapping chamber, until the effects of the mild anaesthetic had worn off. Once she had regained full strength she was placed into the recovery chamber for subsequent release upstream.

"Salmon, length 84.5, weight 5.65kg, slightly coloured, no marks." A second fish was handed over and the routine repeated. It was six o'clock on a grey and rain swept morning in early June. The three of us working the trap were tired and cramped after a cold night. The first rule of trapping wild fish is to take every step possible to ensure their safety and the trap had been manned constantly throughout the twenty-four hours for which it had been operated.

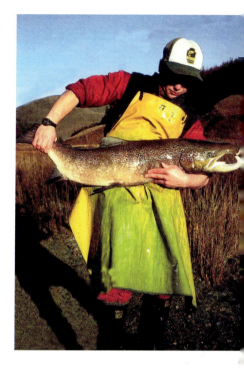

From the fish counter downstream of the trap, we knew that between ten and twenty large salmon were likely to be in the holding chamber. The counter was normally over ninety percent effective for fish of this size but operation of the trap affected fish behaviour and caused a degree of uncertainty about the accuracy of the counts recorded. We expected all of the fish to be two sea-winter salmon because the counter showed that all of the fish were far larger than the average run of Ribble sea trout or grilse. June was also early for the main grilse and sea trout runs, so we were confident that the fish would all be late running spring salmon. This was encouraging because reported catches of this scarce component of the Ribble stock had declined to almost nil over the past decade.

"Salmon, 82.5cm, 6.70kg, lice," Sampling wild salmon and sea trout was the highlight of our jobs in the NRA fisheries' team. We all enjoyed collecting biological data about the stocks under our control, surveying juvenile populations in the spawning tributaries, checking for tagged fish and, later in the year, collecting brood stock for the hatchery. On a day like this, however, doubled up within the confines of the trap, with the rain sheeting down and water soaking through our inadequate waterproofs, even the pleasure of direct contact with the fish paled. The three of us were functioning like numbed automatons as we followed the familiar sampling and recovery routine.

I took scales from the fish and was just about to slip them into the sample wallet when I noticed that they were different to those of the previous two fish. The scales were much smaller and more difficult to remove than those of the salmon.

"Hold on a second," I said, "can we re-check the last one please?"

The fish was laid out carefully again on the measuring board. As I had suspected, the upper jaw stretched well beyond the back of the fish's eye, the rear edge of the dark tail was

Chapter Ten – Silver Ghosts

flat and its wrist thick and muscular. A dozen large, intensely black spots gleamed against the silver sheen of the scales, confirming that this was a special fish indeed. A sea trout, fresh run from the estuary and weighing nearly fifteen pounds lay before me. As always happens at moments like this I felt the calm, rational mask of the scientist slip as the excitement of the life-long angler broke through.

We double-checked the weight and length, took several photographs and some additional scales, to confirm the identification later in the laboratory. Those scales would map the fascinating story of the life of the sea trout, from its juvenile existence in a Ribble tributary, its migration to sea as a smolt and its subsequent returns to the river to spawn. She was helped to recover and then released into the holding chamber and another fish anaesthetised. This too was a sea trout, a little smaller than the first but still far larger than any anglers had reported from the river, or any that I had ever seen before.

There were fourteen fish in the trap that morning if I remember correctly, of which eight were sea trout weighing between eleven and fifteen and a half pounds. They were all fresh run, immaculate specimens that the angler in me could only dream of encountering with rod and line. It was clear that this was a sample of fish from a cohort of the Ribble sea trout stock that was previously unrecorded. Here was direct evidence of a group of very large, old fish, running the river in late spring.

At first, I wondered how these fantastic sea trout could have remained unnoticed by the anglers on the river. Eventually, I realised that this was a result of that old chestnut, the self-fulfilling prophecy. No one was fishing for these fish because no one knew of their existence and no one knew they were there because no one was fishing for them! Few spring salmon had been caught from the river in over a decade, so few anglers ventured out at this time of year. Those that did were fishing exclusively for salmon, as the presence of the large sea trout was unknown, and the anglers probably left the water before dark, when the sea trout would start to move. Furthermore, we had trapped under ideal conditions on a falling flood. Although a large proportion of the fish we had caught were large sea trout, the total population of these fish in the river was probably very small.

Consider the futility of fishing for a small population of large sea trout in a river the size of the Ribble. One would have no way of knowing where in the system they would be at any time or even if they had returned to the river at all. Imagine, then, the chances of presenting one of these scarce fish with the right fly, in the right place, when it was in a mood to take. The odds of the National Lottery suddenly seem very attractive!

You would have to be slightly mad to spend nights fishing with so little chance of success. Completely mad in fact, but I have never been known to let sanity interfere where fishing is involved. Besides, these sea trout were no mere rumour or myth. I had held and seen some of them myself, read their scales and returned them alive to the river, to join the other silver spirits that I could picture so clearly in my imagination, ghosting through the cold water towards the summer holding pools. No angler who had seen so many fantastic fish at one time could resist the challenge of trying to catch one.

So it was that the next week found me thigh-deep at the head of a noted pool, some way downstream of the trap, fishing with an anticipation and intensity I had seldom felt before. Despite the futility of the odds against me, I expected each cast to produce the electric shock of contact. Every sense was keyed up for the lunge and draw of a take. I knew the river here well, as it was the NRA's own day ticket length and I was responsible for its management. The most likely pool was where the Hodder joined the Ribble below a boulder strewn length of shallows. Here there was water deep enough to hold fish while they compared the acid based waters of the Hodder with the limestone flow of the Ribble and decided which was their natal stream. The banks were free of trees and an easy cast sent the Stoats Tail searching sweetly along the crease of the river junction, where the currents met and resisted their inevitable convergence.

Conditions were perfect. The river was fining down after rain yet still coloured like rich brandy. The sky held a crescent moon that defined the shadows and made the river gleam enough to guide the cast, yet was not so bright as to deter the fish. Bats flitted through the cool night air and the musk of a fox drifted on the slight breeze. Earlier I had heard it calling, probably a vixen leading her cubs. The noises of the night were overlaid with the splash and bubble of the river that pressed my waders within a cold fist.

Almost on the stroke of midnight, the passage of the fly had been interrupted sharply and the rod pulled over as a fish took hold. There was no need to strike as the fish hooked itself against the flow.

Rod and line thrummed as the fish swept across and down the pool, using the press of the water to counter the resistance of the rod. I thought for a moment that the impossible had happened but then the fish cruised into the slack water down stream of me and I could tell from the lacklustre fight that this was no sea trout. My hopes were raised again briefly when a large silver flank rolled at the surface, gleaming in the moonlight, but then died as I drew a chub over the rim of my net. It must have weighed nearly Five pounds and in season, on appropriate tackle, I would have been thrilled to catch such a fish. Now it was simply a disappointment and I returned it to the river with hardly a second glance.

Cast, follow through and retrieve. Three in the morning and the cold push of the river had sapped my warmth and energy, so that it was becoming hard to concentrate. My casting was becoming lethargic and sloppy. Suddenly, there was a crash from the tail of the pool and the water rocked as a large fish cleared the surface. Sea trout! Again the fly tracked its familiar course along the crease but now with renewed intent. Five casts later the passage of the Stoats Tail was checked for a second time as it came level with

the submerged boulder and the shadow of the rod hooped over. No surge through the pool met the strike on this occasion, just a deep, hanging resistance, like holding a kite in a strong wind. Suddenly, a tremendous pull made the reel cry out. A large, unseen, unstoppable force described a tight circle within the heart of the river and returned to the slack behind the rock. Then came a second sharp pull that thumped the rod flat to the butt and she was gone. The line floated free, the loose end frayed and twisted, and the Stoats Tail was consigned to history with the silver ghost that had claimed it as her own.

I never came close to catching one of the large Ribble sea trout again. Now, living in Somerset and too far from the river to make a return visit practicable, I suppose I never will. I would dearly love to hear of one of those large sea trout being landed. Perhaps someone may be inspired by this story to try or perhaps another, more fortunate angler has already succeeded. As for myself, the image of those majestic silver ghosts lives on in my imagination and I'm left with the bittersweet memory of a loose line fluttering in the pull of a cold, dark river.

The Severn Oaks Syndicate

The Great Berwick Estate lies just upstream of Shrewsbury on the River Severn. It is a classic country estate with a large and rambling house that has been allowed to go slightly to seed because of the expense of its upkeep. It looks like somewhere that a modern day Miss Haversham might live, pining away her days, whilst waiting to be buried in the private church which would still be decked out in the faded flowers of her jilted wedding day. Berwick is a farming estate and there are a number of large Victorian farmhouses and a series of smaller cottages for the agricultural labourers, gamekeepers and other estate workers. Berwick, then, is a throwback to a grander time and just passing through the main gateway onto the estate is enough to trigger some deep seated race memory that makes you want to doff your cap.

I first visited Berwick as an angler when I lived just outside Lancaster and worked for The National Rivers Authority. The estate was a two hour drive from home and I had to pass over the prime barbel fishery on the River Ribble to get there, yet as soon as I saw the Great Berwick water I knew the effort was worthwhile. My friend Bill discovered Berwick at a time when a Lancashire fishing club leased the fishing rights and he had bought us both tickets for the year. The members were match fishermen and because the Berwick fishery was so far from the club's home waters it was only fished once or twice a year, when the club charabancs descended on the estate and disgorged a crowd of match anglers for a competition.

For most of the season the members neglected Berwick completely, apart from one or two more dedicated specimen anglers, who had realised that the fishery provided seclusion and had untapped potential for its barbel and other coarse fish.

The small car park was a long walk from the river. The path led down an overgrown estate track, through some coppiced woodland which was alive with pheasants, and eventually emerged on a steep bank that overlooked the bottom end of the fishery. Below us the sinuous silver ribbon of the Severn flowed through open grassland for as far as we could see, before it dived into the dense woodland to our left. The open view of the floodplain was punctuated by a number of large oak trees, relics of a parkland landscape that added a sense of timeless maturity to the scene; it was love at first sight.

The path led down a steep flight of over a hundred steps, which brought us out at the far side of a meadow that we crossed to arrive, at last, at the bottom boundary of the fishery. "Those steps are going to be murder on the way back!" said Bill. I couldn't care less about the prospect of the trudge back to the car, though, because I was completely captivated by the river. The banks were treacherous and steep but between them the Severn rolled and boiled past us in an unending dance of pirouetting eddies and sweeping turns as it glided over the gravel dance floor of its riverbed. The river was about twenty yards wide and its powerful current flowed clear apart from a slight tinge of colour, like a beef consommé. Upstream, the river swept past a bank of overhanging willows for about a quarter of a mile and beneath their trailing branches the clear water was four or five feet deep, just deep enough to obscure the bottom of the pools and give them that essential sense of mystery. Every dip in the riverbed and each of the extensive clumps of streamer weed looked likely to hold barbel and chub.

I wandered slowly upstream, resisting the urge to cast because there was so much to explore. When I reached the last pool at the top of the willow line, however, it looked so seductive that I could resist no longer and I quickly tackled up my Allcock's Super Wizard with a simple link leger and cast a lump of meat out to the crease, where the smooth flow from the pool above plunged into a deep pot formed by a fallen branch from the crack willow above me. I felt the swan shot trip and rattle across the gravel

and then a decisive thump, followed by a long, determined draw as a fish took the bait. I tightened and the rod swept over and then locked into an arc that pulsed with the energy of the river and the fish.

The barbel made a number of long runs across the river, running between the weedbeds and then turning into the flow as it tucked itself beneath the waving fronds. I could picture it, spreading its pectoral fins and angling them against the current, as it used the force of the river to clamp itself to the gravel. Each time it found sanctuary I managed to tease it up and turn its head again, setting it off on another run. I felt it tiring and clamped down, lifting it up into mid water for the first time and then it gave up and I bundled it into the edge and into the mesh. It weighed just over Five pounds and looked as bright and fresh as a newly-minted penny.

Bill knew of a hot swim about a mile upstream and he set off to find and fish it. I followed more slowly, checking out each likely spot on the way. Up until that day I had only fished two rivers for barbel; the Ure, which had few fish and where a single barbel in a day was all I expected to catch, and the Hampshire Avon, which I'd always found deceptively difficult to get to know. The Severn was different altogether and it seemed that every time I cast into a likely looking spot, I had a bite immediately. The river was prolific and every barbel fought long and hard and was in perfect condition. By the time I reached Bill, I'd landed four more fish but none of them were very large (I think the best weighed about Six pounds).

I found Bill sitting beside a fabulous long glide, where the golden gravel of the riverbed gleamed through the gaps in the swaying beds of ranunculus. Over on the far bank the flow had carved a deep hole beneath a trailing willow that simply screamed barbel. I crept down next to Bill who was gazing at the river, with his rod in the rest beside him, pointing at the sky. We had a whispered conversation about how great the swim looked and all the time I watched his rod tip, expecting it to slam over at any moment. Then I noticed that Bill's bait and end tackle were lying on the ground at his feet. "Haven't you cast yet?" I asked. "Not yet," Bill replied, "I'm just building myself up for it!"

I left him to it and walked back downstream to a lovely glide on the near bank, where the river swept out of the shallows and scoured a lovely long slack under some willow bushes. I knew the swim would hold fish and I cast a big lump of meat out into the flow and tracked its course as it tripped over the clean gravel to rest under the thickest part of the willow tangle. The bait hadn't even settled when I felt a slight knock on the line and then a firm thump, which I struck at once. I knew immediately that this was a better calibre of barbel than those I'd already landed that day and instead of the fast, darting runs of the smaller fish the strike connected with a solid, ponderous power that just circled slowly and surely around the swim before dragging the rod over and lodging itself solidly beneath the willow again. Slow and steady pressure from my Allcock's Super Wizard eventually told and I felt the barbel move slowly up the margin towards me. As soon as the fish was under my feet I crammed on as much pressure as the tackle could take and felt the fish lift and turn before another strong run took her back down to the willow again. She was tired now, though, and the next time I brought her level with me I held her and soon a lovely, fin perfect barbel of nearly Ten pounds was ready for the net.

Bill also caught a couple of lovely barbel before dusk settled and we had to leave. The trudge back up the steps to the car park would indeed have been the gruelling slog that Bill had predicted, except that our success buoyed our stride and I hardly felt the cramp in my muscles when I collapsed, gasping for breath at the top. Over the years I came to hate those steps with a vengeance and I'm sure the flight got longer every time I fished. The steps were so quick to descend and so hard to climb that it felt like the river was trying to trap us on its banks.

Bill and I enjoyed a couple of seasons' superb fishing on the club ticket but then we heard the bad news that the club had lost the fishing rights because of the amount of litter left on the riverside after their matches. Sensing an opportunity, I wrote to the estate with the proposal that my friend Keith and I wanted to take on management of the fishery and run it as a small syndicate. Our proposal led to a meeting with the owner and before the start of the following season we had secured a lease of the fishery. There was even better news because we had also persuaded the estate owner to allow us to fish the stretch at night (something never allowed before) and to build a syndicate hut in a small copse near the river.

The Severn Oaks Syndicate came together like driftwood collecting in an eddy of floodwater and before long we had a group of eighteen like-minded friends with whom to share the fishery. Slowly we all got to know the water and before long new areas had been explored and new swims found and named. The slack beneath the willows where I landed the near double proved to be a consistent swim for the larger barbel and I named it the "Withy Glide". We soon realised that the willows upstream and downstream, where the shallow water was enriched with oxygen, could be equally productive on hot summer days and the "Upper" and "Lower Withy" were born.

We found another fantastic pool and glide that we named the "Aquarium" because the water was so clear and the swim was always full of fish. I spent an hour here watching from the bank as one of the members fished the far bank willows with a swim feeder, after wading out into the near margin to make the cast easier. Each time he filled his feeder before the cast he inevitably dropped some hemp and casters into the shallow water around his feet and when he was concentrating on his rod tip, two huge barbel appeared from some cover downstream and cruised up to feed on this spilled bait. Every time he reeled in, the fish drifted back downstream to their hiding place and the angler was completely oblivious to the company of these two barbel as they fed. I suppose the biggest fish would have weighed about eleven pounds and the lesser one about nine. I didn't like to disturb the scene by making the angler and barbel aware of each other's presence.

Bill's swim turned out to be the most prolific on the fishery and big catches of barbel and chub could be taken here, either legering or on the float. Keith enjoyed an amazing day fishing this swim, on which he caught a mixed bag of more than forty barbel to nearly nine pounds and some big chub, all taken on trotted maggot and caster. The river here was a comfortable wading depth across to the far bank "pot" and it was a lovely swim to fish on a hot day, as the cooling Severn flow swept past and the barbel fed with abandon.

I was fishing this swim in chest waders one night when I heard a commotion in the river below me and something large and unseen splashed past along the far bank of the river. Soon afterwards I felt an almighty thump against my legs and a shower of spray soaked me. I turned, just in time to see a big boil on the surface of the river, as my assailant shot away upstream. Then a bow wave appeared and arrowed towards me down the flow. As the bow wave reached me and an unseen creature turned beneath the surface, the muscular tail of an otter smacked into my legs for a second time. I started to back out of the river but the otter attacked twice more before I reached the bank. As soon as I reached dry ground, the bitch whistled and two silver arrows on the moonlit surface of the river traced the passage of her cubs as they swam upstream to join her.

The top boundary of the fishery was just above the largest and deepest corner on the whole of the River Severn. Called the "Ell Hole", it was a right angled bend where the river had carved a deep (some said bottomless!) pool beneath a sandstone and shale cliff that towered nearly two hundred feet above the river. I never found out how deep the "Ell Hole" actually was but the farmer swore that entire trees had fallen in over the years and been sucked under by the vicious currents and lost without trace. There is no doubt that it was a daunting place to fish, reached only by wading to the pool through the shallow glide below or scrambling precariously down the cliff face.

I never managed to get a bite fishing in the depths of the pool itself but the run into the bend was a good spot for big barbel after dusk and the run out from the bend was one of the best barbel swims on the fishery, holding large numbers of fish of all sizes. I would have loved to have taken some scuba gear up to the "Ell Hole" but I never found time to do this. There is a similar big pool on the Ribble that I know, which is a noted place for finding Roman artefacts, thrown in to appease the river gods. I imagine the Ell Hole might hold all sorts of interesting archaeology and it would have been an exciting but slightly risky place to explore underwater. I once saw a huge pike of at least thirty pounds in the pool and an encounter with that alone would make the risk worthwhile.

Photo courtesy of David Miller

I called the next sweeping bend downstream of the Ell Hole the "Swallow Glide", in memory of a summer evening I spent perched on a willow branch above the water whilst dozens of swallows skimmed past between my legs, feasting on the swarms of gnats and taking an occasional drink from the river. I was perched on my branch because it was the only place from which I could present a bait to a brace of big barbel that had taken up residence under the willow roots. I'd spotted a golden flash deep in the pool as one of the two fish turned in the sunset and I spent an uncomfortable hour up the tree trying unsuccessfully to tempt one to take a lump of meat. I failed to induce a take and in the end both the barbel drifted off downstream as the light faded, leaving the pool to the dancing swallows and to me.

The tail of the Swallow Glide was where a good friend of mine, Dave Nicholls, caught his first barbel. Dave joined the syndicate primarily to explore the fishery's potential for brown trout and salmon because he was a keen fly fisherman. The desire to catch a barbel soon caught hold, however, and I showed him how to tackle up for barbel, how to cast with a centerpin and where the likely spots were. Dave always seemed to be unlucky, though, and the harder I tried to put him into some productive barbel swims the longer his run of blanks became. In the end, after many days spent trying to catch a barbel under my inadequate supervision, Dave vanished for an evening and wandered up to the Swallow Glide alone, where he waded out into the tail of the pool and caught fourteen barbel fishing a Czech nymph on his fly rod! Dave died tragically last year from a brain tumour and I'm glad I have a photograph of him returning the biggest of those Swallow Glide barbel, to remind me of a wonderful time spent in the best of company.

The fishery was often at its best in the most unlikely of conditions. I loved to fish a big winter flood and when the Severn had almost burst its banks and was running a metre or more above its normal level the barbel fishing could be spectacular. Under these conditions, the barbel congregated in the slacks and eddies in the margins of the flow and it was easy to find them. Often when the water was high and coloured they fed with abandon and it was always possible to catch a big barbel or two.

Sometimes though the conditions weren't just challenging, they were downright dangerous! The Severn in full spate is an elemental force of nature and not to be treated lightly. I spent a long weekend at the Severn Oaks with Dave Nicholls that really brought home to me just how dangerous the river could be. We had timed our visit to coincide with an autumn flood because we had plans to test out the untapped salmon fishing potential of our part of the river. We called the phone service that recorded the river levels at Welshpool and thought we would arrive at the river just as the peak of a big autumn spate had passed. This would give us two days of fishing as the river fined down after the flood and we were confident that we would catch some good barbel in these prime conditions. We were also hopeful that we might see some salmon moving and we had fly rods and spinning tackle with us to cover this eventuality.

What we hadn't taken into account was the sheer volume of rain that had fallen in the Welsh mountains that week. Far from falling, the river was still on the way up when we arrived at the syndicate hut and set off to fish on the first evening. There were two or three swims that we knew well by now, which we could reach safely in chest waders even when the water was lapping the top of the riverbank. In fact these conditions were when these swims were in their prime for a big barbel.

I'd caught two Eight pounders before I realised the river wasn't just lapping into the field any longer, it was positively flowing in. Not only that, it had filled an old, dry cut-off channel across the field between us and the hut as well. The cut-off had done its job well and we were stranded, cut off from the safety of the higher ground where we had built the hut. Suddenly, we weren't just paddling across a soggy field, we were in real danger, wading knee deep through a river that had grown to be over three hundred yards wide and that was getting deeper and wider by the minute. We made it back to safety in the end but it was pretty hairy, especially when we had to cross the deeper channel, where the water was over waist deep and pushing through like a steam train.

We spent the next day and a half stranded in the hut, drinking tea and putting the world to rights in between long walks to photograph the flood and marvel at nature's power. When the river did drop, not long before we had to leave, we caught another barbel each and Dave landed a Four pound chub from the middle of a field, where he found it feeding in the eddy created by a cattle trough! We also saw two grilse moving and then Dave found a salmon stranded in a depression in one of the fields. We carried

the stranded silver fish back to the main channel and released it to continue its ascent of the river to spawn.

On our way home we drove through Shrewsbury and were stunned by the devastation in the town. The car parks by the river were more like marinas and we could just see the tops of the roofs of the lines of abandoned vehicles. A floating Thai restaurant moored in the river above the Welsh Bridge had gone down with all hands and the roads were covered in silt.

The estate owner had taken quite a liking to us and two years into our lease he let us extend our fishing downstream below the main house. The "new" river ran through an overgrown wood that concealed the remnants of some wonderful abandoned architecture from the estate's heyday. We found an old ice house, an ancient pump house for taking river water up to the mansion and, best of all, the crumbling remains of a fantastic Gothic boathouse that was falling sedately into the river.

The boathouse had a wall running parallel to the riverbank that created a safe harbour for the boatmen to load and discharge their passengers. This harbour had an entrance that pointed upstream, so that the boats could safely navigate out into the flow of the main river. There was a small building that was linked to this harbour by an ornate, covered veranda that had a small flight of steps to take the ladies and gentlemen down to their punts or skiffs. It was easy to ignore the fallen masonry, the silted harbour, the rusting ironwork and the encroaching ivy. Whenever I fished the "Boathouse", I would squint slightly and picture the Edwardian ladies with their parasols and flowing summer dresses, sipping champagne and laughing genteelly as their beaux escorted them down to the harbour and set sail. I missed several good bites thanks to such flights of fancy but the Boathouse became my favourite swim on the river. I used to love fishing from the remains of the veranda and sipping a glass of port as the sun set across the river; it was my tribute to the vision of the people who built this lovely relic of a bygone age.

Despite its early potential, the Severn Oaks water never really produced the huge barbel we hoped to find there. That doesn't mean they weren't present, just that we didn't fish long enough or hard enough to find them. In fact, the biggest factors in our failure to catch a monster were that there was simply so much untapped water to cover and the fact that the syndicate was relaxed, unpressured and not in the least bit competitive in its fishing.

Keith caught the first double from the stretch, when he landed a short, stocky Ten pounder from the "Log Jam", the swim where I caught my first Severn Oaks barbel. My own biggest was just over Eleven pounds and, as far as I'm aware, the record barbel landed in our time on the fishery was a superb Twelve pounds Eight ounce fish caught by Dave Foley. I've lost touch with Dave, which is a massive shame because he was really great company in which to pass time on the riverbank. Dave was so swept away by his first visit to the Severn Oaks water that he left an old claw-bail Mitchell 300 on the roof of my car as a present, with a little note of thanks for the invitation to join the syndicate. That sort of generosity of spirit epitomised the Severn Oaks Syndicate and I have many happy memories of my time there.

As is the way with such things, time and lives moved on like the river itself, taking us away from the pools where we fished and carrying us off down different glides to new waters. The core of the syndicate are still good friends and still meet from time to time, and the syndicate itself lives on under a new management. For me, though, the move down to Somerset took me too far from the river to allow me to give the management of the syndicate the attention it demanded and deserved. Ashmead also came to dominate my time, which made that rare resource even more difficult to find.

After deciding to give up my membership and step down as a leaseholder, I made the journey up to the Severn Oaks and fished its waters one last time. I spent a day walking and fishing the entire beat from the lower boundary, up past the Boathouse, the Pump, the Ice House, the Log Jam, Withy Glides, Aquarium, Swallow Glide and Ell Hole. I savoured every cast I made and every memory I passed along the way. In the field by the copse that housed our hut, I discovered that one of the seven great oak trees that inspired the syndicate name had fallen and it lay rather sadly on its side, like a monument to the passing of an era. When I found it, I knew it was time to leave and I turned my back on the river and slogged back up those bloody steps for the last time.

Alchemy

" An early, unscientific form of chemistry that sought to change base metals into gold and discover a life-prolonging elixir "

I've always been an all-round angler, brought up on the writings of my childhood hero and now sadly missed friend, Bernard Venables. I didn't get to know Bernard until I was in my thirties, when he became the President of The Golden Scale Club, but his alter ego, Mr Crabtree, taught me from an early age to enjoy the wide variety of fishing available to the British angler during the course of the year.

I've always loved the contrasts in fishing. The rise of a wild trout to the fly; the thumping bite and fight of a barbel; the flash and swagger of the perch and the subtlety and majesty of a large carp - each bring their own distinct challenges and pleasures. I love the beauty of the surroundings into which each species leads me, from lily covered pools to brooding highland lochs, and from sparkling mountain burns to meandering lowland rivers.

The main flow of my fishing each year eddies around trout in the spring, carp and barbel in the summer and autumn and pike during the winter months, but I also get diverted into side streams and backwaters containing salmon, chub, perch, tench and grayling. I enjoy the variety but if I had to limit myself to just one kind of fish, I'd pass my days next to a classic estate lake, casting for wildies. There is something magical about conjuring a bar of purest gold from the depths.

I caught my first wildie when I was seventeen, from an ancient monastery pond that lay hidden in the depths of the Somerset countryside. I'd already caught a few mirror and common carp into double figures from the River Parrett near my home and my carp angling addiction had developed to a stage where every rumour about the existence of a carp pool had to be explored. I once cycled over sixty miles in a day, from one promising splash of blue on the Ordnance Survey map to another, in search of my dream water but every one turned out to be a figment of the cartographers imagination or a silted up, stagnant remnant of a once lovely estate lake.

The Monastery Pool was one of the few blue dots on the map that didn't turn out to be an illusion. The pool was roughly circular and covered about three acres, with no area greater than three feet deep. I fished there for the first time on a glorious autumn day and the woodland surrounding the water glowed with a gold made even brighter by the contrast with the kingfisher-blue sky.

I had sweetcorn and lobworms with me, both of which had proven to be effective baits for the Parrett carp. I fished a single rod (my lucky MkIV); casting the scarlet tip of my quill to join the collage of reflections about ten yards beyond the rod tip. Whilst the reflections danced continuously in the light breeze, my quill remained obstinately still as the hours slipped past.

Have you ever sat for an hour or more watching the tip of a motionless float against the restless, shifting backdrop of a lake? The effect is quite mesmeric and when you finally drag your eyes away from the float, the movement of the water remains imprinted upon your eyes, so that the whole world is deliquescent and appears to have become liquid. When I looked up eventually from the float, everything seemed to flow around me and the hard facts of life (including my straight rod and motionless float) ebbed, drifted and melted into my surroundings. I had become completely absorbed by this hallucination when the float sailed away and, as a result, I missed the only bite of the morning.

After lunch another angler joined me on the bank. He was obviously a local who knew the water well because he made a bee-line for a particular swim and, without even glancing at the lake, set up a complicated leger rig that he used to cast a large lump of crust out into the middle of the pool.

No sooner had the crust bobbed up to the surface than the water near to it swirled and rocked and it disappeared with a gurgling suck. From a distance I watched the angler battle with a demon that tore all over the place in its fury at being hooked. I'd never seen anything quite like it and it seemed to take the angler forever to bring the carp to the net.

In no time at all, I stripped my quill from the line and hurled a half-ounce bomb with a three foot tail out across the water, baited with the remains of my last sandwich. It was the first time I'd ever fished a surface bait and the tension became almost unbearable as first one large shadow and then another appeared beneath the bread, eyeing it suspiciously but with clear intent. I think the earlier disturbance had made the carp a little wary but before long one of them edged towards the crust, prompting the second, slightly smaller carp to lunge forward and engulf it before it lost its chance of an easy meal.

The shocking speed and power of that fish will live with me forever. Within a heartbeat, the carp had stripped twenty yards of line from the reel, changed direction and run another five before crashing out through the surface like a tarpon. How the small hook held I will never know but my reactions simply couldn't keep pace with the fish and I had no control over the fight at all. My old Mitchell 300 couldn't handle the onslaught either and it simply exploded under the pressure. I had to handline the carp into the margins where it thrashed the water into a maelstrom before I finally managed to scoop it into my landing net. My Mitchell never recovered and I still have it on the shelf at home, a shattered memento of my first wildie.

My first wildie; it weighed just less than Five pounds but it had fought harder than any double figure King Carp I'd ever landed. It was beautiful, with small, regular scales of a deep bronze along its back that gave way to purest gold on its flanks and butter yellow on the belly and at the base of every fin. The fins themselves were almost scarlet, shot through with a lighter orange, and the symmetrical tail was enormous, each lobe almost as large as my hand. The wildie positively bristled with attitude and, even in defeat, it quivered with wild defiance. Somehow, the carp's whole demeanour was so much more vibrant and alive than that of the docile King Carp I had caught before. It was a bit like the contrast between a wild buffalo and a dairy cow.

In that moment I was hooked as surely as the carp and I have never been able to break free from the hold that fishing for wildies has over me. I returned to the Monastery at the first opportunity, yet I never cast a line there again. The pool had been drained and dredged and the carp removed by a new owner who wanted to stock it with some "proper carp" instead of the "stunted" fish it had contained, so that he could charge anglers proper rates to fish, rather than stunted day-ticket prices. I was devastated and although I now live less than half an hour from the pool, I will never go back.

So, what is a wildie? In his book "A History of Carp Fishing", Kevin Clifford disputed the idea that any true wild carp are to be found in England today. He suggested that most, if not all, so-called "wildies" are no more than feral, under-nourished common carp. It is difficult to debunk this view and I think he is right in many cases but I believe that true wild carp can still be caught from some secluded sanctuaries that have evaded the invasion of the Kings. All of the wildies I claim to have caught have had clear characteristics that conform to those set out in the scientific literature and I am certain that some of their haunts haven't been stocked since the early 1700's, which is good enough for me! The only way to be really sure would be to carry out some genetic tests to compare our wildies with wild carp from the original source populations in Eastern Europe.

Perhaps the most comprehensive study of wild carp and their history is a paper published in 1995 by the Canadian fisheries scientist Eugene Balon, in the scientific journal Aquaculture (a friend of mine, Nigel, found the paper and sent me a copy recently). Balon traced the origins of wild carp back to populations in the Black, Caspian and Aral seas, from where he mapped their spread eastwards into Asia (tracing their evolution into the ornamental Japanese "nishikigoi", which Balon romantically calls the "swimming flowers") and westwards across Europe and into Britain, probably early in the 16th century. As with so much of value, Balon credits the Roman Empire as being responsible for their spread, as a food source, from natural populations in the Danube Delta.

- "What have the Romans ever done for us?"

- "What about roads?" "What about sanitation?"

- "What about wild carp?"

- "Ah, now you're talking!!"

Balon described the characteristic features of the wildie, including the long, torpedo- shaped body, large, regular scaling and typical colouration. Without delving into the complex meristic characteristics that a scientist would use to determine whether or not a fish is a true wildie (scale counts, the fin rays, the size and shape of the pharyngeal teeth and so on), the most significant outward sign is probably the almost straight transition between the head and the top of the body, without the humped shoulder of the domesticated King Carp.

Interestingly, Balon also noted that wild carp are more mobile, stronger and nimbler than their domesticated counterparts because of their adaptation to life in the rivers from which they originated. These characteristics also account for the wildies strength, stamina and lightning speed when hooked. Balon described the physiological differences that underlie the wildies better performance. Wildies have been shown to have more red blood cells and haemoglobin than domestic carp and a better blood supply to feed oxygen to their muscles. They have far higher blood sugar levels, more fat in their organs and more glycogen in their liver, which gives them greater stamina than the plodding Kings. They also have more vitamin A in the eyes and liver than the domesticated strains (Steffens, 1964). In short, wildies are truly the international athletes of the carp world.

After the loss of the Monastery, I didn't catch another wildie until I joined the Golden Scale Club and became close friends with Mike Winter. Mike founded the Devon Carp Catchers Club with Larry Beck in 1958 and is known to everyone in the Golden Scale as "Prof". I'm sure that Prof knows every wildie water west of Dorchester and we have spent many happy years fishing some of them together (although one or two are so secret that Prof has never divulged their whereabouts).

Going back to the wildies strength and speed, Prof and a friend of his once measured the run of a hooked wildie at an average of over 15 mph and estimated that its top speed, against the pull of a fully bent MKIV, must have been over 20mph. They also calculated that the spool on Prof's Elite must have been blurring around at 2700 rpm to keep up! No wonder my old Mitchell melted…. Prof has recounted this story and many other tales of his wildie fishing in his lovely book called "Along Fisherman's Paths", published by Medlar, and I would recommend it to anyone with an angler's soul.

It's thanks to Prof that I have followed my love of wildies to some of the most beautiful pools in the southwest. Along the way I've learned that traditional wildies respond best to simple, traditional ways. Bolt rigs, hairs and boilies should play no part in wildie fishing and their fighting prowess cannot be appreciated on any rod of more than a 2lb test or line of more than eight pounds breaking strain. No, wildies should be sought with light tackle (preferably with a quill float and a centerpin) and simple baits such as sweetcorn and bread.

Another thing I've discovered about wildies is that they love Swamp Snot. Swamp Snot is a great term coined by the American angling writer John Geirach to describe the coagulated scum of algal residue, dead insects, leaves and other detritus that often forms on the surface of old estate lakes. In my experience, wildies are only found in lakes that produce Swamp Snot and the snot draws the wildies like a magnet, as they are attracted to the rich supply of food that is trapped and held by this natural, floating glue.

Chapter Twelve – Alchemy

Swamp Snot lead me to my first double figure wildie. Some Golden Scale Club friends had gathered to fish a lake that is steeped in angling history and mystery, during the traditional opening week of 1996. Demus and I were sitting on a high bank above the shallows when a warm breeze picked up from nowhere, pushing the surface film before it.

"Just look at all that Swamp Snot, Skeff," said Demus. We could also make out the dark shadows of several large carp that were drifting down-wind with the scum. They appeared and disappeared beneath patches of it, like barrage balloons drifting between the clouds. As the carp followed the Swamp Snot, so we took our stalking rods and followed the carp.

In a damp and rather gloomy corner of the pool, I found that a snot bed several yards across had collected around the base of a tiny island. I waded out as quietly as possible, but several bow waves still sped away on my approach. Coagulating vortices were left in the scum, marking the positions in which the departing carp had lain. Through these windows formed in the snot I could see that the scum was over an inch thick and had the consistency of the head on a pint of real ale.

I settled down quietly with my back against a willow and flicked some dog biscuits out into the snot one at a time, so that they sounded just like the beech-nut husks that were falling periodically from the encroaching trees. Almost at once I began to notice humping and tiny movements in the scum that were clearly not caused by the breeze. Gently, and so slowly that it was almost impossible to detect their movement, a pair of cream coloured lips engulfed a biscuit. In another area, the biscuits were silently disappearing one by one, as a carp sucked them down from below, without disturbing the Swamp Snot at all. The biscuits span in little vortices that led into the carp's mouth. Elsewhere, a dorsal spine flickered upwards and a scaled back rose briefly through the filth, before vanishing again without trace. As I adjusted my senses to these small signs of life, I became aware that the water in front of me was alive with fish. Some were passing so close to me that I could have reached out easily and touched their flanks.

I baited with a single biscuit and cast so that my line passed over the end of a twig about four feet away. The biscuit was lowered into the Swamp Snot without any tell-tale nylon touching the surface. Five minutes passed, ten, twenty, and then the Swamp Snot beneath my bait bulged slowly upwards. I could picture the carp, scanning the layer of scum for the food that its sensitive taste organs had detected. There was a sound like the remnants of a thick milkshake being sucked into a straw and the twig vibrated as the line tightened.

"Ready," I thought. "Steady, NOW!"

There was a sudden boil on the surface, as the hook struck home and the carp sent spume flying into the air with a great sweep of its tail. The rod slammed over and the centerpin rasped, as the incredibly fast, powerful carp dived for some sunken branches to my right. Side strain and pressure from above only just turned it in time. There was a horrible grating sensation of line on wood, before the fish turned suddenly and the line cut left into open water.

The carp sped through the water in a series of long runs, punctuated by rapid, apparently random changes in direction. At one point, the fish leapt out of the water, like a golden salmon, shaking its head and thrashing its tail. I waded along the margin to reach a better stance from which to control the fight, wolf-whistling as I went. By the time Demus reached me, the battle was won and my sagging net cradled a fish I had been chasing for over fourteen years; a double-figure wildie of Thirteen pounds Four ounces. As Demus took its portrait, the sunlight played across its bronzed flanks and the carp gleamed.

Chapter Twelve – Alchemy

I caught my largest ever wildie from the same pool in 1998. Sitting at the end of an oak branch, some twenty feet above the surface of the lake, I watched the wildie cruising lethargically around a sunken snag below me, its dorsal cleaving the surface. The wildie swam with bored sweeps of its tail, until it drifted directly beneath my perch and revealed its enormous length for the first time. I stalked the carp for nearly two hours before fooling it into accepting a floater, drifted hard up against the snag. The whole world exploded when I set the hook and I remember nothing of the fight but snapshot images of tails and scales and flying water, yet somehow I brought it to the net. At Fifteen pounds Eight ounces it remains my largest wildie and by far my best ever carp. Beside it, the thirty, forty and fifty pound Kings that have graced my net pale into insignificance.

I'm sad to say that even the wildies of this sanctuary are threatened with extinction because of the introduction of King Carp into the pool. Wildies simply cannot compete with the larger domestic strains that are such efficient feeders. In every water I know where the ancient wildies have been forced to compete with stocked mirrors and commons, they decline and die out eventually. Even where they do manage to hang on for a few years, the purity of the strain is compromised. In fact, Prof and I are now struggling to find a wildie water within casting distance and I know of none in the area that remain "pure". Prof knows of a pool in Devon that has remained unstocked since 1830, so perhaps there is hope that I may one day fulfil my greatest angling dream and catch a pure wildie of more than twenty pounds. If I ever do, I will die a happy man.

It is a tragic indictment of carp anglers that we don't value the wildie in its own right and its important place in our angling heritage. Size, it seems, is all. Wildie waters are already rare and are disappearing fast as, one after another, they are stocked with domestic carp. Without action to save them, the wild carp will soon be extinct in Britain and hundreds of years of natural heritage will have been destroyed. I am ashamed to say that carp anglers will have been the cause of this desecration.

If you know of a wildie pond that has survived the pressures of the modern carp scene, please treasure it and keep it safe and secret; although you might think to drop me a line…..

References.
Balon, EK., 1995. Origin and Domestication of the wild carp, Cyprinus carpio: from Roman gourmets to the swimming flowers. Aquaculture., 129: 3-48.
Steffens, W., 1964. Vergleichende anatomisch-physiologische Untersuchungen an Wild- und Teichkarpfen (Cyprinus carpio L.). Ein Beitrag zur Beurteilung der Zuchtleistungen beim Deutschen Teichkarpfen. Z. Fisch., 12: 725-800.

A Fool and His Eel

Some years ago, my friend Steve Maynard, who owned Ashmead, told me that he needed to sell the lake for a number of reasons. He didn't want to put Ashmead on the open market but wanted instead to find someone who would respect the unique qualities and history of the pool and who had the vision and commitment to protect its future.

Tom Squires, the previous owner of Ashmead, had sold the lake to Steve on a similar basis, having decided that Steve was the perfect person to protect the lake, and Steve wanted to take a similar approach, recognising that the future of Ashmead was more important than simply making the biggest possible profit from the deal. Steve asked if I would be interested in buying the lake and I will be eternally grateful that he thought that I was the right person for the job. Everything fell into place and in the following April my wife Shona and I took over the freehold of the seventeen-acre wetland.

Property ownership is an interesting concept when it's applied to somewhere as special as Ashmead. Ownership gives us direct control over the future of the property to a degree, but we are dependent upon our membership to finance our plans and to cover the costs of caring for the fishery. With this in mind, we carefully selected members who had a genuine empathy with our objectives and we tried to involve them in everything we did and in every decision we made. We needed members who wanted to be a part of Ashmead's long-term future, rather than anglers interested only in catching the 'target' carp before moving on. Only if our anglers had a real sense of commitment, and had pride in the fishery, could we succeed in our aims. We keep this same philosophy alive at Ashmead today and we select new recruits to the syndicate from candidates recommended by the existing members, to ensure the unique atmosphere of the fishery is maintained.

We are also aware that everything we value about Ashmead is the product of centuries of empathetic management by previous owners, from the Duchy of Cornwall, through to Tom Squires and Steve Maynard. We see our role as that of custodians who have been entrusted with the future of Ashmead for a brief time and we are determined to hand it on to the next generation in good shape.

In the context I have just described, my job as a senior conservation manager with The National Trust has interesting parallels with our management of the lake. My role in the Trust is essentially to help develop our land management policy and provide professional advice on the management of the

Trust's estate. In fact, I've just been leading a team to develop a comprehensive Freshwater Fisheries Management policy for the Trust for the first time.

The Trust owns its property inalienably, which in simple terms means that it can't be sold but is held permanently 'For the benefit of the nation': 'Forever, for everyone….' as the Trust strapline puts it. 'Forever' is a concept that takes almost a leap of faith to grasp, especially when you are making decisions that will affect the quality of some of our most precious landscapes for generations to come.

Some important philosophical ideas underpin everything that we do in the Trust. In terms of my own work, the most fundamental of these is our definition of 'conservation' (the Trust's core purpose) as 'The careful management of change'.

The Trust's conservation philosophy embraces the idea that even our wildest British landscapes have been influenced by man and that carefully managed change is inevitable and essential, if they are to be protected for future generations.

The same philosophy underpins the management of Ashmead under our stewardship. In fact, one of the first things we did when we bought the wetland was to plan an exciting transformation that would not only restore and protect the nature of the site, but develop the full potential of Ashmead as one of the best carp fisheries in the country.

When we bought Ashmead the ancient wetland had two main areas consisting of Goat Willow Pool and the wider wetland area. Steve Maynard created Goat Willow, a separate three-acre pool in the heart of the wetland, in 1995 and it is this lake that held the huge carp for which the fishery is famous. The remaining fourteen acres of channels, bays, reedbeds and open water had silted up over the decades and had been stripped of fish by otters visiting from the River Yeo.

The first thing we did as owners of the pool was to set out on a major project to restore the entire wetland area and to reconnect it with Goat Willow. Our plan was to give the Ashmead carp room to continue to grow and to create a unique fishery where you are as likely to catch a forty pounder from

Chapter Thirteen – A Fool and His Eel

beneath the rod tip whilst stalking the channels, as you are during a session fishing the areas of open water. One of our future aims is also to set up a breeding programme, to secure the long term future of the Ashmead stock and to make the Ashmead strain available to other fisheries.

Since we bought Ashmead, the fishery has continued to answer the dreams of those who fish there. At first, just three of us fished the lake, whilst Shona and I planned for the future and pulled together the core membership of the new syndicate. I couldn't resist the temptation to be selfish and to spend some time fishing at Ashmead on my own, to absorb the atmosphere, reflect on the past and plan for the future. We also invited two local friends, Alan Gaylard and Martin Head to fish. Both had supported us in putting our plans together and giving them some exclusive angling gave us an opportunity to thank them for their help.

I fished my first session as the new owner of Ashmead that February, sharing the lake with Alan for a night. There was a lovely winter sunset that painted the landscape with a rose tinted glow that matched my mood perfectly. Alan had already settled on the North Point when I arrived in the evening and as I wandered around to see him, I spotted an area of disturbed silt off the east bank. A mild wind pushed into the area and I elected to set up there in the ideal conditions, fishing two rods into open water amongst the remnants of last autumn's weed. I catapulted out some hemp and the water had barely settled when a carp head and shouldered over the spot. Brimming with confidence and happy with the world I settled back to wait.

It turned out that the rosy sunset had been misleading. From the west, a black bank of cloud built steadily on the horizon, blotting out the last, lingering glow of the day. The weather front hit the lake just before night fell, sending a wall of rain sweeping across the lake on the back of a vicious squall of wind. I only just managed to get my shelter up in time.

The storm was wild and I spent the first few hours of darkness clinging to the ribs of my brolly as gale force winds threatened to blow it away and expose me to the torrential rain. Then the storm passed as swiftly as it had arrived, revealing a bright winter starscape that twinkled in the still, damp air.

Just after midnight I had a steady run, which accelerated when I picked up the rod and bent into the fish. The carp hung deep and I made little impression as it swung left and headed for the margins of an island about twenty yards away. I had nothing to do with the fact that the fish stopped short of the safety of the marginal reeds but for some reason it boiled on the surface and turned, cutting back to my right and away from their sanctuary. I think it just felt safer in the deeper water.

The carp hugged the bottom of the deep bay, circling steadily and sometimes making a longer, more purposeful run through the remnants of the weed. I merely hung on, powerless to do anything other than maintain the bend in the rod and apply as much pressure as I dared. After twenty minutes impasse I was beginning to doubt that the carp would ever tire. I'd been wolf-whistling to get Alan's attention to help with the net and he finally appeared out of the darkness just as the carp showed the first signs

of weakness. Even so, it was another ten minutes before Alan finally lifted the mesh around the frame of a huge mirror.

When Heady first learned that I had bought Ashmead, he commented that it had been fate that I had caught Single Scale (the water's first fifty-pounder) the previous summer. He said the lake's largest carp had obviously wanted to show her approval of the change in ownership. Now I laughed out loud (Alan must have thought I was mad!) because here she was again, gleaming in the torchlight. She was down in weight at Forty Eight pounds Eight ounces and in fine condition, having evidently spawned successfully the previous summer. We took one quick photograph and returned her.

Single Scale was clearly feeding well in the mild weather because Heady caught her again a week later (his largest carp to date). Normally this carp is caught once, or at most twice in a season but the lake had hardly been fished whilst I'd been negotiating the purchase and she was clearly hungry and less suspicious after the break from any angling pressure.

A few weeks later, Alan caught a lovely, deep-bodied mirror of nearly Thirty Four pounds and I was full of confidence when I returned on 25th March for an overnight session. I set up in the south west corner, where I had seen fish bubbling during the previous week. I positioned one bait at the base of a long marginal ledge to my left, pinning the line to the top of the ledge with a backlead, so that the slack line followed the contour of the slope and left little chance of spooking any browsing carp. A second was cast to open water to my right near an old weedbed. As I sorted out the tackle, a carp rolled off the back of a nearby island and a third bait was dropped on the spot, tight to a clump of iris. I felt the lead hit hard clay with a satisfying thump that indicated that feeding fish had cleared the area of silt.

Each rod was baited with a large boilie and fished over a small handful of free offerings and some hemp. These days, all the reputable firms produce good baits that will catch fish if applied correctly and I think location and approach are far more important than the bait used. I've used pretty much the same type of boilie from Bill Cottam at Nutrabaits for the last eight years with complete confidence. It has a superb, wholesome smell, with the spicy overtones of Madagascar Clove and it is an exceptional bait that has caught me carp from a number of very difficult waters; it stands out, it's different and the carp love it.

In common with many other syndicates, most of the anglers fishing Ashmead in the past clubbed together on a going bait each season. I've always ploughed my own furrow and like to use a bait that I know the carp have not seen before. I remember a story in Rod Hutchinson's book, 'The Carp Strikes Back', about the pursuit of a particularly large carp on a little-fished pit. Rod quickly established a bait that had the carp feeding enthusiastically and he soon hooked and lost a big carp. Instead of persevering with the same bait, as most anglers would do, he changed to another immediately, just in case the carp he had hooked and lost had been the one he was after. It is that sort of thinking that sets anglers like Rod apart.

I had a fast run off the shelf within an hour and after a fast and furious fight landed a beautiful common of Twenty Eight pounds Eight ounces. The carp was as fresh as a sea-liced salmon and I don't think it had seen a hook before. I returned it chastened and wiser after taking its portrait.

Everything was quiet that night, apart from a tawny owl hooting in the oaks behind me. It turned cold and a sheen of frost glistened in the dawn sunlight. I knew I had to go at lunchtime and I sat back to enjoy the morning and scan the water for signs of carp. A gang of long-tailed tits distracted me and I spent an hour watching them fighting for warmth in a willow thicket. Two of the tiny birds huddled together on a twig and a third then muscled in between them. Others fought their way into the centre of the line, to benefit from their companion's warmth, until the twig collapsed under their combined weight. They flew off in a flurry of feathers, only to start the whole process again on a new bough.

Midday came and I'd already packed away most of the gear when I had a run on the rod cast to the island. The carp kited on a tight line and I thought it would snag the tackle on the right-hand rod, so I moved quickly up the bank to avoid any tangles. I could see the flanks of a large mirror carp gleaming in the clear water, as it ploughed up and down the margin until it tired and came to the net.

I unhooked the carp and placed it carefully into a sack so that I could sort out my camera for a photograph. As I lowered the sack into the lake, I noticed that the top of the right-hand rod had pulled around and that the previously slack line was taught. Thinking I'd snarled the line during the fight after all, I secured the sack and picked up the rod to free it, only to find a powerful carp attached. The carp exploded from the swim and I later found that it had stripped the teeth on the anti-reverse switch of my Mitchell 410, such was the power of that first run. I was unprepared for action and the carp made it through the gap between two of the islands before I had the wits to turn it. I had a few hairy moments before I managed to bring it back into open water and eventually into the net.

What a brace! The mirror weighed an impressive Thirty Five pounds Twelve ounces and the second carp was an incredible golden common that was shaped like a huge wildie and at Thirty Six pounds Eight Ounces was the largest common I'd ever caught.

A week later I returned to the same swim for a two-night session that produced a catch that I don't believe I will ever surpass. On the first morning, I hooked an immensely powerful carp that fought hard for every inch of line. I knew which fish it was from the fight and I felt a little guilty when I hoisted Single Scale onto the mat for the second time in less than a month. I took little pleasure from the capture and apologised as I returned her.

Then, in the afternoon, I had a fast run on a single hookbait cast to a bubbler that I'd spotted in open water. The carp had been circling slowly over a bed of silt, pausing now and then to feed and making small frothing patches of bubbles that marked its route. I watched it for half an hour before flicking out a light lead with a long hook-length into its path, so that the bait settled with a minimum of disturbance onto the soft lakebed where the carp was sure to find it. I simply held the rod and waited for the slack line from the rod-tip to draw tight.

The strike pulled the hook into a solid resistance and the rod quivered briefly under full pressure before the fish succumbed and I slipped my net under a common carp that looked even longer and heavier than the common of the previous week. The balance confirmed that the weight of my biggest common had now climbed to Thirty Seven pounds Fourteen ounces. Its scales were larger and much darker than those of the Thirty Six pounder of the week before, looking more bronze than gold. It looked a real powerhouse of a fish yet the fight had been slightly lethargic and lacklustre given its size.

The next day I hooked another far more powerful carp from the same spot. Alan, who was fishing from the point opposite, came around to assist with the net and he spotted the large half-moon scale on the carp's shoulder as it surfaced. "I know which fish this is mate," he said. "Take it easy, you don't want this one to come off…." It was Moonscale, as impressive as ever and bristling with energy, at a weight of just under Forty Three pounds. In just two days, I'd landed the three largest known carp in the lake. As Heady said, it was as if the senior Ashmead carp all wanted to meet their new owner.

There was still one carp that I desperately wanted to see on the bank, a large common that had not been caught for more than three years. Rumours suggested that the carp had died or been taken by a marauding otter but I thought I'd seen it mooching around in the shallows a couple of years before and believed it was still alive.

I popped down to the lake for a walk one lunchtime, taking a rod with me, just in case a chance of a fish presented itself. Carp were feeding hard over a silt-bed near the south bank, smoke-screening and bubbling furiously as they rooted in the mud after a hatch of natural food. I cast a halibut pellet to them on a simple lift-style float rig and spent the next ten minutes on tenterhooks as browsing carp brushed the line, making the float duck and dive but without indicating a clear take worth striking.

Out of the corner of my eye I spotted a disturbance on the surface and, turning my head slowly, I saw a common cruising along the margin towards me. The carp swam right up to me and buried its head under a small patch of weed at my feet. It looked like a good double and when it tilted its head up and started to suck nonchalantly at the weed, I reeled in carefully, removed the float and shot and lowered the bait gently onto the weed near the carp's mouth. It sensed the bait immediately and teased the fronds of hornwort apart until it could suck in the pellet. It was then that I realised I had a problem; the carp was too close for me to strike properly as it was no more than a foot away from where I was standing. Instinctively, I reached out and grabbed the line and simply gave it a sharp tug with my hand; an unconventional but effective way to set the hook!

The carp rolled and smashed the surface with its tail, soaking me from head to foot, and thrust away into the silty water. It suddenly felt far more substantial than it had looked on the surface. During a determined fight, the carp continued to grow in stature and when I finally managed to bring it to the net I realised that I'd hooked the common for which I'd been searching. I weighed the carp carefully at Thirty Five pounds Eight ounces and when I looked at my watch, I found that I'd been fishing for just twenty minutes.

Of course I was delighted to catch such a stunning carp but even more pleasing was the way that the capture seemed to confirm that the patriarchs of Ashmead approved of their new guardians and the omens for the future of Ashmead looked good. Somehow, this fool had managed to catch his eel and hang on to it yet, even now, whenever I wander the banks of Ashmead, I still can't quite believe my luck.

Crumbleholmes Demise

After years of searching, I have almost given up any hope of stumbling across the perfect tackle shop. I suppose this chapter might be looked upon as a crie de couer, for someone to tell me where such an establishment can be found. Opinions as to what makes a good tackle shop will vary from angler to angler. In much the same way that personal preference might favour one rod over another; carbon fibre over cane or glass; fixed spool over centerpin; or even bream over barbel (heaven forbid!), one angler's ideal tackle shop would be another's idea of purgatory.

Just recently I made a visit to a shop that I have known all my life, which is as close to my ideal as any I have yet found. It would, in fact, be perfect, if only it sold fishing tackle! Mr Crumbleholme's hardware shop is, or was, on the main street of the sleepy Somerset village of South Petherton. Sadly, the proprietor died recently and when I last visited, the stock in his emporium was being run down in preparation for closure. I took my wife Shona to the shop, so that she could experience the atmosphere before it passed into folklore and became a distant memory to those villagers alive during the "Crumbleholme era".

Crumbleholme's sold everything! It was a family joke throughout my childhood that Crumbleholme's was somewhere you could buy anything from a Jay-cloth to a Jacuzzi. Shopping there was a magical experience. You were spellbound, from the moment you first glanced through the cluttered window, to the time when you finally escaped, clutching the item you came for and several additional purchases that you would never need.

The window was the lure, the web that enmeshed the shops' victims as surely as any spider's trap. Exciting, amusing, alluring, confusing; mops and brushes loomed large over shelves, where real lead soldiers fought farmyard animals across a tundra of buckles and buttons, string and tape. Gaudy mantle-piece ornaments posed alongside kitchen utensils and pots of paint. Flower pots were stacked into impossible towers next to tins of dog food, rolls of fabric and bottles of multi-purpose cleaner. Always, tucked into some corner, prominent enough to catch the eye but placed discretely enough as to appear unintentional, was the one thing you required. Even if the particular item you wanted wasn't there, you would always spot something of interest just as you turned to leave, which would encourage you onwards into the shop.

The trap shut with complete finality when you went through the door. It was always stiff to open, requiring a tug and a shove to break the seal against the undersized frame. It would catch against the floor and the old brass bell would clang and jingle, alerting the predator within. Once inside, the door would slide closed easily behind you with a smooth whisper; so silently that you didn't realise the trap was sprung until the catch snapped into place, with a final, doom-laden click.

Inside, the shop seemed vast. A central stand of display cabinets formed the focal point of a maze of shelving that led the unwary deeper and deeper into the dark recesses of the store. Customers were known to have disappeared for days at a time, before stumbling back onto the street, dazed, confused and looking ten years older. "All I wanted was a tap washer," they would mumble, as the ambulance took them away. Some were simply never seen again. Villagers in the square would be overheard talking; "Have you seen Phyllis recently?" "No my dear, she went into Crumbleholme's last week …." They would nod knowingly and glance furtively at the shop.

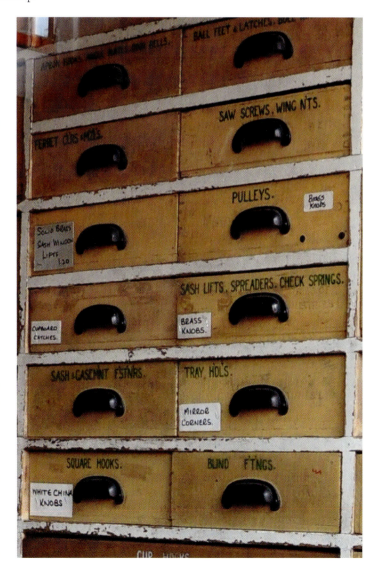

Mr Crumbleholme was the very epitome of the small shopkeeper. As the Aberdonian saying goes, "he wasn't tight with his money; just careful." His brown overall was probably of pre-war origin and he wrote out the itemised bill with a pencil stub so small, that he seemed to have graphite implanted into his finger. He charged fifty pence a week for any postcard occupying the prime advertising space in his window, whether it promoted an item for sale or a charity jumble.

I'm certain that he had a photographic memory, honed and focused over decades of hoarding. Mr Crumbleholme never discontinued a product line until it sold out completely. It was common to find tubs of mangle grease, covered in dust or boxes of radio valves, left over and redundant after the invention of the transistor. The banks of drawers were covered in layers of old hand-written labels that chartered the history of their contents over the decades. If you peered through the shop window at one prominent stack of home-made drawers just inside the glass you could even see one that was labelled "Ferret collars and muzzles" (or rather "FERRET CLRS & MZLS" in Mr Crumbleholme's shorthand). Mr Crumbleholme knew where each and every one of these items resided, even those that had not seen the light of day in twenty years. Ask him for anything, no matter how obscure and he would shut his eyes for a fraction of a second and then go straight to the racks of tiny drawers. "I'm sure I had a delivery of those in April '73......Ah yes! Here we are..."It is very sad that this great institution has been lost, because it is certain that it will never be replaced. Somehow, visiting B&Q won't be quite the same. I am now not only on the lookout for a tackle shop but a hardware store as well. To me, the requisite features are the same for both. I am a kleptomaniac when it comes to fishing tackle (I'm sure that most anglers are). A good tackle shop should not just be somewhere to visit to purchase tackle; it should provide counselling and support for our kleptomania. The shelves should be laden with weird and wonderful gadgets to be picked up, admired and discarded until next time. As with Crumbleholme's, one should be able to ask for obscure items, such as a low-bridged, chrome and agatine intermediate, without feeling ridiculous. What is more, there should be a better than even chance that the shop will have one in stock.

More importantly, the shop should have soul. Old, crumbling fish should stare accusingly down from cracked glass cases. The shop should smell of pipe tobacco and maggots, boiled hemp and damp. It should be the sort of place one can walk into in muddy boots and feel quite at home. Davis Angling, which serves the Royalty on the Hampshire Avon, is as good as it gets...

The character of the proprietor is an essential ingredient. The shopkeeper should welcome you in, pass the time of day and then leave you in peace to play with the toys he has provided for your entertainment. From time to time, he should sidle over to impart some great secret to you, sotto voce. "Wonderful hooks those, caught a twelve pound barbel on one from the weir last season....." or "Here, try a sprinkle of this in your maggots; it drives the roach wild....." or (if you are very lucky) "Do you fancy a cup of coffee?...." I was greeted recently in a well known Pall Mall establishment with a cool "Can I help you?" accompanied by a hard stare at the slime trail left by my footwear across the gleaming threshold. In these circumstances it is best to pretend to be looking for the optician's and leave quickly.

Good fishing shops should be cherished. Like good pubs, village Post Offices and old fashioned hardware shops, they are an endangered species. The scourge of the mail order tackle company poses the same threat to the local tackle shop as that which the supermarket giants pose to the souls of our towns. Convenience and discounted prices are the basis upon which such abominations survive.

Why should we pay twenty pounds more for a rod, ten pence more for a loaf or a pound more for a box of nails, in order to cover the high overheads of a small, town centre shop? To me, the answer is a simple one; I happen to like and value personal service. Equally, I like and value variety, character, eccentricity and camaraderie. All of these are negated by the impersonal commercialism of internet, mail order and supermarket. It is like the contrast between the richness of a mixed deciduous woodland and the hard sterility of conifer mono-culture. That which is financially more attractive in the short-term may leave us all impoverished in the future.

From the angler's point of view, the problem is also a practical one. We need our tackle shops, so that we can buy our pots of worms, our half pint of maggots, our packet of float rubbers; all those little essentials for our day on the bank. Like children in a sweet shop, we must have an outlet where we can go with our coins clutched tightly in our palms, to sample the excitement of "penny tray" shopping. The problem is that the pennies spent in this way must fall a long way short of the cash flow needed to sustain a shop in this day and age. Unless we visit those same shops with our cheque books out, in search of that new bivvy, rod or reel, they will be forced to close. It is impossible for the small tackle shop to compete on price alone or to carry the vast range of stock available through the mail order giants. Those that survive do so through specialisation or simply through the good will of their customers.

A good example is given by one of the best tackle shops I've ever known. There used to be a great shop in Chorley in Lancashire, where the coffee pot was always bubbling. The brew was usually lukewarm and served in a mug that someone should have preserved for medical science because of the diversity of the bacteria it carried, but the welcome was always genuine. John, who ran the show, was a very knowledgeable and respected carp angler and the contents of the shop reflected this. The place was only small but it was full of fancy gizmos and I could play happily in there for hours! There was a terrific display of electric bite indicators; each capable of operating at a range of volumes and tones that would satisfy an organist. I'm convinced John practiced Oasis riffs on them when the shutters were down.

The only problem with the shop was that a nation-wide carp bait making service was run from the premises and sometimes it was possible to find the shop blindfolded from six streets away, by following the reek of N-butyric (blue cheese apparently!) or Monster Crab. The development of this type of specialist service obviously helped the business but the shop was still a traditional tackle shop at heart. I am sure John's personality and the respect local anglers had for his experience kept the shop alive. John specialised to a degree in the provision of modern carping paraphernalia but he was equally helpful to anglers with other interests. He always gave me a ribbing about my "panda fodder" rods when I called, but he couldn't have been more helpful when it came to catering for my idiosyncrasies about tackle.

Chorley Anglers rightly became a focal point for the anglers in the area. To the regular customers, the provision of tackle and bait was almost secondary. They came for advice, for the latest news on the local waters and for the good natured banter. They came because a visit to the shop was a good second best to being beside the water with a rod. John has become a very good friend but his shop is long gone, closed when a large company that needed his understanding of fishing tackle development ensnared him with an offer that his shop business couldn't match.

There must be hundreds of similar shops up and down the country but I fear they are in decline. How many of us enjoy the time spent in these establishments, try out the rods that they stock but ultimately go online to place the order and save ten pounds on the purchase price? Is the loss of the shop really worth so little?

My local tackle shop in Somerset is nearly as good as Chorley Anglers used to be. The guys behind the counter are friendly enough and they keep the shop well stocked but I have to confess it's a little too tidy for my liking and I've only scrounged one coffee in the last ten years. That said, it's a thriving business and at least I can be reasonably certain that I'll still have a local tackle shop to visit in five or ten years time. The secret of its success is evident in the recent change of name on the front of the shop; the "Yeovil Angling" sign has been replaced with one that reads "Tackle.co.uk". At least the owners, who are both friends of mine, are good local anglers and I'm sure their commitment to the shop will remain, even if the internet takes over as their main line of business.

With the passing of each small tackle shop, we lose not only a convenience store for our everyday items of tackle, we lose another small piece of the soul of the angling community. It is the same as South Petherton losing Mr Crumbleholme's.

The Grizzled-Wing Adams

Every trout angler has a favourite pattern of fly, the one to start the day with, the failsafe when the fish are uncooperative, the pattern that fooled their largest fish. Mine is the Adams, tied to the definitive prescription with a grizzled wing. It was Demus who put me on to this fly when he gave me one at a Golden Scale Club AGM at The Swan, on the upper Hampshire Avon one May. "I've had three this week," he said, "all on this," and he handed me a small, non-descript grey fly. "I rate it more highly than a Klinkhammer!"

Non-descript: The Grizzled-wing Adams is almost impossible to describe because it has no feature that makes it stand out amongst the plethora of insect imitations that rust and gather dust in my fly box. Not for the Adams the brazen flash of colour of an Alexander nor the elegance of the Greenwell's Glory or burliness of the Grey Wulf. No, the Adams lies self-effacingly in the corner of the box. It stands apart only on close inspection simply because it does not stay idle long enough for the hackle to gather dust or the hook to lose its gleam.

Non-descript: Therein lies the Grizzled-wing Adams' magic. Riding precariously in the surface film, it could be mistaken for almost any natural fly afloat on our rivers. It may not have the precise detail of the more refined imitations, the clinching feature that will draw the most discerning of chalkstream trout but, by the same token, there is nothing in its make up to arouse suspicion and cause rejection.

I can only marvel at the quality of the flies that I've seen tied by the country's top fly dressers; imitations so precise that I half expect them to jump out of the vice and fly away. I could never use such a fly though because I'm not an entomologist and couldn't be certain that I had selected a pattern that imitated the insect upon which the trout were feeding. The downfall of precise imitation is that it is destined to fail unless the angler is correct in this judgement.

In his excellent Chalkstream Chronicle, Neil Patterson talks of the over-riding importance of the overall shape and imprint of the fly and I agree whole-heartedly. Bird watchers refer to the "GIS" of a bird, an overall impression of shape, size and flight that allows them to recognise the most fleeting glimpse of their quarry as it darts away. I think GIS stands for "general impression of shape" and that neatly sums up what I look for in a trout fly. A trout has what, three or four seconds in which to take or reject a passing fly? Seen against a broken and distorted background, it must be the general "feel" of the fly that triggers the fish's response most of the time, rather than specific detail.

The other reason my fly box lacks refined flies, is that I could not afford to buy them and would never wish to lose one if I had made the investment. My casting is intuitive rather than skilful and I'd go so far as to say I'm pretty clumsy with a fly rod. I also love to fish those tight, seemingly impossible places into which other anglers are too sensible to try and thread their line because the trout in such spots are vulnerable and over confident. This combination is a certain recipe for lost flies and having a work of art attached to the tippet would be a liability.

In the same way, I dream of one day owning a handcrafted piece of cane by Edward Barder. I have actually flexed one of Edward's fly rods on the Kennet carrier at the back of his workshop and fallen instantly in love with its feel. We even discussed price and where one might get a mortgage. To have actually bought the rod though would have been taking a step too far. Each time I thought to use it, the sound of the tip cracking against a riverside willow would echo in my imagination and it would be left in the rack. No, a Barder rod is too precious, too beautiful, too damned expensive, to be of any use to a clumsy oaf like me. I prefer my old Allcock's (I have a three-weight "Halcyon" and five-weight "Marvel", both bought through the local paper for £10) and a box full of flies that wouldn't break the bank or my heart if they all ended up dangling from the branches of trees.

Chapter Fifteen – The Grizzled-Wing Adams

Anyway, getting back to the Grizzled-wing Adams, if I was limited to one fly for all of my fly fishing, this would be it. It has become a talisman that I believe weaves a magic that will save a blank on even the hardest day.

The Adams' magic last saved a blank on a very enjoyable but very difficult day I spent on the Frome at the kind invitation of Tony Hayter. I don't have many angling heroes but Tony is definitely one of them and I find his outlook on the management of trout fisheries inspirational. Tony was the creative force behind The Wild Trout Trust with Charles Rangely-Wilson and his waters are simply a joy to fish. Tony is wonderful company and I can only marvel at his skill with a fly rod. To watch Tony casting the perfect fly into a tiny run between the ranunculus beds on the Frome is to watch an artist at work.

I only caught one trout on my day out on the Frome and it was only small but it was a sharp finned wild brown that was worth a dozen pellet-fed stock fish three times its size. The trout epitomised the perfection of the lovely chalkstream to which I returned it, after taking its photograph on a dense bed of floating streamer weed with its bright daisy-like flowers. The Adams' was the trout's downfall and it added the sparkle at the end of an already perfect day on the river.

I first used the fly Demus gave me when I was invited to fish as a guest on a very pretty stretch of the Bybrook, a small tributary of the Bristol Avon. The late summer evening was close and still, the thick scent of dog rose hung in the air and swallows scythed through the clouds of midges that cloaked the stream. It was one of those evenings when the threatened thunderstorm would have provided a welcomed relief to the tension, the heavy rain diluting the atmosphere and allowing the world to breathe.

As soon as I saw the water I wished I'd packed my little three-weight rather than its larger brother. I usually take the five-weight Marvel on the first visit to a river because it offers greater versatility but I much prefer the dainty three-weight Halcyon. The cane of the Halcyon is twisted and set from years of abuse but the rod still responds like a natural extension of my arm, sending the fly floating out magically to land with a dimple in the precise spot pictured in my mind's eye.

I once described this rod as casting with a watchmaker's precision but, on reflection, that isn't true. Watchmakers depend upon refined tools and my Allcock's "Halcyon" is anything but refined. The secret of the Halcyon's accuracy lies more in a forgiving nature, which compliments my intuitive casting perfectly. The result is a little Zen in nature and I can picture the fly landing and being taken by the trout before the back-cast is completed. Somehow (don't ask me how!) this image is translated fluidly during the forward cast into an interaction of body and rod that produces the desired result. Well, twice in every ten casts at least, which is good enough for me.

The five-weight felt unduly cumbersome as I wandered the Bybrook, peering into tiny pools and scanning the water for rises. Upstream dry fly only was the syndicate rule, which is a little refined for my more catholic angling tastes but the Bybrook is no Test or Itchen. The riverbanks were not too manicured and alder, willow and hawthorn crowded in on alluring little pools and glides. The rich sward of the bankside meadows was uncut and the river itself was verdant with swaying weed. I put down several fish with badly cast Greenwell's and Ginger Quills and had my sedge ignored by several others before I finally tied on the Adams.

I found a tiny hatch pool where the flow from a sharp weir frothed beneath a cave of alder. A good trout flashed yellow in the tail of the pool as I arrived. It was in an almost impossible position, on the fringe of a mass of roots and under a canopy of interlocking branches that trailed into the surface of the stream. I studied the lie and watched the fish's movements before deciding on an approach that might just work. The only possibility was to flick the fly upstream from a short backhanded cast, extend the line in flight and then drop the tip sharply to the right, so that the fly flicked over on a loose line. If all went well and the Adam's curved under an arch in the foliage, the trout would have about two seconds to make up its mind before the line snagged in the alder.

I practiced the cast twice in the field before approaching the river. "Right", I thought, "here goes nothing…" Back cast, fly clipping the leaves behind me, forward, don't snatch but draw the rod down and across sharply… The fly alighted perfectly and was greeted and engulfed by the trout. Strike! And draw swiftly, rod tip beneath the surface and the trout's tail beating the branches. Miraculously, the trout came free and was dragged unceremoniously into the net after a desperate, thrashing fight.

It was a classic brown trout, testimony to the quality of the syndicate's stock management. Low level, "trickle" stocking with top quality browns only meant that the stocked fish augmented rather than replaced the indigenous trout population. The low rate and density of stocking also allowed the trout to adapt to their new habitat and establish feeding territories. The net result (if you'll pardon the terrible pun) was that every fish landed was fin perfect and it was difficult to tell stocked and wild fish apart.

The Adams accounted for three more fish that evening, each capture involving a tactical war of nerves as challenging as the first. By the time dusk slipped away from the river and my host suggested that we should follow suit, the Adams was little more than a crumpled grey ball of fluff. The silk was broken near the eye of the hook, the hackle was beginning to unravel and the tail was a clipped stump.

The fly had acquitted itself well and since then the Adams and I have shared many adventures and caught many fine fish. It accounted for my largest fly-caught chub from the Severn and fooled some of the most fickle trout that I have ever encountered on the Oakley stream, a carrier of the River Test at Mottisfont.

I can remember the evening on the Oakley Stream perfectly. It was early summer and the last vestiges of the Mayfly hatch were coming off the glassy surface of the chalkstream in ones and twos, rather than in swarms. I'm sure the trout were gorged as well and there was only a sporadic rise to greet the emerging Mayfly. "No thanks, I'm stuffed… Oh alright then if you insist, just one more but then I'm going on a diet…" It was going to be hard fishing.

The Oakley Stream forms part of the Mottisfont Fishery, which is owned by the National Trust. The Mottisfont Estate has a good length of single bank fishing on the main River Test as well as fishing on the Oakley, Abbey and Rectory beats of a lovely little carrier.

FM Halford leased the Mottisfont fishery and it is here that he developed his rather dogmatic views on fly fishing. In fact the banks of the Oakley Stream were the birthplace of the cult of upstream dry fly fishing. Halford was famously at odds with G.M. Skues who fished the Itchen at Barton Court. When the trout dictated that they wanted to feed on the nymph rather than the imago, Skues was happy to comply and fish a nymph pattern, rather than waiting for the trout to come round to the dry fly dogmatist's view about what they should take. I believe Halford became so obsessed with catching trout on the dry fly that he thought it was unethical to cast until you had seen a fish rise. I definitely lean more towards G.M. Skues much more pragmatic perspective!

Halford left a legacy of his time at Mottisfont in the form of his fishing hut beside the Oakley Stream and the Trust has restored the hut and the small garden Halford created. To sit outside the hut, with the swallows flitting along the river, is to slip back into the age of the English country gentleman. In fact I wouldn't bat an eyelid if Halford himself strolled down the river bank and asked if I'd seen any rising trout.

I may ridicule Halford's obsessive approach to fly fishing, but I admire his views on fishery management. Halford liked wild fishing and he railed against any stocking policy aimed at providing easy sport for the angler. Much of the Test has been stocked with large brown and rainbow trout in recent decades, in the belief that anglers expect to catch on every outing to justify the cost of a day's fishing.

When I was first involved with the management of the Mottisfont Fishery, I worked with the local team to completely revise the management of the river and to establish a more natural fishery. The driving force behind the management at Mottisfont is Phil Marshall and he has focussed on restoring the water habitats on the estate, to benefit the trout, salmon and other wildlife, such as the rare Southern Damselfly and the estate's colony of Barbastelle bats.

The Trust now attracts anglers to Mottisfont who want to experience good quality fishing in a natural environment that Halford would have recognised and appreciated. The Trust has a fishery to be proud of and I'm very pleased to have played my part in helping this change in management happen.

On the evening in question, I fished the Oakley Beat from the Halford hut upstream. By the time I'd fished the beat through, using every mayfly imitation in my fly box, I was despondent. I'd moved only one fish, which inspected the fly carefully in a nice run between two weedbeds. The water gathered pace and sparkle as it danced across an area of shallow gravel that had been created by the restoration work and the trout had taken up station where the flow slowed into the next pool. The trout dropped downstream and carefully studied my drifting Mayfly before veering away and shooting back to its lie. No other trout even inspected the flies I offered them and I might as well have been casting a feather duster for all the reaction I was getting.

I stopped to have a cup of tea in the hut, hoping that a glance through the catch log might give me some inspiration. I looked through my fly box one last time and then I remembered the Adams that Demus had given me. I tied it on without much expectation but on the first cast a trout rose and took it at the tail of the garden pool. I was so astonished that I missed the fish by a mile but I started to fish with a renewed sense of purpose. I missed another brown just below a footbridge and then landed a sparkling fish of about a pound from the same spot.

The best fish took with a slow roll after I'd made a testing backhand cast upstream, turning the fly around the branches of a hawthorn towards the tail of a dense bed of crowfoot. I knew immediately that this was a big brown from the lunging, determined runs upstream. I had to let it go or it would have smashed the light leader and when the backing knot rattled through the rod rings I followed it, splashing through the margins of the carrier. I got it in the end, a golden brown with large spots that shone like ebony as I returned it to the chalkstream.

That session on the Oakley Stream has been mirrored countless times elsewhere and I always tie on an Adams when the trout are in a fickle mood. It has become a lucky charm that I rely on whenever a blank is on the cards. The worry is that I might find myself on the river one evening without an Adams in my fly box and then I'll be faced with the certainty of an empty creel.

Greylags at dawn

Wild cries carried in a wilderness of wind
In the thundering breath of the barren spaces
That blows and strikes the senses like an unrelenting hammer
So that only the cries and the space and the wind are real.

Shadows ghosting through the half light
Turning on pinions arched to clasp the sky
The sun rise rusts the heather and casts shadows from the lazybeds
Tombstones of abandoned toil, reclaimed now by the wild.

Monarchs of the lowering winter skies
Wild nomads claiming all this world your own
Over layers of history on the rugged edge of man's domain
You swoop, as ancient and unchanging as the land.

When summer comes and brings the endless days
And man returns to wonder at this place
You will be gone to seek another lonely haven in the clouds
And all that will remain are echoes of your cries.

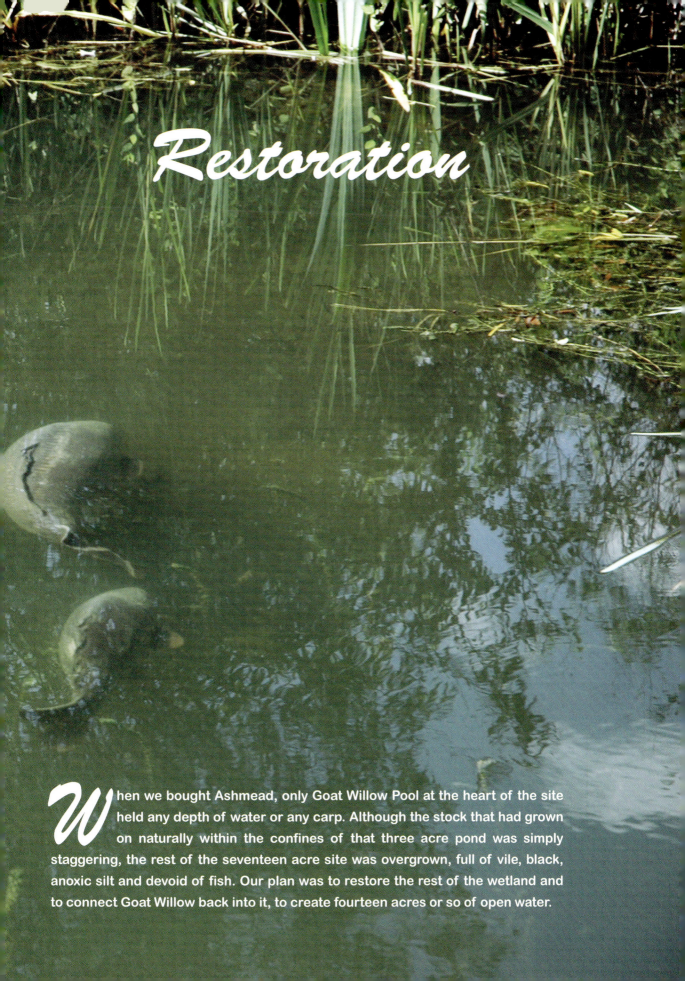

Restoration

When we bought Ashmead, only Goat Willow Pool at the heart of the site held any depth of water or any carp. Although the stock that had grown on naturally within the confines of that three acre pond was simply staggering, the rest of the seventeen acre site was overgrown, full of vile, black, anoxic silt and devoid of fish. Our plan was to restore the rest of the wetland and to connect Goat Willow back into it, to create fourteen acres or so of open water.

My main interest in Ashmead lies in its history and importance as a wonderful piece of Somerset countryside, and the opportunity to restore and manage the wetland as a whole meant far more to me than just the creation of a fishery. Ashmead is an ancient and timeless piece of landscape. It is the lowest lying land in the area and it was beyond the skill of the engineers who installed the huge pumps that drain the Witcombe Bottoms to dry the area out for agriculture. Instead, it has always been maintained as an area of sedge and its primary use has been for wildfowling. In fact, I suspect that it might be an old duck decoy pond, designed specifically to allow wild duck, such as teal, widgeon and mallard, to be harvested.

Decoy ponds were once common features in the Somerset wetlands in the 18th and 19th centuries. They consisted of a pond surrounded by woodland designed to entice wildfowl to land and designed in such a way that the birds could then be trapped. Once they landed, the ducks were enticed to enter narrow channels, or "pipes", at the corners of the pond. This was sometimes done by using a small red dog to chase the ducks by weaving in and out of a series of willow hurdles beside the channels. The ducks mistook the dog for a fox and would swim towards it as a flock to chase it away, only to find themselves lured into trap nets set at the end of the pipe. The pools on the levels were often rectangular with five or six pipes and sometimes an island for the duck to roost on, as an additional attraction to tempt them in. The earthworks of some decoys can still be seen today and some are Scheduled Monuments in recognition of their historical and cultural importance.

In preparing to write this chapter I've just read an entry from my diary that I wrote in the early spring of 2008, just after the last diggers had left the site:

"I am sitting beside Tom's Pond, a pool that is so clear that I can see the clay bed six feet beneath the surface; so clear that the beetles rushing around industriously in the depths might be flying through air rather than swimming in water. The presence of the beetles indicates that the pool will not remain this clear for very much longer and I'm enjoying it in its pristine state whilst I can."

That entry in my diary takes me straight back to the point when the diggers had finally left the site and the pool had just filled naturally with rainwater over the winter months. The clarity persisted only because the rainwater that filled it was sterile and devoid of life, yet the environment into which the rain fell had already tainted its purity and the crystal clear water had allowed sunlight to penetrate the depths and work its mysterious alchemy. So far the winter chill had kept the lid on this natural chemistry set, but I knew the boundless energy of the sun would inevitably bring life to the pool and once life began the water would never be as clear again.

In places the water already had a greenish tinge, a bit like a cress consommé, that showed that unicellular algae had already started to grow and reproduce. These provide grazing for a multitude of microscopic herbivores that in their turn are prey to carnivorous invertebrates that roam the water column like a pack of aquatic lions hunting their freshwater Serengeti. The beetles I could see were carnivorous evidence that the lesser links of the food chain had been forged already. Within weeks of the water filling the restored wetland, a complex ecosystem had miraculously appeared, conjured from the potent ingredients of pure water and spring sunshine.

The clay bed was covered here and there by a film of the filamentous green algae Cladophora sp., better known as silkweed or blanket weed, because of its texture and massive propensity for growth. Blanket weed has the ability to dominate and smother any water where a mature ecology that includes larger rooted plants has not developed, and this virgin pool was an ideal habitat for this pioneer species. Any virgin water will pass through a number of ecological stages before it develops a mature and balanced ecosystem with large rooted water plants as well as the "lesser" algae and a rich diversity of insects, amphibians and fish.

Eventually, every stillwater will silt up, become encroached upon by marginal vegetation and revert to mire and ultimately dry land. This natural cycle meant the pool in front of me was in an advanced state of decline and well on the way towards a boggy death when we bought the wetland. Over many decades of neglect, natural processes had replaced the water with several feet of thick, black silt. We needed to intervene to reverse the natural cycle, remove the silt and restore the original lakebed, to ensure the pool remained as open water for another century at least.

We also needed to prime the creation of a healthy ecosystem capable of supporting fish. This was a question of nudging the natural processes along after the dredging was complete, by establishing an environment capable of sustaining the complex ecosystem needed for the fish to thrive and creating the diverse habitat they require to hunt, hide and reproduce. It was a bit like extensive organic farming or gardening.

Ashmead held a population of fantastic carp when we bought the lake, all derived from a single stocking of fingerlings into the wetland in 1971. So, in terms of the carp fishery we took on a "work in progress", rather than starting off on a stocking policy from scratch. Indeed, Ashmead will never be stocked under our stewardship unless we suffer some catastrophe that wipes out the existing carp. We know the Ashmead carp have the genetic potential to grow to an enormous size and that their incredibly rich environment is no limit to that potential, so all we had to do was to restore their environment and control the number of carp present, to optimise their potential.

The initial restoration process was more akin to a mugging. It was a messy, brutal, invasive attack that left the site reeling, battered and bruised. Nature is tremendously resilient, though, and twelve months on, the reed beds and meadow lays on the banks had already started to recover and the water itself looked incredible and full of promise.

It all started with an evening in the pub. My great friend, Alan, has always been close to the heart of Ashmead and we often argue about which one of us fished the water first (Alan thinks I probably did whereas I'm sure from his description that he found the lake a year before me). When it came to planning the restoration, two heads would definitely be better than one, especially as Alan is a builder by trade and has a solid practical understanding of slues, bulldozers and spoil. I had my fisheries management expertise to rely on and so, between us, we felt we had the bases covered.

We sat down with dozens of aerial photographs of the area, a red marker pen and a pint or two of fine Somerset beer. Over the course of about three hours, we produced plans of the final layout of the fishery. We discussed and discounted one option after another, until we were finally satisfied with the result. We wanted to retain as much of the original atmosphere of Ashmead as possible and to create an intimate fishery with the same tight channels and bays we remembered from our youth. We knew we needed to create some areas of more extensive open water to satisfy modern carp fishing techniques and we planned the layout of the many islands to create secluded swims, where each angler could enjoy a feeling of privacy and solitude. The other consideration was that we wanted to create as much water as possible in which the carp could thrive, whilst still retaining all of the dredged material from the restoration work on site.

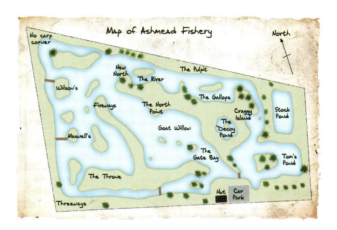

By the end of the evening, the final result looked more like a maze than a plan for a lake and I was delighted with it. The footprint of the wetland was pretty much unchanged but the fishery that would emerge from the neglected waterways would be tremendous. All that remained to do now was to carry out some test augers to check for the depth of the clay lake bed and then to get in the contractor and start work.

When we started the restoration, the old channels held over eight feet of sludge in places, all of which had to be dried, removed and then incorporated into the bankside clay. We had a fourteen ton slue working on site for nearly three months doing the work. Typically, the rain started on the day the digger arrived and we had endless delays because of the weather. We persevered, though, and it was magical to see the channels and bays taking shape as the silt was removed, back to the original clay lake bed. It was like watching the hands of an expert art restorer reveal the vibrant colours of an old master from beneath centuries of grimy old varnish.

Our restorer and artist was Gary Coombes. Gary is a proper Somerset countryman, who is a champion hedge layer and during the winter months makes the most fantastic walking sticks as a sideline. In the drier months, Gary drives an ancient and battered Case slue for a local contractor, Les Peel, and between them they must have dug and maintained just about every pond and ditch in Somerset over the years. Les is well into his eighties and his digger doesn't look much younger, but Gary can handle that old workhorse like a skilled sculptor. I spent hours watching in admiration as he made fourteen tons of ancient machinery twist and turn, one minute gouging out big bucketfuls of sludge and the next smoothing and shaping the clay banks with the finesse of an artist using a pallet knife.

The restoration of one area required a big bulldozer to be brought in, fitted with swamp tracks to prevent it sinking into the soft bed of the lake. This was Alistair Bear's idea of heaven and our youngest son spent every possible waking moment sitting in the cab with Gary, chugging up and down on this monstrous Tonka toy with his face split from ear to ear by a huge grin.

Most importantly, many years of experience had taught Gary just how far he could push the digger and bulldozer without getting them stuck in the silt he was trying to clear. Thanks to this experience Gary managed to reach areas of the water that I would never have thought possible and the finished work is testament to the old adage that it is the workman, not the tool, which makes the difference. I'd meet up with him at six each morning and we'd discuss the day's work ahead, planning the positioning of swims and features, using the design Alan and I had dreamed up in the pub. By the time I got back to the lake after work, Gary would invariably have done something completely different because he "thought it would be better like that" and, given that I was paying for the work on the basis of an hourly fee rate, I seldom disagreed.

There were some areas that Gary's old Case simply couldn't reach and we had to bring in specialist equipment from Kingcombe Aquacare in the form of a fifteen metre long-reach digger, to complete the work. Kingcombe are at the top of the tree when it comes to specialist contractors for this sort of restoration work and they have the kit to tackle the most difficult of challenges. There was a problem,

though, in that the driver of the long-reach had only been with the company a few months and although Jim was fine on hard, level ground, he didn't have Gary's experience when it came to dealing with eight feet of sludge. On the very first day, the machine went down with all hands and Jim only just managed to bail out and take to the lifeboat before the ooze flooded the digger's quarter deck. It took them two days to dig the thing out and for a while we thought it might become a permanent feature in the lake. We now have "Jimmy's Bay", just next to the entrance, named as a fitting testament to Jim's resilience in the face of an embarrassing disaster!

To finish the job, Kingcombe used two machines working in tandem; a seven ton machine driven by the experienced and slightly mad Chris Keeble, which he used to push the sludge over to the long-reach driven by Jim (now placed firmly and safely on solid ground!). Chris would plough the smaller slue into impossible depths of ooze with an insane gleam in his eye and then fight his way back out again, working the silt around him and somehow clearing it away, like some sort of deranged hippo clearing out a watering hole.

Big boy's toys! It was a summer of mud, sludge, stress and endless fun! By the autumn, the heavy work was complete and the restored lake had begun to fill with crystal-clear rainwater (Ashmead is purely rain fed and has no streams or springs supplying it). The last task for Gary was to remove the bund between Goat Willow and the restored area, when the water levels had equalised, giving the Ashmead carp access to their expanded universe for the first time....

The moment of the breakthrough was really thrilling. There was always a slight lingering doubt about whether or not the restored area would hold a depth of water compatible with that of Goat Willow but the rain-filled pool seemed to be keeping its level well. The biggest unknown was how the fish would respond to their strangely expanded universe. Would they stay hunkered down in Goat Willow? Would they wander out in ones and twos through the new channels? Would they all pass out with shock, when they realised that their three-acre world had magically grown five times larger?

Several of the members came down to witness the event and we were amazed how quickly the carp spread out to explore their new surroundings. Within an hour we had seen slightly bemused fish cruising through the crystal clear waters in every part of the restored lake. In one narrow channel, Alan watched a mid-thirty common swim into the bank, head-butting it at full tilt. It paused and seemed to shake itself before spinning around and accelerating into the bank opposite. The carp was clearly used to the more spacious confines of Goat Willow and it lay stunned and bemused for a while before it realised that the world hadn't suddenly closed in around it but that it could follow the channel on into more open water.

Other, more confident carp seemed intent on discovering every nook and corner of the fishery as quickly as they possibly could. One minute they'd be up in Tom's Pond at the eastern end of the fishery and the next minute someone would spot the same carp dashing along one of the channels at the opposite end of the wetland. The carp must have been as exhausted as I was, trying to keep up with them!

Now that the restoration is complete, Ashmead is a complex and intimate fishery. There are about fourteen or fifteen acres of water but its unique configuration means that there is over a mile of bank. There are three main areas of open water, each extending to about three acres and dotted with islands. These are linked by a series of channels and bays that create a labyrinth within which the carp can hide.

The starting point for good fishery management must always be the environment of the fishery. Only when the water quality and quantity are at their best can any fish stock hope to reach its true potential, and investment in the restoration of Ashmead focused on creating the perfect environment for the carp.

We created shallow areas, with a range of depths, to provide spawning habitat and suitable areas for the offspring of the carp and other fish to feed in relative safety. These areas also have a critical role in providing a wide range of habitats for invertebrates on which the fish depend for food. The wider, deeper and more complex the food web that can be sustained naturally by the water, the more robust it will be in the face of harsh winters and dry summers, ensuring the security of the carp's food supply.

As a result of this careful planning, Ashmead is now rich with food, with plentiful supplies of snails, swan mussels, hatches of insects and fish. I am convinced that carp are far more predatory than many anglers think. A couple of years ago I was watching a large shoal of rudd sunning themselves when a shadow rose up slowly beneath the shoal and a thirty pound common tilted up, opened its cavernous mouth and sucked in a mouthful of three-inch fish, before slowly sinking back down to the lakebed. With a pulse of its operculae, the common crushed its feast with its pharyngeal teeth, sending a shower of sparkling scales out through its gills. The rudd scattered but after twenty minutes the shoal reformed in the same sunny spot as before, having forgotten about the carp that was still lying like a shadow across the lakebed. Slowly, the common loomed up again and slurped in another mouthful of living fishmeal; a process repeated again and again over the two hours that I spent watching in complete fascination.

The natural food web has taken time to establish in the restored areas of the fishery but, after two years, the dredged areas are now probably even more productive than the carp's original home within the confines of Goat Willow Pool. Before the restoration, it seemed that several of the carp in Goat Willow had reached the maximum size sustainable in the three acres in which they lived. The evidence suggests that the carp are responding well to the restoration and the additional water they now have to exploit. Many of the fish are starting to pack on weight again, after several years of "freewheeling" around the plateau imposed by their previous environment.

The rich environment of Ashmead does bring some headaches as well as benefits, the biggest of which is the phenomenal weed growth we have each year. Now I don't mind weed and, particularly in a shallow water like Ashmead, where much of the lake is within wader depth, it isn't too much of a problem in terms of the fishing.

The weed is a key part of the ecosystem and it gives the fish shelter and holds much of their food, but Ashmead is so productive it can become hard to see where the grass of the banks ends and the lake begins, because of the amount of weed.

At some point in the past, someone introduced the Canadian pondweed, Elodia crispus, into the lake. This weed grows incredibly quickly and has an abrasive stem, so that the dense beds formed each summer can result in lost fish no matter how careful you are once a carp is hooked. We gear the weed management around tipping the balance away from the growth of the Elodea sp. and in favour of less problematic weed species, such as the prolific but less abrasive hornwort.

We never seek to remove all of the weed but manage it in a rotation, removing blocks of weed that become particularly bad and allowing other, less dense areas to remain. In this way, the lake remains fishable throughout the year but the balance of the ecosystem isn't upset. Removing too much of the weed brings the danger of an algal bloom and oxygen crash. We favour the backbreaking but selective and effective manual removal of the weed, rather than any chemical treatment. Using a combination of a highly effective home-made weed cutter and manual pulling to remove the weed by the roots is really hard work but achieves the desired result. The work parties always provide a bit of a social occasion as well, fuelled with a few beers and one of Shona's excellent stews or chillies.

Although complete, large areas of the fishery looked like the Somme after the diggers departed and it was time to kick-start the natural colonisation of the muddy banks with a few sacks of wildflower and grass seed mixes and some judicious planting. Whilst dredging the lake we were careful not to track over more ground with the diggers than was essential and also to avoid damaging as few plants as we could. As a result, we only needed the wild seed mixes to boost new growth in those areas that had suffered the greatest disturbance. We mixed the seeds with damp, coarse sand in a bucket, to make them easy to spread by hand, harder for the birds to find and to prevent them simply blowing away. I found my baiting spoon was the ideal tool for spreading the seeds and a good flick of the wrist would give a good, even coverage of seeds over a wide area. The banks were richly fertilised with the silt removed from the pool and the pace at which nature bounced back to reclaim the ground has been simply staggering. Within a year, waist-high rushes and a colourful blaze of wild flowers, including everything from foxgloves to ragged robin, appeared to replace the bare mud.

Some of the flower species that appeared posed a bit of a mystery for a while, as they hadn't been present before the restoration work and didn't feature in any of the seed mixes we applied. I eventually discovered that one of our members, Jill, had been carrying out some undercover restoration work of her own, planting a packet or two of wild flowers every time she came up to fish. This has added an element of unpredictability to the excitement of watching the banks mature and flourish. Ashmead has rewarded Jill for her kindness and she has been one of the most consistent fish catchers since the syndicate opened, with a succession of large commons to over Thirty-Seven pounds falling to her rods. I'm sure she gets as much pleasure from the butterflies visiting the wild flowers as she does from the carp.

Whilst most of the conservation works following the completion of the dredging involved planting and nurturing the wild plants, there was also a lot of tree surgery required. The banks of Ashmead hold dozens of crack willows of a variety of ages and sizes that have grown like weeds over the years. Traditional willow management requires them to be pollarded every four to eight years, to prevent their limbs from splitting and breaking. Even the ancient, original pollards around the lake (some of which may be well over 100 years old) hadn't been touched in decades and their condition varied from the unsightly to the downright dangerous.

Willows are important for wildlife and only the oak tree supports a wider range of insects, which in turn provide food for birds and bats. Old pollards are particularly valuable and their decaying core provides an ideal roost for several bat species, as well as a home for insects and fungi. The invertebrate communities that depend upon rotting wood are amongst the most threatened in Europe because we have become so obsessed with tidying up our countryside. Several species have such specific requirements that they are found only in the mouldering hearts of old willow pollards.

With this in mind I set about the task of bringing the willows back under control, starting with those that were actually dangerous but aiming eventually to put in place a rotation of pollards that I could then manage in succession in future years. The bonus of a four-year pollarding rotation is that it will also provide us with an endless supply of wood for the wood burner at home. The next step is to install a back-boiler so that we can axe our oil bill and hopefully benefit from free heating and hot water this winter!

Pollarding crack willows is not something to be undertaken lightly. Down here in Somerset, the willows are known as "widow-makers" because of the readiness with which they split and their propensity for rotting from the inside out, so that even an apparently healthy limb can be a death-trap. Gary, who drove the digger for me during the restoration work, told me a horrific story of an incident just a year or so ago when he was working on a site with willows that they had to fell to make room for the diggers to operate. One of his colleagues was working on a tree when his saw suddenly fell silent and Gary turned, just in time to see him thrown ten feet through the air and into some bushes. A large willow branch he was cutting had split and "bounced", catching him under the chin and when Gary reached him he found that it had "stripped the poor bugger's jaw and face right off".

I'm an experienced chainsaw user but with this story ringing in my ears, it was with great respect and all of the right safety gear that I approached the first tree! Four days and many pollards later, though, I thought I had the hang of it and whilst I wouldn't say I'd grown complacent I was pretty confident about what I was doing and a bit more relaxed; a little too relaxed as it turned out.

At the end of one particularly long and tiring day, I approached a large old pollard at the far end of the lake, thinking "Just one more and I'll stop for the day…" How many accidents happen as a result of that thought running through a tired mind? I notched the first limb and started the felling cut but I'd hardly made an impression on the foot-thick timber when the crack willow lived up to its name. With a noise like tearing cloth, a long split appeared in an instant, running lengthwise up the centre of the branch. The limb fell but as it was still held by the uncut timber it twisted and pulled back on itself, so that twenty feet of timber landed vertically on my left foot, burying it up to the ankle in the soft clay.

I shouted for help but the guy who had come down with me for the day couldn't hear me. I'd had the presence of mind to kill the saw when the branch started to split but now I had to fire it up again because the branch, which was about forty feet long and a foot in diameter, was still wedged vertically on top of my foot and tangled in the adjacent trees. I cut through it so that it fell away from me and then dug my foot out from the ground with my hands. Adrenaline is a fantastic pain killer and strangely it didn't hurt at all, which worried me; I knew it would be bad…

I took off my boot and sock and the foot ballooned instantly to the size of a rugby ball and turned an interesting shade of purple, the toes sticking out at all sorts of strange angles. I had the presence of mind to roll down to the water's edge and submerge the foot in the icy lake, before wriggling around so that the slope of the bank elevated it. I had been shouting (ok, screaming!) for help all the time but with no response. With some difficulty, I managed to retrieve my mobile and call my wife Shona. "Now I don't want you to panic but I've had a bit of an accident…"

An hour later I'd hobbled around the lake with the support of an improvised willow crutch and Shona had whisked me away to hospital in her truck. I eventually passed out just as she helped me through the doors of A&E. I came to with half a dozen surgeons and nurses gathered around my bed discussing the injury. It was clearly causing some interest and excitement and I found out later that they thought I had completely severed the metatarsal bones from the back of my foot, which is a rare and challenging injury. Just then, the X-rays came in and after a quick look, I heard one of the surgeons say "Oh! Just three smashed metatarsals, never mind!" And with that they all left, never to be seen again. I nearly shouted out after them "Sorry! I'll try harder next time…"

I now have a titanium plate holding my foot together as a memento of the event and even more respect for the old willows. You can't make an omelette without breaking a few eggs or rather you can't restore a carp lake without breaking a few legs... If you are ever on a work party and considering taking down a willow as one of the jobs for the day, my advice is to think long and hard about calling in a professional instead.

With the main work on the fishery completed, we celebrated the opening of the first season on the restored Ashmead in style, with a syndicate barbeque. It was a great night but I enjoyed the following evening even more. When everyone else had crept off home to nurse their hangovers I went back down to the lake for a walk on my own, taking time to enjoy the place and reflect on two years of hard work. Of course I took a rod.

Beneath a weeping willow in Tom's Pond, where I had caught my first Ashmead carp nearly thirty years before, I found a group of three carp cruising along the margins. A year ago the water here had been inches deep but now we had removed eight feet of black sludge and the carp seemed to float suspended in the air, such was the clarity of the pure, rain-fed water. A scattering of small pellets soon had one of the fish nosing at the surface film and it took my hookbait confidently. It was a joy to play the carp as it plunged through the deep water, flashing, golden scales reflecting the sunset. The carp fought well but it tired in the end and rolled into the net.

The portrait of that carp still makes me smile as broadly now as I did at the time. The common weighed just over Thirty pounds but that carp represented so much more than its size and stunning looks alone could encompass. The carp bristled with new found energy in the same way that Ashmead itself seemed to glow with new life; it was Ashmead's "thank you" for the success of all the planning, investment and hard work. The restoration of Ashmead was complete and the result was even better than I had dreamed.

The Strange Case of the Attingham Salmon

One of the joys of my work for the National Trust is that the Trust not only owns and manages an incredible portfolio of fisheries, it also has wonderful libraries stuffed with angling books, fantastic angling artwork, collections of vintage tackle and even a Robert Adams designed fishing lodge at Keddlestone Hall. Every now and again I stumble upon something that is simply breathtaking.

I imagine that every angler knows that Miss Georgina Ballantine holds the British rod-caught record for the Atlantic salmon, with the fish she caught from the River Tay on 7th October 1922. The story of her battle with a 64 pound cock fish, taken spinning on a dace deadbait from the Glendelvie beat where her father was the ghillie, has passed into angling legend.

The Ballantine salmon was a truly astounding fish but the fact that it is so well known has as much to do with the nature of Miss Ballantine herself and her ability to spin a tale, as with the shear size of the fish and her skill at spinning a bait. She recounted the story in a classic article, published in the Fishing Gazette in 1923, which drew the spotlight onto her achievement. I would encourage anyone who has not done so to read her tale, which has been reproduced in several angling anthologies.

In simple prose, she shared with her reader the thrill of hooking the fish, the excitement of the fight and her gritty determination to see the battle through to the end, even though it lasted for more than two hours and ran on into the darkness of that October night. The exchanged conversations with her father during the course of the story are recounted in the Scots dialect and really give a feeling of Miss Ballantine's strength of character, the dour temperament of her father and the sullen majesty of the salmon.

The fight took the boat that she and her father shared far down the river and they beached it at least once during the course of the fight, before the fish forced them back out onto the water. *"…Evidently our progress downstream was farther than father had anticipated, as I immediately got into hot water; "Dinna lat the beast flee doon the watter like that, 'ummin". With few remarks and much hard spitting, we again boarded the boat, this time keeping in mid-stream for fully half an hour."*

At one point she tells of how her *"…left arm ached so much with the weight of the rod that it felt paralysed, but I was determined that whatever happened nothing would induce me to give in."* It seems that her father didn't offer much encouragement. *"Man, if only the Laird or the Major had ha 'en him I wouldna been sae ill aboot it." "Encouraging remarks such as these, I swallowed silently. Once I struck the nail on the head by remarking that if I successfully grassed the fish he must give me a new frock. "Get ye the fush landed first and syne we'll see aboot the frock," was the reply. (I have kept him to his word and the frock has been ordered)."*

Eventually the salmon was exhausted and *"…the gaff went in successfully, which brought him to the side of the boat. A second lift (no small weight, over ½ cwt) brought him over the end, into the floor of the boat, father, out of puff, half-sitting on top of him.*

Reaching for Mr Moir's "nabbie", I made a feeble attempt to put him out of pain and was afterwards accused of "knockin' oot ane o' the poor beast's een!" We were met at the bridge by the old lady, my mother. Her greeting showed how anxious she had been during our absence - "Guid's sake, I thocht ye were baith i' the watter!"

Larger fish than Miss Ballantine's record have been caught, including one of 70 pounds from the Tweed caught by the Earl of Home in about 1730 and a 67 pound fish caught on the Nith in 1812, by the "notorious poacher" Jock Wallace. In the first chapter of his classic book "The Atlantic Salmon. A Vanishing Species" (Faber and Faber, 1968), Anthony Netboy mentions a world record salmon of 103 pounds from the River Devon in Scotland but gives no further details. These larger salmon failed to meet the strict criteria required for a rod-caught record to be recognised (I would be surprised if the "notorious poacher" Jock Wallace troubled himself with the inconvenience of a fishing rod at all!).

The Nith at Dumfries produced another monster in 1957, which was caught by a 65-year-old retired British Rail engine driver Mr W Service. A James Ross of Edinburgh recounted the story in a letter to Trout and Salmon Magazine in 1994. He remembered tailing the salmon for Mr Service on the steps on the Wee Green, after a two and a half hour fight. The salmon was taken to Gunyeon and Douglas' fish shop in the High Street, where it was found to weigh 65 pounds exactly. The shop owner, "Spuggy" Douglas, weighed the salmon with Mr Ross and Will Blythe (another engine driver) as witnesses. Apparently "Spuggy" paid £8 2s 6d for the salmon; 2s 6d a pound! According to Mr Ross, *"none of us even considered a claim for any record then, or since"*. There must have been salmon steaks for sale in the shop for months afterwards!

Other large salmon have been caught but none to challenge the status of Miss Ballantine's record. The early 1900's seem to have been a golden period in which several such "portmanteaus", as these huge fish were called, entered our rivers.

On 21 October 1924, Mrs "Tiny" Morrison landed a salmon that weighed 61 pounds from the Low Shaw Pool on the River Deveron. Like Miss Ballantine's monster, this fish was a male and it is thought to be the largest ever caught on the fly (a 1½ inch Brown Wing Killer).

Other huge fish include the "Kelso" fish of 57½ pounds that was taken at Floors Castle on the River Tweed and a spring salmon of 59½ pounds caught from the Wye by Doreen Davey in March 1923. Doreen Davey shared the task of playing the fish with her father. They passed the rod back and forth between them for almost two hours, before finally landing the salmon by the light of a fire that had been lit by her father's chauffeur. This Wye fish is the largest Spring salmon caught in Britain and had a length of fifty-two and a half inches and girth of twenty-nine inches.

One would have thought that all of the largest salmon caught in Britain would be known and well documented and yet, on a wall of the Tenants Gallery in the basement of Attingham Hall, hangs an unmarked case that contains a truly remarkable specimen. I believe it to be the largest salmon ever caught fairly on rod and line in Britain. It is certainly the largest salmon ever caught in England and I believe it to be the largest ever caught on the fly. It is a salmon to shake the foundations of both Miss Ballantine and Mrs Morrison's pedestals.

The Attingham salmon came to my attention through a strange sequence of coincidences that started with a visit to the Trust's West Midlands Regional Office, which occupies part of Attingham Hall. I was passing the time with the Regional Rural Surveyor, Hugh Devlin, when the conversation turned

to fishing and Hugh asked if I had seen the big salmon hanging in the Tenant's Gallery. When he said that he thought the fish weighed "about 60 pounds", I must admit that I dismissed the statement immediately as a bit of an exaggeration. After all, no fish of anything like that weight had ever been caught from the Severn to my knowledge.

Then, the following week, I received a copy of an email from Peter Nixon, the Trust's Director of Conservation, which was headed "Attingham salmon". The message read, *"When I saw Richard Adney last Saturday he mentioned the huge stuffed salmon at Attingham which came from his father. He said that there is still alive a 90 yr old, called Mr Godbehere I think, who witnessed the capture of the fish. I think Richard said he lives in the Potteries. It would be good if someone, a volunteer maybe, could visit Mr Godbehere to record his eyewitness account of the fish's capture."*

I volunteered immediately and in February 2005 I travelled up to Attingham to meet Richard Adney with a view to finding out more about the salmon.

The first thing I did was to go and see the monster for myself. The salmon hangs on the end wall of the Tenant's Gallery, forming the focal point for the room. The understated black case with a plain blue ground serves to emphasise the grandeur of the fish within and the enormity of the salmon is stunning. The taxidermy is far from perfect and the fish has a jaded and desiccated appearance, commensurate with the age of the case, but it is easy to imagine what it must have looked like when it was landed fresh from the river, its flanks shining like quicksilver and the huge tail beating the air.

Rumour had it that the salmon had been caught from the junction pool, where the River Tern joins the Severn, within the boundaries of the Attingham Estate. Large fish gather stories and another rumour suggested that the salmon wasn't caught on rod and line at all but that it had been caught in a net. Now I had the chance to find out the truth behind the rumours and I set off to find the man who had witnessed its capture, almost a century ago.

Richard Adney is a local farmer who rents some land at Attingham from the Trust. Richard told me that his Great Uncle, Thomas Allen, had caught the salmon in the early 1900's but he knew few details about the fish. It had remained in the ownership of Mr Allen's housekeeper until her death, at which time it was left to Richard's father and subsequently to Richard himself. Richard had tried to find out more about the salmon and, at one time, the Environment Agency had measured the length and girth of the salmon and had taken some scales from the fish for study. In 1991, The Times ran a short article about the fish but the provenance of the salmon had been impossible to authenticate and the salmon slipped back into anonymity until it came into Trust ownership.

The key to unlocking the mystery of the salmon was a ninety-one year old local man called Thomas Langley. His cousin, Thomas Godbehere, was the nephew of Thomas Allen's housekeeper and, when he was an eight-year-old boy, he had been with Thomas Allen when he caught the fish. Now aged one hundred, Tom Godbehere lived in a local residential home and he had agreed to meet us to recount his memories of Mr Allen and the salmon.

I have only met one other person who was a century old and I wasn't sure what to expect when one of the residential home staff showed us into Tom Godbehere's room. I certainly wasn't prepared for the energetic welcome that Tom gave us as we were introduced. If I hadn't known his age, and if a telegram from the Queen to celebrate his hundredth birthday on 4th December 2004, hadn't been on display on the windowsill, I would have placed him closer to seventy years old than a hundred.

Any fears I had about Tom Godbehere's ability to remember events that had happened more than ninety years ago evaporated as the two cousins caught up with family news and reminisced about people and places they knew. Whilst both of them sometimes had trouble recalling names or recent events, their memories of their youth were vivid and detailed.

Tom Godbehere's mother was the sister of Tom Langley's father and their common grandfather was born in 1849. They recalled how Tom Langley's father had "practically built Cressage Bridge" across the Severn and brought all of the materials for the bridge to the site using horses. They shared memories of the many tramps, often soldiers returning from the Great War, who used to frequent the farms in the Atcham area. Tom Godbehere recalled "…one chap in particular called Tom Morris, who used to spend a lot of time in the blacksmiths shop doing a bit of striking for the blacksmith" and how he would always appear at the blacksmiths looking for work in the winter months because "…There was always a warm hearth after the fire had gone out to lie on, to keep warm over night."

Eventually, I steered the conversation around to the subject of the salmon and its captor, Thomas Allen. Tom Godbehere had a glint in his eye as he described Mr Allen. When he was living at Eaton Constantine as a child, he spent a lot of time with Thomas Allen and "…practically lived at Mr Allen and Aunty Nell's" (his housekeeper). He described Thomas Allen as "…a big man" and "…a wonderful sportsman of every description. He was good at everything, sporting. He was a wonderful chap. We used to get on together like nobody. He almost thought of me as a son or a grandson or something."

Richard handed an old, sepia-tinted photograph to Mr Godbehere, who recognised Thomas Allen instantly. He also remembered the dog in the photograph clearly. "Yes. That's Mr Allen. I can see him now and that is the house at Dryden. The name of that dog was Judy. He told it to do something once and it disobeyed him and he let fly and he shot the damned dog! But it was far enough away to do no harm. Oh, he was a character Mr Allen was, a true character."

Tom interrupted me as soon as I mentioned the salmon. "I was there when it was caught! He took at least two and a half hours to get it out the river so they could net it. 63½ pounds it is..."

I asked him what he recalled about the day and he remembered that it was a pleasant, autumnal Tuesday, with the river at normal levels and that Thomas Allen hooked the salmon at midday. "Aunty Nell took it into Shrewsbury to the taxidermist next morning," he told me. "That's how the salmon came to be here in that damned big case,"

"So they weighed it the following morning?" I asked. "And it weighed…"

Tom interrupted my question again, "63½ pounds."

"So," I checked, "it had been dead for as much as twenty hours before it was weighed, so it would have been heavier when it was first caught?"

"Oh yes," Tom confirmed, "possibly heavier."

Tom remembered the length of the salmon as 53½ inches (I measured the fish later and made it 54 inches). He also remembered the fight in vivid detail. Thomas Allen had been fly-fishing opposite Cound Lodge near Eyton Rocks on the River Severn (seven kilometres downstream of Atcham Bridge as the salmon swims) when he hooked the monster. "Oh I was running up and down the bank," Tom told me, "and he got him in the river up to here [chest deep] two or three times. But he was a wonderful sportsman of every shape and form, Mr Allen was. He was in the river up to his chest several times. Cor, I can see him now."

"It must have been quite a sight when you first saw the fish?" I asked. "The size of it?" "You've no idea," replied Tom. "I think he was so astounded when he saw what he'd got hooked that he didn't say anything. He was just so astounded at the size of the damned thing."

He told me how John Bright, Mr Allen's cowman, who had been cutting thistles in a field near the river, came down to see the fish and helped to land it. Apparently, quite a crowd had gathered on the bank opposite to watch the battle.

When I asked him directly about the rumour that the salmon had been caught in a net, rather than on rod and line, Tom was dismissive. "I was there!" he said, simply, and his description was so clear and detailed that I'm sure that he was.

When I asked if Thomas Allen had thought about claiming the salmon as a record, Tom replied, "Oh no. He had just caught a salmon and that's all that mattered to him. As I say, Aunty Nell got in the trap, the horse and trap, next morning and took it to the taxidermist in Shrewsbury and it was stuffed, and so the damned thing's there today."

"You didn't think of eating it?" I asked. "It was a pig," Tom replied. "If someone put a salmon of sixty-three and a half pound in front of you, it would want a bit of chewing!"

Tom had trouble remembering the exact year in which the salmon was taken but he thought that he had been eight or nine years old. Then, as we took our leave, he spotted a facsimile of a poster on the wall in the entrance hall of the home and remembered that the salmon had been caught in the same year that he heard the news about the ship in the poster sinking. The ship in the poster was the Titanic and the year was 1912.

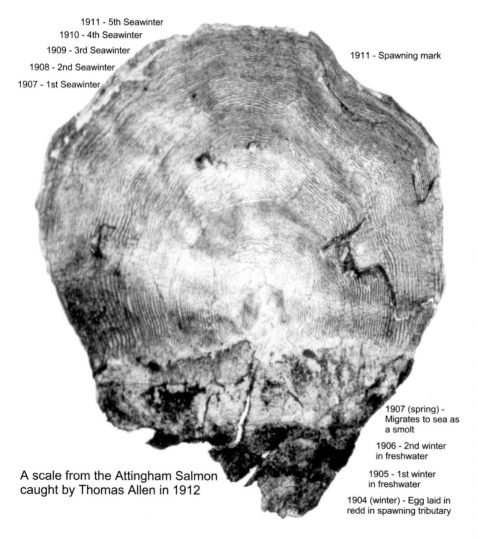

A scale from the Attingham Salmon caught by Thomas Allen in 1912

Having established that Thomas Allen caught the salmon by fair means on rod and line, I now set about finding out as much as possible about the fish itself. I contacted the Environment Agency and tracked down Ros Challis, the Ecological Team Leader who had carried out the earlier study of the salmon. Ros was very helpful and found the scale sample she had taken from the salmon at that time.

Salmon retain their scales throughout their lives, unless they are lost through injury or disease, and they lay down new material at the exposed edge of the scale as they grow. The result is that salmon scales show a series of concentric growth rings or circuli, similar to the rings of a tree.

Growth in salmon is temperature dependent and they grow more slowly during the winter months than in the summer. In winter, when growth is slow, the distance between the rings is small and in summer when the growth rate increases with water temperature, the circuli have more space between them. The result is that a winter "check" can be seen clearly on the scales, as a dark band of rings packed closely together. The number of winter checks is related directly to the age of the fish.

Salmon also grow far more slowly when they are juveniles in freshwater than they do in the food-rich environment of the oceans. This means that the scale of an adult salmon will have a densely packed "nucleus" of circuli that reflect the freshwater stages of its life cycle and a set of more widely spaced rings that reflect its marine growth

It is possible to derive even more information about the life cycle of a salmon from its scales than just the number of winter's growth in the riverine and marine environments. The distance between the winter "checks" is directly proportional to the increase in length of the salmon during each growing season. This means that it is possible to calculate the length of the salmon at each stage in its growth from juvenile to adult, from the distance between the winter "checks" and the length of the fish when the scales were taken.

When a salmon returns to freshwater to spawn, it stops feeding and growing. At the same time, the exposed edges of the scales start to erode. The result is that salmon that have returned to a river to spawn, survived the ordeal and returned to the sea as kelts, show a distinct spawning mark on their scales. Atlantic salmon survive spawning in very low numbers (seldom more than ten percent of the population) and the vast majority of salmon that do survive are female.

Scale reading is more of a black art than an exact science but an experienced fisheries scientist can interpret the pattern of rings on a scale and work out the detailed life history of the salmon from which it was taken.

The scales of the Attingham salmon were not of the best quality and were quite difficult to read, due mainly to their age. However, they were sufficiently clear to show that the salmon had spent two years growing in freshwater before migrating to sea as a smolt. It then spent four years at sea before it returned to the river to spawn for the first time. The salmon survived spawning and returned to the sea as a kelt. It was making its second spawning run when Thomas Allen caught it.

The fork length of the cased salmon is Fifty Three and a Half inches and the girth is Thirty Five inches. Using a standard formula for calculating weight, these measurements give an estimate of between 64 and 67 pounds. The girth measurement may not be representative of the live fish because the girth

> The request to anglers in last year's report to provide the Board with particulars of the number, size, sex, and weight of the salmon they catch, and some of the scales, has not met with any response. A circular has recently been sent to all licensees for salmon rods and lines, and promises have been received from a considerable number that they will send to the Board particulars of the fish they take next year.
>
> Some particulars of the salmon in the Severn District during 1913, taken from the Bailiff's reports, will be found in Appendix V.
>
> LARGE SALMON.
>
> The number of fish of 35lbs. and over is again high, and those weighing 40lbs. and upwards are the same as in the previous season.
>
> A list of large fish with dates and places of capture will be found in Appendix VI.
>
> The number of salmon over 35lbs. in weight for the last 11 years has been:—
>
> | | Male | Female | Sex un-ascertained | Total | Heaviest |
> |------|------|--------|--------------------|-------|----------|
> | 1903 | 6 | 1 | — | 7 | 52 lbs. |
> | 1904 | 7 | 0 | — | 7 | 41 |
> | 1905 | 11 | 4 | — | 15 | 55 |
> | 1906 | 10 | 3 | — | 13 | 45 |
> | 1907 | 4 | 1 | — | 5 | 45½ |
> | 1908 | 3 | 3 | — | 6 | 44¾ |
> | 1909 | 6 | 2 | — | 8 | 49 |
> | 1910 | 12 | 1 | — | 13 | 43 |
> | 1911 | 9 | 2 | — | 11 | 52 |
> | 1912 | 16 | 7 | 11 | 34 | 46 |
> | 1913 | 20 | 5 | 5 | 30 | 50 |
>
> TROUT.
>
> The season for trout has been on the whole a good one, especially in those waters where trout are protected, and coarse fish kept under.
>
> FRESHWATER FISH.
>
> The average catch of each fisherman was probably less than in recent years, but some very good catches were reported.
>
> EELS.
>
> The eel season was bad. As in all seasons when there are a number of freshes about the end of the summer and the early autumn, the eels descend in driblets, and no large catches are made while the contrary is the case when a flood comes at the end of September after a spell of dry weather through August and September.
>
> LAMPERNS.
>
> The season for these was also poor. There were much fewer about than usual.
>
> TWAIT.
>
> There were no twait, not only in the freshwater, but hardly any in the estuary; it was from some unexplained cause the worst twait year for years.
>
> ELVERS.
>
> The number taken as compared with ten years ago are substantially less, and it would appear that the runs of elvers were small.

may have been distorted when the fish was set up. However, this estimate is consistent with the weight of 63 ½ pounds given by Tom Godbehere, particularly when account is taken of weight loss during the considerable time between the capture of the fish and its delivery to the taxidermist the following morning. It is interesting to compare these measurements for the Attingham salmon with those of the other portmanteaus given above.

The salmon catch statistics for the river Severn at the turn of the twentieth century make interesting reading. In the late eighteen hundreds, the Severn was a prolific salmon river. As Tom Godbehere put it "in those days the Severn used to be one of the best salmon rivers in the country." Catches declined rapidly during the first three decades of the twentieth century, because of industrial pollution, over-exploitation by nets and the creation of weirs that formed barriers to salmon migration. The salmon rod catch plummeted from a peak of thirty three thousand in 1910 to less than five thousand in 1930.

The single most important contributor to the Severn's decline as a salmon fishery was insidious, chronic pollution. Sewage discharges from villages in the upper catchment degraded the quality of the spawning tributaries, washings from a sugar mill polluted the Tern and acids from the numerous Kidderminster factories polluted the Stour, which joins the Severn at Stourport. The worst offender was the city of Gloucester, which discharged all of its untreated sewage into the estuary. This barrier of untreated human waste was the last thing that the smolts faced as they left the river on their migration to the sea and the first obstacle that greeted them when they returned as adults.

Thomas Allen was fortunate to be fishing the Severn when the river was in its prime and he caught his portmanteau just before the degradation of the catchment caused the salmon population to decline. The average rod catch from the Severn between 1990 and 2003 was just three hundred and thirty nine salmon. With a peak catch for this period of six hundred and forty three salmon in 1996, the Severn fishery is but a parlous shadow of its former glories.

Ros Challis traced further information about the Severn salmon fishery at the turn of the twentieth century from the records of the Severn Board of Commissioners, which are kept at the Environment Agency's Tewkesbury office. Thomas Allen's name appears only once in the records, as the Commission's representative for Sallop. He attended the Commissioners annual meeting just once on Thursday, 3rd October 1912 (the same year that he landed his monster). Why Thomas Allen didn't publicise his triumph is a mystery but the Attingham salmon doesn't appear in the annual lists of largest salmon caught from the Severn, recorded in the Commission's minutes.

The records of the Severn Commission show that several salmon were caught each year from the river during the early twentieth century that were of a size unheard of today.

So, will the Attingham salmon and its captor, Thomas Allen, ever replace Miss Georgina Ballantine and her 64 pounds Tay fish in the record books? I discussed the likelihood of this happening with a member of the British Record Rod Caught Fish Committee. Despite the strong circumstantial evidence that Thomas Allen's salmon was heavier than Miss Ballantine's when it was landed, and the existence of an eyewitness account of its capture, the evidence is not robust enough to satisfy the Committee's strict guidelines. Thomas Allen caught his salmon ten years before Georgina Ballantine landed her record and so, even taking the weight of 63 ½ pounds, he should have held the record for that period. However, it seems that too much water has passed beneath Cressage Bridge to establish the Attingham salmon as the current official record.

Unless the gaps in the circumstantial evidence can be filled with certainty, we are left with a number of questions. Was Thomas Allen's salmon the largest ever caught on rod and line in Britain? Was it the largest fly caught salmon from British waters? Was it the record salmon from an English river? You can judge for yourself but I for one believe that the answer to all of these questions is yes.

Would Thomas Allen mind that his fish was not on an official list? I don't believe for one moment that records and publicity were important to him, or he would have told the world about his salmon at the time. As Tom Godbehere put it "Oh no. He just caught a salmon and that's all that mattered to him."

Every angler should visit the Tenant's Gallery at Attingham Hall, to see the case that hangs there. The magnificence of Thomas Allen's salmon speaks for itself.

Icebreaker

The folklore predicted last winter's arctic blast far better than the weathermen. Last autumn the trees were laden with berries and a slight frost coated the grass in our meadow one night in September. A September frost heralds the new Ice Age.

I'm glad that the omens were right. I loathe damp winters and much prefer a season of crisp, clean frost and snow. In fact, I love the winter as much as any other season and the first snow usually has me pining to be in Scotland with my crampons and ice axe, stomping over the snow fields of some remote mountain. I love those crisp, cold winter mountain days when the air is as clear as crystal and the musical melodies of the tumbling burns carry for miles across the hillside.

Winter carp fishing can be fun too, if you adopt the right attitude and wrap up like an Eskimo. The chances of catching always seem remote but that makes any success even more pleasing. Winter carp fishing teaches you to find satisfaction in the smallest of pleasures and landing just one decent fish can make you smile for a month.

There is a lake near our cottage where I am always confident of hooking a carp, no matter how harsh the cold. I took my friend Dunkeld there a few years ago during one of his visits south from Aberdeen, having boasted that I could catch a carp on the surface there in a blizzard. I could tell he wasn't hopeful of success, as he complained that the weather was even colder than it had been at home. "Perhaps we should try for a chub instead?" He asked.

Even my optimism faded slightly when we found icebergs in the margins of the pool. Yet when I flicked out some floaters, one disappeared almost immediately in a great swirl. Within half an hour we had several carp going crazy for the dog biscuits. Two of them were even coming like great icebreakers, smashing the glazed surface to get at floaters trapped on top of the ice. Eventually, I hooked one but lost it at the first plunge of the rod, when the line was severed neatly by the razor-sharp ice on the surface of the pool.

I used to put the carp rods away for the winter to concentrate on other species, although even the rivers can be difficult during an icy winter like the ones we have had in the last couple of years.

I remember fishing the Hampshire Avon near Downton one very cold December day in 1983. The sky was as grey as slate and threatened snow. Chris Yates was with me and another Golden Scale Club member called Berol. Chances looked as bleak as the weather and we all agreed that we had to be mad to be fishing, but that didn't matter because I had another companion to keep me warm, my girlfriend of the time who was called Sarah.

My memories of the day are like a series of frozen snapshot images, as clear and sharp as shards of fractured ice: crackling puddles under clumping feet; trying to blow "smoke rings" with our breath; the razor cut of the wind; icicles in the rod rings and the bleak, yet beautiful frosted landscape. Through it all flowed the river, viscous, dark and seemingly without life. Indeed, it looked like the river itself might slow to a standstill and freeze at any moment.

We set up below willow tree, where a deep, slow eddy looked like it might be home to one or two chub. If it had been, Sarah soon evicted them by stamping her feet to get warm. I wasn't in the least bit put out by this as I didn't really want to catch fish anyway and within a few minutes there were two of us snuggled up in my old overcoat and my rod had been abandoned to fish for itself. I'm not sure what Berol and Chris made of the two of us behaving like a couple of giggling love-struck teenagers but then again, I didn't really care. After all, at least I was warm and, as I said earlier, the river looked devoid of life.

There was life though. An iridescent roach of about a pound attached itself to the end of Chris's line and we gathered around to witness the miracle but it fell off just short of the net. Then, just at last light, my old cane Wizard slammed over and the centerpin raced but by the time my frosted brain had clicked into gear and Sarah and I had untangled ourselves, the fish (probably a chub) was long gone. I remember us all getting chilblains by the pub fire and laughing into our drinks. Hardly the most productive day's fishing but an enjoyable and memorable one just the same.

Sometimes the conditions are not just difficult, they are impossible. In the mid-eighties, I remember escaping from Liverpool, where I was studying, to drive home for the last day of the traditional carp season. It had been an icy spring and I wasn't going to bother to make the six hour trek back to Somerset but on March 13th a mild, westerly airstream swept in across the Wirral and finally drove out the Siberian cold that had settled over the country. My studies had kept me away from fishing for nearly three months and the arrival of the warmer air was all the encouragement I needed to make the journey.

I left Liverpool at about six in the evening and by the time I reached Somerset the last day of the season had arrived. I grabbed a rod and the bare essentials of tackle and headed straight for a lake a few miles from home. As I left the car, I noticed the bright full moon and I paused briefly in my excitement as I realised how cold the air was. The mild air I'd left behind on Merseyside didn't seem to have reached Somerset. The lake was still and the full moon reflected perfectly in the strangely calm water and cast a bright, ethereal light on the scene.

There was no need for a torch, the night was mercurial and I tackled up by touch alone. One, two, three swings of the rod and I sent the tackle sailing out into the night, towards the centre of the pool. There was a pause as I waited for the splash but all I heard instead was the Chink! Chink! Chink! of the lead, as it bounced and skated across the surface of a lake still frozen under an inch of ice. I felt so foolish that it put me off winter carping for years.....

My first taste of winter carp fishing success came whilst fishing as a guest on a lovely estate lake in Wiltshire. The lake is one of a chain of waters within the romantic grounds of an 18th century manor house. The water was shallow and very clear and on first inspection it seemed devoid of fish of any kind. Even at the dam end the lake can't have been more than five feet deep and I could see every inch of the silty bed; it didn't seem possible that the water could hold the number of large carp that made the lake one of the best syndicate waters in the county.

After more than an hour spent creeping slowly around the pool I found several carp patrolling along a marginal reedbed in the shallows, where the water was only two feet deep. I didn't spot these fish directly, I suddenly noticed their shadows, cast upon the lakebed by the bright winter sunshine. The lake had frozen the night before and it amazed me to find active carp in such shallow water, as I had assumed that any fish would have favoured the deeper spots by the dam. Now, in hindsight it made perfect sense for the carp to be up on the shallows. The melting ice would have produced a layer of cold, heavy water that would sink into the deepest areas, driving the fish up into the slightly warmer waters of the shallows. Here, the weak winter sunshine would add to the warmth and encourage greater activity, despite the recent freeze. These days I always look to the shallows first in search of winter activity.

There were four fish cruising the margin, their flanks brushing the base of the reedmace. They made their way from the shallowest corner along the reeds to a small bay beneath the oak tree from which I first spotted them, pausing to upend and feed in the thick silt beneath me before returning along precisely the same route, to disappear into the reflected glare from the ripple at the head of the pool. All of the carp moved incredibly slowly and with hardly a flick of a fin and I would have missed them if it wasn't for the dark shadows they cast.

It took the carp nearly half an hour to complete their circuit from the bay to the head of the pool and back. I set up my rods in the swim opposite and then climbed the tree again, waiting until all four fish had vacated the area before returning to my tackle and casting a hookbait some thirty yards over to the reeds. The cast fell about a foot short but I was quite confident that the carp would scent out the bait, encouraged to forage by the light scattering of free baits I introduced. I fished a single hookbait on the second rod in the open water area visited by the carp at the opposite end of their patrol route, having waited for them to reappear in the bay below the oak before making the cast.

I was brimming with confidence but a clear, frosty night passed without as much as a line bite. At dawn I awoke to find two limp, lifeless lines running from the rod tips into a margin glazed with cat-ice. A fresh brew of tea warmed me enough to get up and creep round to the oak and I'd just taken up my perch in the branches when the same four carp appeared, following precisely the same route along the margin as before. As I watched, the large mirror leading the group tilted gracefully down and picked up

a boilie that had been lying tight up against the reeds. Almost all of the free bait had disappeared and all that remained was my hookbait and half a dozen other baits, scattered a foot or more out from the margin. Although the carp must have been aware of these baits they obstinately ignored them, never deviating from their chosen path.

Once again I waited until the fish disappeared from view before shinning swiftly down the tree to recast the margin rod. Again the cast just fell short but this time I wasn't going to accept anything less than a perfect drop. On the fourth attempt, the lead hit the wall of reedmace, bouncing off to land less than an inch out from the roots. Just ten minutes later I had a fierce take and after a long, powerful fight I drew a Twenty Six pound common over the net cord. I remember the depth of gold in the carp's scales and the way they simply glowed in the winter sunshine; until that moment I hadn't appreciated quite how much the colour of the fish deepened during the colder months and how beautiful the effect could be. I also learned the importance of location and, more importantly, of precise presentation when fishing for carp in the winter; a mere foot on the cast had made all the difference and saved a blank.

Ashmead has always been an excellent winter venue. Like the Wiltshire water, Ashmead is relatively shallow, averaging just four feet and with nowhere deeper than about eight feet. It is also quite sheltered, despite the open northern aspect that gives commanding views across the bleak winter landscape of the Somerset levels. The high banks and surrounding willows break the power of a northerly wind and hold the heat of the weak winter sunshine. The water warms quickly and the carp remain active throughout the winter in even the harshest conditions.

In fact, some of the most productive winter days I've enjoyed at the lake have been when a really cold northerly has been blowing. In these conditions the carp lie up in the lee of the islands and high banks like ships at dock, resting in the areas of calm water created by the wind shadow. I've caught lots of carp with frost lying thick as snow on the ground but although I've caught with the temperature as low as minus four, I still haven't landed a really big carp in the snow.

Careful observation is the key to locating the pockets of fish and accurate presentation is essential, as the carp will probably not move more than a few feet to investigate a bait. These conditions are the only time I will confidently cast a rig directly to a group of fish, without expecting them to melt away because of the disturbance. Even though the carp are lethargic they will still feed at some point during the day and provided I've found some carp to fish for I'm pretty confident of a take.

Ashmead has always had a reputation as a hard water but last winter was exceptional and for quite a while the water was very hard indeed; hard enough to walk on in fact. We had nearly four inches of ice in January and a friend of mine recorded a temperature of minus $14^{\circ}C$ in his garden one night.

I was amazed to see how quickly the carp became active after the thaw. One Sunday morning I had been walking around on the ice, yet on the following Monday one of our members hooked a small common from the spot where I had been standing. On the Thursday morning of the same week, one of the members landed a superb common of Thirty Seven pounds, hooked in just two feet of water. My theory that the carp move into shallow water after a thaw, to escape the cold, dense water created by the melting ice seemed to hold true.

My own fishing last winter was very limited, with work and the freeze conspiring together to prevent me from getting out onto the bank. I enjoyed a couple of blank sessions before Christmas and then sneaked a carp out on the only visit I managed.

I'd been visiting the lake regularly for short walks with my black lab Archie, timing my trips to coincide with those times when a sudden change in temperature caused the pool to either freeze or thaw. Watching the water at these times revealed the areas that tended to freeze last and those that consistently thawed out first. These slightly warmer areas tended to be either in the sheltered bays underneath a bit of tree cover, or in shallow open areas that caught the most sunlight during the course of the day. One area in particular, in a swim called The River, was consistently the first and last part of the complex to hold a significant area of open water, when the rest of the lake had a covering of ice.

Careful observation showed that a group of carp were visiting the swim on a regular basis and this was where I chose to fish, trickling in small amounts of my favourite winter bait for several days before the session. I arrived at five o'clock, just as the last pale blue in the sky gave way to the indigo of night. I lowered the single hookbait into the margin beneath the skeletal branches of an ash tree and walked the rod back to the swim, ensuring the loose line followed unobtrusively along the contour of the bank.

I flicked the rig on my second rod into the small open bay to my right and covered the spot with a mixture of hemp and crushed boilies. To be honest I shouldn't have bothered with two rods, as the ash tree was the only spot that I felt was likely to produce a fish and the second line only increased the risk of spooking the carp before one took the bait.

I'm sure it was my imagination but I was convinced that I could hear the lake freezing as the night went on. The creaks and groans were probably made by areas of ice moving on the slight breeze. The night coincided with the advent of a new moon, which rose through the branches of a tree behind my swim, like an image created by Magritte. Venus hung in the sky nearby and I watched as the pale blue evening light gave way to indigo and then black. I tried to count the stars as they appeared and kept track until there were a hundred or so above me, but then someone carelessly spilled the Milky Way across the night and in the blink of an eye the few hundred stars I'd been trying to count gave way to countless millions, which shone brightly across the wide Somerset sky. When I looked through my binoculars even more could be seen across timeless distances that gave me a sense of vertigo. It was one of those fantastic nights that really makes you feel glad that you are a carp angler and I sat up until dawn, completely absorbed by the majesty of the sight above me. On nights such as that I really don't need to catch a carp; they merely provide the excuse for being there.

The only sign of life had been a barn owl that ghosted past in the early hours but then, at eight in the morning, I had a steady run on the rod fished beneath the ash tree. The carp fought hard for every inch of line and several times it nearly made it into the willow roots of the island margin opposite my pitch. Each time it tried for their sanctuary I plunged the rod tip into the water and applied every ounce of side-strain the line could take, to roll the carp off balance. I did briefly feel the awful grating sensation of the line rubbing against a root, but the tackle was sound and she rolled into the net in the end. A deep bodied, heavily scaled mirror of Twenty Three pounds Twelve ounces put the icing on the cake of a wonderful winter trip.

I spent the rest of the morning chatting to Jody and we had just got onto the subject of wildlife, when he told me that he'd seen a raptor harrying some pigeons in between the goat willows, in a lethal game of tag. We ran through the possibilities and decided that the only likely candidate was a peregrine falcon, as Jody was adamant that the bird had sickle shaped wings, rather than the rounded wings of the sparrow hawks that frequent the pool.

A couple of days later I found the wing bones of a pigeon in the grass next to the path, stripped of their flesh with surgical precision before being discarded. I kept a close watch over the next few days and eventually found the falcon resting in the branches of one of the Scots Pines next to Toms Pond. I had good views of the slate grey plumage, mottled breast and golden raptors eye through the binoculars, but she spied me and took flight before I could get close enough for a photograph. Peregrines rank right up there with the Merlin as my favourite birds of prey and I've always had a fascination for them. My interest is possibly inspired from reading TH White's book The Goshawk when I was younger and in fact, if I had the time available, I'd love to train and keep a raptor.

A couple of years ago when we were staying in a small croft in Scotland I found a Merlin that had shattered its wing by stooping into a new deer fence in pursuit of some prey. We took the bird into an animal rescue centre in Ullapool where it stood a chance of making a recovery and return to the wild. Memories of its glaring, defiant eyes will live with me forever.

I thought last year's winter would have a devastating effect on the wildlife at Ashmead. The willow saplings that had been gnawed for the scant nutritional value of their bark suggested that some of the small mammals had struggled to find adequate food. The lake stayed frozen for weeks and the countryside was blanketed in snow. The harsh conditions arrived so early and lasted for so long that I was sure they would have an impact on the wildlife, but that didn't seem to be the case.

There were as many mice and shrews around as ever for the barn owl to hunt and the kingfishers and other birds have been flitting around all summer in their usual numbers.

It's always something of a relief when winter ends and the Ashmead carp start to feed in earnest and show themselves in the first of the warm spring sunshine. I've gone for months without seeing a sign of a carp swimming around in the lake and it is amazing to see the way they can simply disappear so completely in such shallow and clear water. The fact that they do still feed and can be caught if you do

find them is a comfort to their worrying guardian at times.

There are plenty of times in the winter when I'll be out wildfowling rather than fishing and if I do go out I often visit the river in search of some pike, rather than sit it out in hope of a carp. There are even times when I could quite happily sling another log on the fire, pick up a good book and hibernate. But right now, a blizzard is coming! It's time to thaw the rods out and try for that photograph of a large carp in the snow.....

Fishing in Nod

Dipping into the pages of my angling diary last night, I came across a reference to the time when I came close to catching a record carp. Looking back now, I still find it hard to believe that the fish could have escaped to join the many others that haunt the dreams of the lost. The episode happened during a hot summer day, spent at my favourite carp water. Although the day itself was not in the least bit out of the ordinary, the loss of the fish occurred under rather unusual circumstances.

The pool was bell-shaped, lying in a deep fold in the rolling farmland. It had probably lain undisturbed for centuries, apart from the introduction of the carp and the subsequent attentions of the occasional angler. People had come and gone but their impact upon the pool had been negligible and it remained one of the few wild places in an otherwise tamed landscape. The woods in which it nestled were a vibrant mixture of beech and oak, recognised as one of the best areas of mature deciduous forest in the area. Deer, foxes and badgers haunted the woods during the twilight hours, and during the day it was sometimes possible to catch a glimpse of the shy form of a red squirrel, ghosting through the branches.

The day in question was typical of the heat-wave June of 1995. The midday sun beat down upon the canopy of the oaks on the steep bank opposite, making the leaves crackle and scrape in the wind. The brilliant sunlight seared the eye and burnt out the colours, so that it was impossible to focus. I sat, with my back resting against the bole of a beech tree, some hundred feet or so beneath the topmost leaves, and here the air was completely still. Although it was pleasantly warm, the ground held the dampness of decay and a sweet perfume of humus blended with the acid tang of the lake water. Insects droned monotonously but other than their hum, blending with the leaf-rustle, there was silence. No birds called, the nocturnal mammals slept and even the squirrels were quiet. Beside me, my retriever stretched, yawned and snuffled back into his dreams, content in a world of his own design. It was a Dog Day.

The carp, too, were almost comatose. A group of four dark mirrors lay motionless at the surface, just off the skeletal branch of a fallen tree. The only movement was the pulsing of their operculae and the occasional swivel of an eye. In the absence of any current, there was no need for them to flex fin to hold position and one even rested its bulk on the snag to avoid the effort of maintaining its buoyancy. From time to time a small wildie would cruise past in open water, it's back cleaving the surface film, but even this motion did not remove the sense of torpor. The wildie swam with slow, bored thrusts of its tail; interested in nothing and exciting no interest.

My home-made goose quill, resting in the margins, looked less likely to disappear than the tree against which I was leaning. Apart from the brief flutter of a line-bite, nothing had stirred it in nearly two hours. I slowly let my eyes close and drew the warmth of the sun deeply into myself with a yawn. Two more minutes and I would take my rod and net for a stroll, to see if any fish were active under the cool shade of the far-bank oaks. Perhaps a floater might induce some interest, if carefully drifted out to the fish? Then again, there was no breeze upon which to drift one....... Two more minutes.....

At the apex of the pool was an area of marsh, where the inlet stream filtered through a century's accumulation of silt. Even where the ground appeared dry, a heavy footfall could break easily through the thin crust. The risk of plunging waist-deep into the vile, clinging liquidity beneath forced anglers to skirt this area by a wide margin, following the narrow path into the woods before circling back to the water. I found myself on this path now, threading my old cane rod like a needle through gaps between the clasping twigs. The only other items carried with me were the net and some bait. If I was lucky enough to find an interested fish, any other unnecessary paraphernalia would be an encumbrance.

Somehow, I felt as if something was amiss. I wasn't able to put my finger on it, but the familiar tackle and surroundings seemed different. The rod was a favourite old MKIV, which I had obtained many years previously on a cold winter's day beside the Royalty. The rod was usually whipped in a subtle ivory silk, but today it was in buttercup yellow, which clashed violently with the bright purple centrepin fixed to the butt. I remember thinking the reel looked ridiculous. Perhaps the sun was playing tricks, refracted by the glossy leaves of the rubber plants and cacti. Rubber plants? Cacti? Very strange....

I forced my way past an encroaching rubber plant and pushed on, until I came to a well that housed the spring that nurtured the pool. Roughly circular in shape, the well was about four feet in diameter and surrounded by a low wall that was almost lost beneath a blanket of leaf-mould and ivy. I set my tackle down and crept up to take a drink, completely unprepared for the sight that met me as I peered into the depths. The water in the well was as clear as a diamond and floating in it was the largest carp I had ever seen. A great tail, each lobe like an outstretched hand, brushed the stonework on one side, whilst gently mouthing lips kissed the opposite wall. The skin of the carp was the colour of polished ebony and its mirror scales glowed gold in the filtered light. It was huge, monstrous and surreal.

How could such a carp have found its way into the well? Had it come from the main lake through a subterranean tunnel or been stranded by a flood? Who cared? It must be a record. I steadied myself. If I could only get it to take a bait it would be easy to land because the fish had nowhere to go! All I would have to do would be to clamp down hard on the reel and quickly scoop the net underneath the fish. Hardly challenging fishing; in fact a certain record.... Slowly, very slowly, I slunk back from the well to

Chapter Nineteen – Fishing in Nod

my rod. I baited up with a single, enormous maggot, which covered the size four hook with ease, crept forward and lowered the bait into the well, just where I expected the carp's mouth to be. Keeping down behind the wall, so as not to further disturb the carp, I held the line, feeling for a take.

The wait was a short one. Whether the carp was starved of food in its enclosed haven and found the maggot irresistible, or whether it simply inhaled the baited hook by mistake I neither knew nor cared. The line suddenly drew taught and I struck. Water went everywhere as the carp thrashed the well into a foaming cauldron but it had nowhere to run; it was mine.

I reached down for the net and the slight slackening of the line allowed the great fish to turn its head. Suddenly, realising my mistake I heaved, desperate to bring the head back up, but it was too late. With the slow roll of a sounding whale the carp dived, swimming powerfully downwards. I could do little more than hold on, keeping the line chiming at its breaking point and the rod arced towards the shadow of the fish, growing ever dimmer in the depths of the well. Tick, tick, tick; on and on; arms aching and the ratchet of the purple reel counting out the yards of line like a metronome. Then suddenly it was gone and I fell backwards, the world tumbling around me, my eyes springing open.......

When I made my way up to the head of the pool, after a refreshing cup of tea, I found that the rubber plants and cacti had been replaced by more commonplace butterbur and willow. My rod had reverted to its ivory trim and my old Aerial was, once again, the usual gunmetal grey. The well was still there, but it was almost completely filled with silt and the few inches of grimy-black water held no sign of a fish. Perhaps it was just coincidence that, when I eventually hooked a large carp near to the inlet stream, the fish dived beneath a branch at my feet before heading out into the lake. Just as in my dream, the rod tip was pulled inexorably downwards and the line peeled from the drum until, with a resounding crack, it parted.

I have always dreamed so vividly that it can at times be difficult to separate fact from fantasy. The clarity and content of my dreams often reflect the surroundings within which they are forged. The dream I have just described came to me beside the most wonderful carp pool in the country; a place of wilderness and magic. Sometimes, however, even the mundane can be transformed and enhanced under the influence of Morpheus. Some of my most exciting angling takes place behind the rapid flutter of dreaming eyelids. Better yet, I am convinced that dreams can form a tangible link to future events and that their correct interpretation can lead to a point where the imagination and reality converge. Just occasionally, the point of convergence is one where a special fish is looking for a meal and the results can be spectacular.

I haven't experienced this type of convergence very often, which is probably a reflection upon the weakness of the link between my subconscious mind and the natural world. Too much time spent tapping away in front of a computer screen and too little time spent fishing. Certain anglers, like my friends Chris Yates and Mike Winter, seem to exist in a permanent state of commune with a supernatural guide, who leads them unerringly from one momentous capture to the next. Of course, that is not really the case; I am simply less skilled than they and less in tune with my fishing. Even so, I can occasionally predict correctly where and how a particular fish will meet its downfall.

The last such experience took place during a day on the Severn, where I had been pursuing some rather large but very elusive barbel. The night before I was due to make yet another dash up the motorway, I had a vivid dream in which I netted a good barbel from a deep pool beneath an overhanging willow. Nothing too unusual in that, except that the netting operation was made more difficult by the presence of a dead cow, which floated within the willow's trailing branches and which kept trying to chew through the bottom of my net.

The following morning, my usual amble in search of a swim was brought to an abrupt end by the stench of decay. There, trapped in the branches of a willow, lay the dead black and white form of a Friesian cow. The cast hardly had time to settle before the rod slammed over as the fish I had been searching for grabbed the trundled lobworm. The fight was unspectacular but when it came to netting the fish, my net caught on some rusted barbed wire, which lay buried in the riverbank. Holding the rod in one hand I tried impotently to free the tangled mesh with the other, but it was impossible. I tugged viciously at the frame and tore it free, ripping the base of the net. When I eventually landed the barbel, it glowed in the autumn sunshine, just like the fish of my dreams. It weighed a little less than Eleven pounds.

Even if you are too rational and suburbanised to accept the existence of some form of telepathic sense, which harks back to those distant times when our race had to rely upon the hunter's instinct for survival,

you must admit that dreams can be fun. Sometimes they can surpass the excitement of the reality they mirror.

I clearly remember a dream I once had whilst staying at my parents' home in Somerset. I was lying back in a deckchair on the terrace in the back garden, when I fell asleep. Suddenly, I noticed a large carp feeding in the goldfish pond, some thirty feet away across an expanse of lawn. In my dream, a baited rod appeared from nowhere and I flicked the bait in a gently curving arc, to land close to the fish. The carp turned nonchalantly and slurped in the bait, but I lost it during the fight when it swam out of the pool, beneath the grass, and smashed the line around the roots of a rowan tree. The only sign left of the battle, was a line of freshly ploughed earth, tracing the flight of the fish. It was a bit like the earth trail left behind the fleeing rabbit in a Bugs Bunny cartoon.

The wonderful thing about angling dreams is the way in which the most bizarre possibilities can be realised. Having lost a dream-carp under such strange circumstances, I reassessed the potential of my surroundings. I suddenly understood that it was only the paving upon which I slept that was truly solid. The rest of the garden around me was deliquescent, passing continually between the solid and liquid states. What was more, the garden was alive with feeding carp, which had left the confines of the pond to reap the benefits of their strangely expanded universe. Closer scrutiny of a gentle humping in the earth of the rose-bed, similar to that caused by a mole constructing it's hill, revealed the lips of a large common which was trying to slurp down a piece of crust left out for the birds. Similar stirrings were taking place all over the garden, as carp burrowed through the heather-bed looking for worms, basked under the clematis and browsed on greenfly amongst the apple trees.

The dream developed into the most successful afternoon's carp fishing recorded in my diary. I landed ten fish to nearly forty pounds and lost at least as many again during epic struggles, in which the passage of the carp through the soil was mapped by a furrow of fresh earth, cut by the taught line. By the time I awoke the grass looked like a plan of spaghetti junction, with most of the furrows leading to a particularly sharp snag in the lawn-mower shed. I was exhausted when I regained consciousness, and my arm ached.

Only a dream perhaps but the excitement and fulfilment were real enough. Besides, who can really be sure where the divide between the real and the imagined lies? Ever since that afternoon I have checked my parents rose-bed carefully whenever I visit and I always make a point of closing the mower shed door, just in case........

Encounters with Pike

There are days in angling that stay with you forever, golden moments when everything seems to fall magically into place. For me, one such day was 17th February 2006, the day that I became a pike angler. I'd caught pike before, of course (it would be difficult to go fishing for forty years and avoid them completely), but I had always viewed them as ugly, rather stupid brutes that possessed no finesse and demanded none from those who fished for them.

My first encounters with pike were fuelled by Crabtree. What young angler could fail to be impressed by the drama of Bernard's cartoon strip, in which Mr Crabtree and Peter fished for pike on an old estate lake? The Crabtree's fished with live baits caught for them by "Tom the bait catcher". "I've got you 1½ doz. Roach about 4 or 5 inches Mr Crabtree." Ah! Those were the days.... They fished from a boat in a reedy bay and the tension when Peter's old Fishing Gazette bung starts to move erratically as a pike draws near is electric.

My first pike fishing trip, in about 1979, was with a friend called Monty Halls and his dad, who were both keen anglers and lived just up the road from us. Monty's dad was also called Monty (which was a little confusing) and "Big Mont" had heard that there were good pike being caught from the lake in the grounds of Sherborne castle.

We set off on a classic winters day of clear skies and hard frost, just the way Crabtree and Peter would have wanted it. In fact Big Mont and Little Mont might have been Crabtree and Peter, even down to Big Mont's choice of pipe. "And now young Monty, we'll see if we can catch some pike..." "Rather, Dad!"

And there it was, Sherborne Lake, identical in almost every respect to the lake in Bernard's illustrations, even down to the reed lined bays. We didn't have a boat or a bait catcher but we did have the right snap tackle and Fishing Gazette bungs. For bait we had a bag of rather sorry looking sprats, which we cast into every likely looking spot as we worked our way around the lake.

Little Mont was the only one to catch, when a pike struck at his bait in the afternoon. His rod thumped over and on his inadequate tackle it took an age for him to land the fish, but land it he did. At about Seven pounds it was by far the largest fish either of us had ever seen and I remember being very impressed and monstrously jealous. Big Mont arrived on the scene when the pike was already on the bank and the pike's fate was sealed. "Knock it on the head and we'll take it home to be set up. It will look splendid on the wall in the living room." Truly Crabtree at his best and worst, yet we knew no better in those days and the poor pike is presumably gathering dust on Mont's wall to this day.

My own first pike came from the River Brue at Basin Bridge in 1981. Big Mont had made contact with the farmer who owned the land where Cripps River joined the River Brue near Bridgewater and this turned out to be a real pike hotspot. The local tackle shop owner had told us that livebait was the key to success here and we started out by catching some shimmering roach on trotted maggots. These were lovely little fish and I hated the moment when I had to impale one on my snap tackle and start pike fishing. It wasn't that I'm squeamish but it seemed unnecessarily cruel to treat such a beautiful fish in this way.

I think our roach fishing activity must have attracted the attention of the pike, because my bung slid smoothly under on just the second or third cast. I don't remember much about the fight but I was using a lightweight bass rod and I think I probably just hung on without giving an inch of line until Monty managed to engulf the pike in my new Efgeeco net, which I'd bought specially for the trip. I do remember the fish though; a stocky pike of Ten pounds Ten ounces. It's glaring down at me accusingly from above the doorway in the hall as I write because I'm slightly ashamed to say it suffered the same fate as Monty's Sherborne fish.

In fact as I left to go fishing that morning I had made my dad promise that if I caught a pike I could have it set up, just like Monty's. When he agreed, I don't think dad thought I'd catch one and I'm sure he didn't realise quite how expensive the taxidermy would be. Dad stayed true to his word, though, and used his contacts to find the best taxidermist available to set up the pike. I remember very clearly striding proudly up the steps of the Natural History Museum in London with my pike, to meet Dr. Alwyne Wheeler, head of the fish section and one of the world's greatest authorities on fish. Dr Wheeler was also a familiar name to anglers, as one of the gurus who presided over the British Record Rod Caught Fish Committee. With Dr. Wheeler was John Hajiloizi, who was one of the museum's best taxidermists and it was John who was entrusted with the task of setting up my pike. What an experience for a young boy, taking my fish to the Natural History Museum! I felt like I'd just broken the British record...

The highlight of the episode came a few weeks later when we went back to collect the finished specimen. Not only was John Hajiloizi's work absolutely stunning, I also got a tour of the museum's collections with Dr Wheeler. This was in a time long before today's more open access to the archives and collections and it was a rare and inspiring privilege. There, preserved in jars, was shelf upon shelf full of fish specimens, going back to the time of Darwin. Dr Wheeler knew about every specimen, its natural history, where in the world it came from and who had discovered it. There, in the dark collection rooms in the bowels of the museum Dr. Wheeler fanned the flames of my love of fisheries and wildlife and fired my determination to become a Marine Biologist. I owe Magnus (the name we have given my pike), and Dr Wheeler a great debt.

As I said, Magnus is glaring at me right now and I always feel guilty and have to look away whenever he catches my eye. I've always regretted killing him but at the same time he is pretty impressive to look at and, as I've described, his adventure in London did have quite a profound impact on my life.

I also found out something else through Magnus' demise and that was that I hated livebaiting. I decided that if it was true that I could only catch the Brue pike on live baits, then I wouldn't fish for them at all; it was as simple as that. I did fish the Brue a few more times and had some success on dead baits, taking pike to Fifteen pounds, but live baits were definitely more effective. Ultimately, I found the fishing rather dull and uninspiring, despite the ferocious splendour of the pike, and I soon gave up and moved on to more satisfying winter sport, fishing for chub.

For years, pike never entered my thoughts, unless they bullied their way in uninvited. Once on the Severn, for example, I was fishing for a huge barbel I had found, which must have weighed about sixteen pounds. I had it feeding steadily on some hemp I'd introduced onto a small patch of gravel beneath a patch of ranunculus and I cast out a large lump of luncheon meat, full of confidence that I would hook it first cast. From the moment the rod pulled over to the moment I slid the net under the culprit I was certain I had hooked my biggest barbel by far and I swore in disbelief when a pike of a similar size to the barbel slid into my net. I never saw the barbel again and the incident only added to my belief that pike were more trouble than they were worth.

Then, one day in December 2006, I received an e-mail from a friend that contained a photograph of a huge pike of over Thirty-Five pounds that had been caught from his local river. Not even I could overlook a river pike of that size and so it was that I found myself sorting out some pike tackle for the first time in over twenty years. I took my cane carp rods and centerpin reels loaded with fifteen pound line and some wire, crimps and swivels to make up traces on the bank. Bait was to be smelt, fished freeline on a set of trebles in the deep pool where the monster lived.

No one had fished the river for pike before and thoughts of the old adage that big pike thrive on neglect added a certain spice to my first visit. Running through the heart of a very old estate, the river is a noted trout fishery. Its banks are well maintained but on the stretch where I was fishing not overly manicured and the river had a slightly neglected feel about it that I really liked. The refinements associated with the very best of exclusive river trout fishing were there, though, including some wonderful old fishing huts that dated back to the days of Sheringham. One of these huts served as my base camp for the day and I felt like an Edwardian squire as I dropped my light load of tackle under the shelter of the thatched roof. There was a map of the fishery on the wall and some sepia prints of anglers fly fishing the river at the turn of the century. The reach had the atmosphere of an exclusive but slightly shabby old gentleman's club and I fell in love with it at once.

The pike pool lay below a set of extensive shallows and I had a theory that the large females gathered here at the end of each season, prior to spawning on the shallow gravel upstream. The surface of the glassy chalk stream flow boiled slightly where the riverbed plunged suddenly from four feet down to twenty and then ran as smoothly as silk for the hundred yards of the pool. I cast the freelined smelt across the current and let it settle into the depths, before twitching it slowly back to the near bank, where I left it for a minute or two before completing the retrieve.

On the third cast, I felt a sudden resistance and the rod top thumped over. A sweeping strike pulled the hooks home and the surface of the pool erupted as a shocked pike burst out of the river and shook its head violently, before plunging back into the stream. The pike soon gave up and came to the net without much more of a struggle. Although it weighed only Twelve pounds it was quite beautiful and as a result of the clear chalk stream habitat, the markings were far more vivid and striking than any pike I'd seen before. The greens of its back were of emerald and polished jade and its flanks were spotted as if they had been dabbed with brushstrokes of ivory paint. The pike bristled in the net as I returned it.

Time for a cup of tea. I cast out the smelt again and let it settle into the pool before placing the rod in the rest and putting the kettle on. Just as the kettle came to the boil I saw the rod tip nod twice; not a sharp rattle like one of the many large trout resident in the stretch would give but two slow, steady bows towards the river. I checked the line for weed where it entered the river but it was clear. I picked the rod up carefully and touched the line above the reel. It was there again; a short but distinct pull, then a longer, more sustained take and the cane rod telegraphed the ponderous sway of the pike's head to my finger-tips. I wound down and pulled sideways to set the hooks, remembering Mr Crabtree's advice to Peter when he had just lost a big pike, "Your strike was too upright, old boy."

Chapter Twenty – Encounters with Pike

The pike cruised slowly into mid river and the rod pulsed to the rhythm of its tail. This was quite unlike the feel of the earlier double; no fireworks and mad dashes but a heavy, solid, powerful run that bent the rod through to the butt. It held briefly in the current and then turned suddenly and powered away with the fast chalk stream flow. It was like playing a large salmon except that the runs were less panicked, more ponderous and more purposeful. The pike made for the ranunculus beds at the tail of the pool and I'm certain it knew exactly where the safest refuge lay. I couldn't turn it against the flow and had to run along the bank to get downstream of the fish, so that I could bring the force of rod and current to bear in unison. She stopped and hung deep, pondering her next move. It felt as if it was weeded but I knew the riverbed at that point was clear.

Then she moved again, making her way slowly up against the push of the river and the pull of the line, rising up towards the surface as she went. Suddenly I spotted her in mid-stream hanging three feet below the surface and looking as if she was gliding on a current of air, so clear was the water. "Oh my God!" I said out loud. "Am I attached to that?"

Never before had I seen such majesty in a fish. Even the large carp I've caught over the years didn't compare to the first sight of that pike. She was huge, long and muscular and with an aura of wild fury that seemed to light up her scales. The pike burnt with a primeval fire that made me step backwards involuntarily, it was rather like the way big game marine fish, like marlin, "light up" when hooked. Boosh! The surface exploded as she turned again and dived for the sanctuary of the deepest water. I'm sure the hooks would have straightened if I'd been using a fixed spool reel, no matter how good the clutch, but on the pin I eased off the pressure instantaneously and let the action of the cane absorb the full force of that lunge for freedom.

Three times I brought her back to the surface and three times I failed to hold her as she plunged back down into the depths of the pool. Then, on the fourth confrontation, I sensed less force in her dive and she felt for the first time like a dead-weight, using the power of the river to carry herself away instead of her own ebbing strength. When she rose again from the depths it was for the last time and she rolled exhausted, unable to find the reserves to struggle any more. The current now acted in my favour and it swung her across the river to my own bank, where I let her drift slowly backwards into the folds of my net.

The pike was as docile on the bank as I could have wished and she lay quiescent as I removed the treble from her jaw and took her portrait. Her graceful lines and wonderful markings impressed me and it seemed to be almost irreverent to weigh her, although I did of course, steadying the needle at Twenty Eight pound Eight ounces. I returned her carefully upstream, letting the cold chalk flow refresh her gills before releasing her to glide gracefully back into the clear depths.

Time for that tea. I cast into the pool for a third time and the freelined smelt drifted lazily across the current towards the near bank, as I settled back into my seat and reached for a teabag. Suddenly, before the bait had settled, the line started to cut back upstream against the current and I reached for the rod and wound down to meet the solid resistance of yet another pike. The first fish had been erratic but lacking in substance, the second ponderous but full of power; this pike was a mixture of the two. The rod went almost flat as she lunged for the riverbed and then straightened as she exploded upwards through the surface like a leaping salmon, gills flaring and head shaking with rage. I only just managed to slacken off in time as she plunged back into the flow and swept away downstream. This early display of aggression sapped her strength however and after a few short, heavy runs through the pool she was ready for the net. For the third time in just twenty minutes I set up the camera to run off some photographs. She weighed Twenty-Four pounds Four ounces and was very different to the twenty-eight, more silvery, stocky and brutal to look at, with an up-turned jaw that seemed to be set in a permanent snarl.

For perhaps the first time I really understood the fascination of pike and why they have provided the inspiration for so many great fisherman's tales. That pike was the last of the day but the capture of a brace of twenty pounders had given me one of the most exciting days fishing I'd ever experienced. The fish themselves had been astonishing; not the sluggish oafs I remembered from the Somerset drains but sleek, powerful and vibrant adversaries, with an aggressive pride that demanded respect. I knew I'd be back for another day on the river at the first opportunity.

The Golden Scale Club was meeting on the Stour for the traditional last day of the season, to fish for perch. I thought the Secretary was going to choke on his tea when I told him I was going pike fishing instead and would meet them at a pub in Wimborne at the end of the day.

Just like my previous visit, March 14th dawned clear and chill with bright blue skies and a rime of brilliant white frost painting the countryside. I was on the river by ten, fishing the same hotspot with the same simple technique as on my previous trip. Today, though, my kettle boiled four times without interruption before I saw any sign of a pike.

I had just made up my mind to go for a wander upstream when a movement spotted out of the corner of my eye caught my attention. I looked upstream to the shallow run and noticed that a large shoal of grayling was feeding, dimpling the surface of the river like rain. This wasn't the movement I had spotted though and I was just thinking that a coot or duck must have been responsible when a dark shape broke surface and "porpoised" on the tail of the grayling shoal. It was a large pike turning over and I could clearly see the dorsal and large tail as they slid smoothly back into the current. I've often seen barbel rolling like this and believe they do it when they need to adjust their buoyancy when they've moved up from deep water onto a shallow area to feed.

Taking a rod I moved well upstream of the fish and sent my smelt sailing out over the river with a smooth Wallis cast. The joy of using a centerpin for this sort of fishing is that you are in touch instantly after the cast and I felt the smelt fluttering and gliding through the flow as it arced back towards my own bank. Every now and then I gave a little tug with the rod top to give the bait some more life and to give the impression of an injured fish,

struggling as it was washed down in the current. The bait must have moved about ten yards when a huge bow wave took off from the tail of the riffle and converged with its path. A massive vortex appeared where the pike met the bait and the rod flattened dramatically amongst a fury of thrashing fins that reminded me of the Attenborough footage of a crocodile taking a wildebeest in some wild African river.

In such shallow water the large pike went berserk, crashing out on its tail and making a succession of long, searing runs for the sanctuary of the deeper water downstream. Realising she wouldn't make the pool she turned and made the most of the momentary slack in the line to paravane away across the fast current, before making her way up the far bank. She turned again but this time the pressure from the rod edged her off course and within a minute she had given up the ghost and was ready for netting. At Twenty Three pounds Nine ounces, I found myself holding another huge pike up for the camera.

I went for a wander upstream after that, finding some other likely looking swims for future exploration and managing to land a couple of doubles on the way. I settled into a lovely looking swim for the last half hour, fishing a freelined deadbait in a long slack that had formed along the inside of a long sweeping bend. On my last cast of the day, I felt the line pull tight and then hold as a pike took the smelt before it settled. The fight was slow and unspectacular but I was delighted with the fish, which weighed just an ounce under Twenty pounds and shone silver in the torchlight as I unhooked it in the dying light. I headed off to Wimborne to meet the Golden Scale members and buy a celebratory round of drinks.

It had become clear that this lovely bit of river held an incredible head of big pike and I was besotted with the fun of fishing for them. I also realised that there was much more to pike fishing than I'd imagined. Even a few short winter sessions had shown that I could predict the movements of the pike according to water level and temperature, as they moved onto the shallow grayling glides to feed as the temperature increased through the day before dropping back into the slack pools and eddies as night fell. The fishing had an unexpected subtlety, and tuning into the pike's behaviour was very satisfying. Of course, the raw excitement of hooking a big pike also took some beating.

I knew I would return for another session but for now the season had ended and I had to give the river over to the upstream dry fly purists until the autumn. For the first time in my life, I found myself wishing away a summer of carp fishing and waiting with eager anticipation for the onset of winter.

The river was very private, and access to it a rare privilege, so I decided to fish for only three or four days each season. That way the pike would remain unpressured and I wouldn't outstay my welcome. I returned for the first time in December but quickly realised my mistake. Although I caught a lovely pike weighing just over Twenty Five and a half pounds, the fish was incredibly lean and I could see she would have weighed closer to thirty in a month or two's time. Furthermore, it was the only fish of the day and caught well away from the previous hotspot. I realised that the gathering of the larger females for spawning probably didn't get underway until the final few weeks of the season and I chose to delay any further visits until the end of January.

It was a good choice and on my next visit I took another brace of twenties, one on a static deadbait from the deep pool soon after my arrival at dawn, and a second from the shallows on a wobbled smelt, after lunch.

The first weighed Twenty pounds Four ounces and was a very silvery fish with a slender head and short, sneering upper jaw. The large, bright eyes perched in a forward looking position on the top of her head would give perfect binocular vision and allow her to spot any prey movement and judge the

distance of the strike to perfection. The lateral line and other sensory pits on this fish were also quite pronounced because of her colouration. Through these exquisitely sensitive sense organs she could detect the slightest scent of a possible meal or the least vibration from a passing prey. For the first time I really appreciated how well adapted the pike is to locating and catching its food, under a wide range of conditions. As I studied her closely, my respect for this freshwater predator increased still further. Here was a fish that was a perfect killer, so well honed to its way of life and environment that it had evolved little since before the ice age. In fact, early prehistoric fossils have been found that can be readily recognised as pike.

The second fish was just incredible. She was a new best of Twenty Eight pounds Twelve ounces, although she looked like a thirty pounder all the way to the net. She fought long and hard after smashing mercilessly into the wobbled smelt at speed, catching one of the barbless trebles neatly in her scissors as she did so. Short of jumping out of the river and slapping me around the face with her tail, she tried everything she could in her fight for freedom and she still quivered with rage as I held her for a photograph. Deep bodied yet still as graceful as a big cat, she was a lovely olive colour and finely marked in ivory. She is still by far my best pike in every respect.

I've caught a number of other good pike from the stretch but I'm still waiting and hoping for my first thirty pound fish. There are a few pike that stand out in my memory as I write, one of which taught me a serious lesson in handling these fish safely. I was fishing with a friend of mine, Paul Hughes, who I'd taken as a guest. Paul is a very experienced pike angler and I hoped that having him along for a day might give me some pointers in terms of catching one of the real monsters that I'm sure inhabit the river.

We fished hard but fruitlessly all morning but on my way back to the fishing hut for lunch, I saw a large pike roll right under the near bank at the head of a long, gliding pool. I covered it quickly with my bait and she took on the third cast and I soon had a thumping Twenty Six pounder in the net.

Now I'm good at handling pike, having had a lot of experience from my fisheries science days, and I'm confident when unhooking them. This fish had taken the bait quite deeply and had evidently gulped it straight down, something I've found the fish often do when the bait is freelined and they are feeding aggressively. I rolled her onto her back on the mat, knelt astride her to stop her kicking and slipped my hand up under her gill plate to open her jaws. The first treble had lodged above the start of her throat but the bottom hook was loose and, with a quick flick of her head, the pike sank one of the points of the treble deeply into my finger. What is more, the point was the only one of the treble that carried a barb (to hold the deadbait), so there was no way that I could pull it back out.

I found myself attached to over twenty six pounds of furious fish by a wire trace that went in through her mouth and out of her gill cover, to the size eight treble impaled in my finger. Blood was gushing everywhere and the pike was as tense as a coiled spring, looking like she might kick again at any moment. I had the presence of mind to grab my wire cutters and reach in through the gills and snip the trace before she could do so and I withdrew my hand with some relief but with the hook still embedded deeply in my flesh. Luckily, Paul arrived and helped me unhook the pike and return her, none the worse for her part in the ordeal. In fact, she positively glared at me as I held her up for a picture, with the flying treble still impaled in my hand. "Come on then! I can do worse than that if you want to mess with me again…" The pike had the same glaring eye as a Peregrine. I slipped her back and she added insult to the injury by soaking me with a flick of her tail as she shot off.

Paul hadn't realised I was hooked until I asked for his help to remove the treble, after the pike had been returned. He almost fainted when I showed him the damage and explained how it had happened. The treble had penetrated right up to the bend and Paul thought he should drive me to hospital to have it safely removed and the wound treated. I was having none of that though; the pike had started to feed! There was no way we could pull the hook back out by the same way it had gone in, so I had no choice

but to push it right through my finger, forcing it through the muscle and twisting it around until the point and barb broke out through my skin. Paul stayed conscious long enough to snip the hook above the barb, so that I could then feed it right back through and out of my finger, leaving an impressive hole and a lot of gore.

My finger took hours to stop bleeding and I believe I may be right in thinking that pike produce an anticoagulant to help kill their prey. There is a scar there still that serves to remind me to keep my wire cutters to hand and to look hard for flying trebles, whenever I'm dealing with a fish.

I rounded off the season last year with another brace of twenties taken in consecutive casts from the same deep pool. The first of these pike weighed just over Twenty pounds and the second just under Twenty Three. It wasn't these two fish that fired my enthusiasm to return next winter, though, it was the enormous shadow that loomed up beneath the larger of the two pike as I played her, threatening to grab her and drag her back into the depths, just as I got her to the net. That shadow left me with an image of monstrous power, as by far the largest pike I've seen held briefly in the depths of the pool before turning away and disappearing into the gloom. The image will stay with me forever and will draw me back to the river every winter, until I can fish no more.

Salmo Salar: The Leaper

Before you launch into this chapter on salmon fishing, I ought to make it perfectly plain to you that I am not an expert salmon angler. I love going salmon fishing of course but I'd hate you to read any further without explaining that I don't fish for salmon often enough to have anything meaningful to say about tactics and techniques.

I can Spey Cast badly. My fly selection depends on good advice from someone who knows what they are doing, or failing that I stick to a dark pattern for clear water and something brighter for fishing on the back of a spate. I usually fish a floating line because it is easier to cast and I tailor my choice of leader length to suit the wind conditions and avoid tangles, rather than to suit the fish. In short, I am a bumbling but enthusiastic amateur.

What I lack in angling technique I can compensate for in some ways, however, because I do know a fair amount about salmon biology and behaviour. My watercraft is quite good because I've worked with salmon as a fisheries biologist and manager for more than thirty years, so I can usually predict where the salmon will be and when they are likely to run and take, even when my casting and presentation skills aren't good enough to do anything about it.

As I said though, I do love salmon fishing and more especially I love the wild places to which salmon fishing takes me. More than anything though, I am fascinated by the salmon itself; Salmo Salar, the leaper, the iconic, mercurial, embodiment of wild fishing.

Salmon fishing on a wild west coast river in Scotland is an assault on the senses. The wind hits you as a physical blow, an unrelenting force that shakes you to the core and roars in your ears like something alive. The rain stings your face and blinds you, it seeps through the best waterproofs to chill your bones and sap your energy. A dazzling palette of autumn colour assails your eyes and the heady scents of damp humus and peat, of iodine seashore and stone-washed birch, fill your soul with every breath.

And the rivers! Well the rivers are all movement and power. A west coast river in spate is an unremitting thunder of water that carves through the landscape and moulds it to its will. Not even the gneiss and granite can withstand the rivers after the rain and to stand beside the torrent is a humbling reminder of our own transience.

Yet against this flow of power, a stronger, more resilient and far more graceful force of nature cuts upstream. Silver salmon, fresh from the tide and still carrying their saltwater sheen thrust back against the river with seemingly effortless grace, holding station in the pools, running through the rapids and leaping the falls, propelled on towards their death by the irresistible urge to spawn.

I have loved these west coast rivers ever since I first discovered them more than twenty years ago. I've spent many days walking their banks with a rod, hoping to intercept one of their salmon on its

way upstream, yet I can count the salmon I've landed on one hand. My lack of success is not because the fishing itself is particularly difficult. Even though I'm no expert with a salmon rod, I can catch the salmon when they are running. No, the reason I've caught so few salmon is that conditions on the short spate rivers of Sutherland must be just right before the salmon will run and more often than not, conditions are far from ideal. Catching a west coast salmon is almost entirely down to the vagaries of fate.

To catch, you have to be there at the right time of year (autumn is best) and your visit must coincide with the day that the river is fining down after heavy rain. Even on the few days on which I have landed salmon, the conditions have only been right for the fish to run and be willing to take a fly for an hour or two at most. For most of the day the river was either too high or had fallen too far from its peak flood. Within that short window of time you have to be fishing the right lie, with the right fly and presentation to arouse the salmon's ire and induce a take. Oh yes! Finally you have to land the fish and in these small spate rivers the salmon have nowhere to go except downstream. With the powerful flow augmenting their own considerable speed and strength, playing one of these fish is like trying to tame the river itself.

Photo courtesy of Chris Yates

More often than not the rivers are low and showing their bones and in these conditions its best to keep walking and search out some trout lochs to fish instead. I've spent far more days not salmon fishing when I've booked a beat for a day than I have in casting with any real prospect of catching a salmon.

In short, west coast salmon fishing is like playing a game of poker against a croupier who has stacked the deck in their favour and hidden all the aces up their sleeves. That's why I love it so much.

My favourite river by far is the Kirkaig just south of Lochinver. The river rises from the lochs that shine like gemstones, scattered across the peat moors beneath the brooding tower of Suilven. The Kirkaig flows like any other tumbling highland river across the Suilven tundra until it reaches the Falls of Kirkaig, where it flings itself from the top of a cliff and plunges to its doom in the frothing cauldron beneath the waterfall. The Falls Pool is a dark, oppressive and brooding place to fish, yet because it is an impassable barrier to the salmon, it is often full of frustrated fish that can follow their instincts no further upstream.

Fishing the Falls, at the top of Beat 1, is an exhausting and difficult exercise. On the only occasion I've fished the pool, I found it almost impossible to present a fly with any degree of precision because the pool is so deep and awash with current and counter current, flow and undertow that I had no idea where the salmon might be lying or which way they would be facing. To make matters worse, I had to fish from a precarious ledge some six feet above the water. When I did hook a fish I had no way of following it when it surged downstream and out of the pool, so I lost it within seconds of making contact.

If the Falls Pool is an oppressive place, charged with the painful memory of the lost salmon, the remainder of the Kirkaig downstream to the estuary is a pure joy to fish. It isn't easy fishing and I love the fact that you have to scramble over rocks and fight through the bilberries and heather to reach the pools. The river has a rough and tumble character that makes fishing there an adventure and imparts a sense of wilderness and exploration that is just fantastic. The river is small enough to be fished with my single handed Scottie sea trout rod and most of the salmon are small enough to give me a good chance of landing one on the single-hander if I can tempt a take.

I never feel these wild, peaty spate rivers demand any finesse in terms of fly selection and I use just two or three patterns whenever I fish the Kirkaig, alternating between a small, black Stoats Tail when the river is low and clear, a slightly larger tube version of the same fly when it is fining off after rain and a bright fly like an Ally's Shrimp for when the river is coloured or I'm frustrated by taciturn fish that don't want to play. I always fish a floating line, simply increasing the leader length if I want to fish deeper

through the pools. I'm not sure why I'm writing about tactics at all though, because as I said earlier, I'm just a novice.

What I do like about the Kirkaig, though, is that it is small and intimate and I can read a pool with ease and picture the salmon in my mind's eye as they rest in the shadow of the rocks, buffered from the flow by the contours of their surroundings and gathering strength for the next push upstream. I can cast with confidence and expectation that as the fly drifts through the pool on a mended line, the take will come just... past... that shoulder... of rock... There! The thump and draw of a salmon transforms the image in my mind into a living, electrifying reality and on the light tackle the fight is a frantic, instinctive explosion of energy that is resolved only by the final capitulation of the salmon or a plunge of despair (as final as the plunge from the Kirkaig Falls themselves) if the fish breaks free.

I always return any salmon I land to the river. I have spent too much energy working towards the conservation of the salmon to take one for the pot. I've heard the arguments about returned fish being exhausted and unlikely to survive but I believe they have a good chance. I've landed salmon that have been hooked and lost by other anglers and I've handled thousands of salmon without loss in the course of my scientific work, so I'm confident the fish I catch will survive to spawn as long as I return them with care. In any case, they have a better chance of survival than they do if I introduced them to a priest!

I lived in Aberdeen for many years and used to love fishing for salmon on the River Don. Salmon fishing has an image of being very expensive and elitist, yet whilst the best salmon beats are way beyond my pocket, some exceptionally good fishing can be enjoyed on a relatively cheap day ticket if you know where to look. Many of the Don beats were great value for money and on the right day provided a good chance of a fish. I particularly liked the Manar Fishery, just outside Inverurie, which provided fishing on a mile and a half of lovely, varied water with eight named salmon pools for just a few pounds a day. The rods were limited each day but by watching the long range forecast it was often possible to book a day in advance when the conditions were likely to be right for the salmon to run. If the salmon weren't in a mood to take, the trout fishing could be exceptional, so a Manar day normally provided a memory or two to savour.

I did once enjoy a wonderful evening fishing on a very exclusive beat of the Dee, the Don's rather more refined sister river. Through various contacts, I secured a very generous invitation to fish the Park beat of the Dee near Banchory. The Park beat is the most productive stretch of the river and is famous for its good spring fishing. Park has to be one of the most idyllic stretches of fly water in Britain and the beats on the Park Estate provide a peerless quality of fishing. Of course, the quality is reflected in the price for the fishing and if you take one of the exclusive three day fishing packages, a day fishing at Park costs more than a hundred times the price of a day at Manar. The fishing is so far beyond my pocket that I had never dreamed of fishing the river there, yet in the end, due to a great deal of local kindness and good timing, my evening just cost me a bottle of malt whisky.

Is the fishing at Park worth a hundred times more than the Donside counterpart? Well, for a start, I imagine that if you can afford to pay over £3,400 for three days fishing, the price is actually irrelevant. Park is for the wealthy and the fishing includes accommodation in the beautiful Park House next to the river, fine dining and gourmet quality lunches of venison and malt whisky. As a package, Park provides the crème de la crème of salmon fishing and I suppose that in that context it is worth what the clients who fish the beat can justify paying. You can fish Park for as little as £150 for a day in the peak season but the restriction on the number of rods means that the chances of getting a beat without signing up for one of the exclusive package deals are remote. I have to say that if I had to make a choice between fishing Park for one day or spending a hundred days at Manar, I would choose to fish the Park Estate, not because I'm an angling snob but because my own evening there was simply magical…

Everything from the moment I arrived at Park House was sublime. We met by the river and the ghillie allocated the beats for the evening to the small group of anglers. I felt like a tramp that had strolled into the Savoy and ordered dinner. I had my tatty old Hardy Wye fly rod with me (a treasured present from Shona's grandfather) and because I didn't have a salmon fly reel available to me, due to unforeseen circumstances, I had loaded a new floating line onto my 1920's Allcock's Aerial. It was like turning up to race in the Gold Cup at Royal Ascot on a pit pony. I have to say the other fishing guests were extremely polite and welcoming and they didn't laugh aloud at my inadequate tackle, and even though the ghillie failed to hide a look of mild surprise he didn't send me packing. In fact, he allocated the famous Cellar Pool and the Durris Stream beats to me for the evening, which was the equivalent of giving me a personal invitation to trot my pit pony along to the Royal Enclosure.

A heavily coloured October fish caught on fly from the R. Usk.

A fresh grilse, coracle caught from the R. Teifi

Another coloured Usk fish, this one 12 lb.

DAVID MILLER

Of course I didn't even move a fish but that didn't matter in the least. I spent much of the evening simply sitting on the bank and watching the river, enjoying the surroundings and ambience, revelling in the joy of just being there. All evening salmon leapt in the pools but they were in the more sedentary water in the heart of the pool, rather than the in the surge of water at the head or tail. In my limited experience, when fish show like this they are unlikely to take and I suspect they may be trying to shed parasites by jumping. When the salmon are running and in a taking mood they show, instead, in the faster currents, topping and tailing like porpoises, with the same fish showing several times in quick succession as it enters or leaves the pool. Salmon that are likely to take the fly are more determined and purposeful in their movements, as they search out a route upstream.

Although the salmon I saw seemed unlikely to take, I fished each cast through in anticipation of that exhilarating contact. The pools looked fantastic and full of potential and I'm sure that a better angler would have induced a fish to move to the fly. Every cast was charged with excitement and expectation. There is something magical about the very act of casting a salmon fly and the rhythmic, graceful sweep of the rod is like Spey Casting a spell with a wand, to conjure up a salmon from the depths. Standing beside the surging majesty of the Cellar Pool, just the act of fishing itself absorbed me completely and each time a salmon jumped it came as a physical shock that snapped me out of my reverie. As I said, I didn't even move a fish but I revelled in every moment of that evening and I smile at the memories every time I cross Park Bridge.

My closest good salmon fishing these days is on a lovely beat of the Usk, which is co-owned by a very good friend of mine called David. David and I met through fishing when he joined the Crabtree Syndicate that I used to help run and which had the fishing rights on two small gravel pits near Thatcham. The lakes had some big carp in them but they weren't really my idea of an ideal carp lake because they

lay in some industrial ground on the outskirts of the town, surrounded by a tyre bay, a nightclub and a sewage treatment works. When the lease expired on the lakes I happily walked away from the fishery but I'm pleased to say that my friendship with David continued.

David shares my love of traditional tackle and we hit it off immediately. Our friendship now goes far beyond angling, however. Our eldest son, Iain, had open heart surgery at the Bristol Royal Infirmary Children's Hospital when he was three and throughout a very traumatic time in our lives, David was an absolute rock. David is a very senior anaesthetic consultant at the Bristol hospitals and he kept an eye on Iain during his time in intensive care. To this day David probably doesn't realise quite how great a support he was to Shona and me and how much it helped to have him there to reassure us and to answer our endless questioning. David has a calm, gentle and very humorous nature that is suited perfectly to his work and which is also, incidentally, the ideal nature for an angler to possess.

David heard through the grapevine that the riparian fishing rights on a beat of the Usk were being auctioned and he went along to see what they would fetch. I don't think for one moment that he ever expected to acquire them himself but sometimes fate takes a hand. The beat wasn't particularly well known and catch records were sketchy to say the least, so it was a bit of an unknown quantity and a gamble for any prospective purchaser. In the car park before the auction started David got chatting to another man who had come along in a similar frame of mind and, having known each other for no more than ten minutes, they decided there and then that if the rights sold for less than a given sum, they would buy them jointly and split the fishing between them.

To cut a long story short, the Upper Llangybi Fishery of the Usk is now the most relaxed and wonderful piece of salmon fishing I know. I haven't fished the water very often as David's guest but I have enjoyed the time I've spent wading the pools with my Hardy Wye. It has turned out to be a very productive piece of water and the small syndicate that has developed there enjoy some excellent sport. I'd love to join the syndicate properly one day because I always like to contribute equally to looking after the places I fish and I confess that I feel wary of taking advantage of David's generosity. For the time being though, I am very lucky to be able to visit once or twice in a season to enjoy some fantastic fishing in some great company.

The luckiest guest at Llangybi must be my friend David Miller. David is an amazingly talented wildlife artist and I'm very grateful for his collaboration with the pictures he has allowed me to use for this book. David has also fished the Usk as a guest and on his very first visit he hooked and landed a fresh run Twenty Five pound sea-liced salmon that I think still holds the fishery record.

For Sho and me, the greatest enjoyment we've shared through our fleeting association with Llangybi was the fishery dinner to which David kindly invited us a couple of seasons ago. Everyone who fishes the water during the year is invited to share a meal at a local restaurant as the guest of the two beat owners. When we went, the company was wonderful, the wine superb and Shona and I both say we can still taste the food, it was so good. Upper Llangybi is the best of fishing and epitomises for me what angling should all be about: the lovely river and its careful stewardship; the company and camaraderie of the anglers; and always the chance, just a chance, of hooking a salmon, the magnificent King of fish.

The Leaper

Running the flood tide in from the limitless ocean
A quicksilver flow of life compelled
To seek death's bitter-sweet immortality
A lover's embrace on the gravel bed
Of the stream where, long ago,
Bright into the sunlight, life flowed and fought
To find freedom in the relentless spiral
Of the ocean gyres
Of eons past and eons yet to come.

Against the press of mountain fresh that carves the rock
And, thus charged with siren's calls of scent,
Leads back and back again to redds
Where at once all life begins and ends
Its own eternal cycle with the seas
The pure flow of nature's current tainted now
By the illusion we can stand apart
And cut the threads
That bind us in eternity.

All That Jazz....
The Art of Stalking Carp

There can be few experiences in angling as intense as watching an enormous carp sidle slowly over to your bait and suck it in with a pulse of its gills, before moving off, drawing the loose line taught across the surface in its wake. Sometimes, I've been so mesmerised that I've been unable to strike before the carp realised its mistake and spat out the treacherous offering in disgust.

There is simply nothing as exciting as stalking, of getting so close to a feeding fish that you daren't breathe in case it senses your presence. Playing out the battle of wits against natural instinct at close quarters is the ultimate fishing experience. In fact, for me, such close encounters with my quarry are the very essence of what fishing is all about; a direct, undiluted, intensely personal contact with nature.

The art of stalking carp is not something that can be learned overnight, nor is it something that can be taught easily. Success is dependent so heavily upon development of the innate hunting skills and natural intuition that lie dormant within us all, and are a throwback to our distant hunter-gathering ancestry. Indeed, the reawakening of these ancient skills, and the direct link they provide to the natural world around me, is the reason that I love stalking so much and find it so addictive and satisfying.

I will adopt a more static approach to my carp fishing when conditions dictate that it's necessary, but if there is even a remote chance of stalking a fish I'll be off with the minimum of gear to try and catch one. In fact, I find that the "trapping" approach so prevalent in carp fishing today can actually detract from the quality of the fishing. Static sessions dull my senses, and too much reliance on the technicalities of rigs and bait gets in the way of my natural instincts. Bivvies and much of the other clutter of session carping simply drive out the natural world altogether.

The alternative approach, of developing the watercraft needed to stalk your quarry, can be equally productive and is far more satisfying. Stalking is all about presenting the bait to a feeding carp in such a way that it is happy to accept it confidently and at close enough range to allow you to strike before it can eject your offering.

One of the things I love best about stalking is the complete lack of predictability. I see so many carp anglers going through the same old routine every time they fish: spodding out a bed of bait; setting up the bivvy and associated paraphernalia; casting out the requisite three rods to the known hot spots in the given conditions, and then sitting back in the hope that a carp will hook itself. Most carp magazines these days give the impression that this is the only approach a "serious" carp angler has in their armoury, and treat stalking as a peripheral activity for those times when the fish aren't responsive.

This is a classic case of the self-fulfilling prophecy. Most anglers accept the static status quo and buy in (at great expense!) to the idea that the first thing to do on arrival at the waterside is to unload a mountain of gear and set up the bivvy. Given the disturbance that this involves, any sensible carp is bound to be well over a hundred yards away by the time the angler thinks to start fishing. Once the bombardment of markers, bait and leads is over, every carp in the lake must know they are under attack and so it is no surprise that the accepted norm on some waters is that you need to fish sessions of at least forty-eight hours to have any hope of a run.

Similarly, if stalking is restricted to the unproductive times when the carp don't seem to be feeding, it will never be successful as stalking depends upon finding feeding fish. But try creeping down to the lake at dawn, with a single rod and net and just the essential bits and pieces of tackle and bait in your pockets; you might be amazed by how quickly you can bring a carp to the bank.

The session approach is like listening to a concerto that builds slowly, predictably and steadily towards the final epic movement in which you land the carp. In contrast, stalking is akin to following an erratic, crazy, improvised and evolutionary piece of modern jazz from one stunning climax to the next, at a tempo that leaves you shattered and confused. I love immersing myself in classical music but Courtney Pine leaves me buzzing!

When it comes to the subject of tackle, it is essential to have complete confidence in every item. When the thirty-pounder you've spent the last hour watching is hooked and makes a lunge for a sunken tree ten feet away, you must have complete faith that rod, line and hook are up to the task of turning it in time to avoid disaster. Any doubt, any hesitation whatsoever, is often fatal. The more room you give a hooked carp to manoeuvre and pick up speed, the more likely you are to lose the fight, and most of the carp I hook never get to take an inch of line off the reel! In fact I've applied superglue to the slipping clutch of my favourite Mitchell 300, to remove any temptation to give the carp a chance to get moving.

I'm often the butt of friendly jokes about my preference for old tackle; "panda fodder" cane rods, centerpin reels and the like. I don't use this tackle just because of some great sense of nostalgia (although I do enjoy the link back to angling's halcyon past); I prefer this tackle because it is up to the task I set it, whereas most "modern" gear is not. For instance, I hook many of the carp I catch while I'm dangling from the branches of a tree, many feet above the water. The best carbon rod would last for a few seconds at best before it shattered during the acrobatic fight that follows, whereas my old 9-foot J.S. Sharpes salmon blank survived twenty years of being bent and bashed against the branches before it finally splintered last year (I've replaced the tip section and it's going to return to front-line duty this summer).

You can't worry about the survival of your rod and reel when a carp explodes towards freedom. My stalking rod is made up from a stock of old cane blanks I found in the basement of an Aberdeen tackle shop and cost ten pounds, whilst my sabotaged Mitchell cost a fiver from a bring and buy sale. These are disposable items and I never give them a second thought once a fish is hooked.

The powerful through action of the cane means that once I've tucked the rod butt into my stomach, it is impossible to break fifteen pound mono on a straight pull. Just as the singing tension in the line climbs to breaking point, the rod gives another inch and, provided that line and hook are up to the job, I know the rod will cushion any lunge well enough to prevent the hook straightening or damaging the fish by tearing free. I've rolled forty pound carp onto their backs with this gear, which I hooked at such close range that they soaked me from head to foot as a result.

Successful stalking depends upon a simple, almost naïve approach. The more gear you carry, the more likely you are to be spotted or to stumble on the bank; more carp are spooked on the approach to a swim than at any other time. Manoeuvring yourself into position without alerting the carp to your presence is the most difficult and critical part of the whole process. I can't tell you how to be cat-footed but it's self-evidently easier to move freely and quietly without lots of clutter.

Complex rigs are also more likely to disturb the carp on the cast or be spotted when in position and a disturbed carp is infinitely more difficult to tempt than one with its defences down. Heavy leads are the kiss of death and I use a freelined bait for most of my stalking. After all, the plan is to strike into the fish the instant you see it pick the bait up, rather than trick it into hooking itself against a lead. I do sometimes use a float or more complex presentation when the carp dictate that one is needed, but the secret then is to wait patiently until I'm completely certain that all of the carp have left the area before casting.

If you're going to play jazz you must be ready to improvise. I normally tie a size 6 hook directly onto the reel line and for most of my stalking that is as complicated as it gets. Bill Reeves, a really good friend of mine, once went to a North West meeting of the British Carp Study Group at which each member was asked to demonstrate their favourite rig. Lots of in depth discussion took place over various ingenious combinations of different hook lengths, leads and tubing, until Bill sheepishly produced his size 4 Super Specialist, Palomar knotted to an inch or two of 10lbs Maxima. Silence....

"Err, that's it," said Bill, "you put a bait on the hook and then strike when you see a carp pick it up."

"You know, Skeff," he told me, when describing the embarrassing lack of interest in his carefully prepared contribution. "I don't think the other members quite understood the concept...."

Stalking is a bit like playing chess against an opponent who can read your mind and who changes the rules on a whim. Actually it's a lot like playing chess against my nine-year-old, Alistair...

The old adage is to "first find your fish" and once you know a water well, you can predict where the fish are likely to be. In general, carp follow the path of the sun around the water during the day; they follow a new wind (particularly a Westerly or Southerly); they like the cover of snags and overhanging branches; they like the quiet areas of the lake that the session anglers ignore; and they like areas where they can find food, such as silt, weedbeds and the lake margins. As you get to know your water it will be easier to predict where fish will congregate in any particular set of conditions. You can even predict the movements of individual carp because they each have their own preferences and idiosyncrasies.

In fact, one of the other attractions of stalking is that it allows you to get to know individual fish and that is the best way to make large wily carp vulnerable. If you are targeting a specific carp, time spent stalking it is time well spent because it allows you to study the way it feeds, the sort of bait it is likely to take and the areas of the lake it prefers. These observations will help highlight its vulnerabilities and help to bring it to the bank, even if you catch it finally whilst session fishing.

When approaching a swim I try to move as if a record carp is basking on the surface at my feet. Think of the way that any predator moves in nature when approaching its prey, whether it's a hunting lioness or a pike; the movements are slow, rhythmic and slight, with frequent pauses to let the prey settle and observe its reactions. You must place every footstep with care and your movements must be slow and heron-like.

I always wear drab clothing, although I spook far more carp with a sudden movement or the vibration from a clumsy step than as a result of the carp spotting me. You will be amazed at how light a tread a carp can detect through its lateral line. It's always the carp that you don't see that you will frighten first and as soon as one carp has sensed your presence, any others in the vicinity immediately pick up on its anxiety. I've lost count of the number of times I've crept up on a fish only to have another of which I was unaware detect me and shoot off, taking the target carp with it. As I said, the best approach is to always assume that the closest carp is only a foot away and move accordingly.

Watch the fish. If a carp has sensed you, it will normally freeze, dorsal bristling and pecs extended, ready to swivel away from the danger. A spooked carp will slowly sink a little deeper and slink off towards the best escape route into open water. Provided the carp hasn't panicked and swum away altogether, though, it will relax again surprisingly quickly, although you may need to stand poised, motionless like a striking heron for several minutes before you see the tension leave the carp, as it returns to its browsing.

Perhaps the most important bit of kit I carry these days is a small pair of good quality binoculars fitted with polarising filters. These allow me to watch a swim from a distance and observe any carp that are present without being close enough to disturb them. The twitch of a reed stem, bubbles, disturbed silt, a slight movement in the weed or a swirl of the water surface, can all give away fish that may not have been obvious immediately.

It always pays to watch the fish for a good while before casting. The temptation to flick a bait out at the first carp you see is enormous but you really should resist. By watching a carp you will slowly form a picture of its behaviour and this makes it so much easier to present your bait in the best way. Watching the carp in their natural environment and seeing the way they move and behave when undisturbed is also just a lovely thing to do. Carp are

very much creatures of habit and you will discover that a fish will always return to a particular gap in the weed to sunbathe, or to a particular spot in the margin to feed, often visiting these spots repeatedly as part of a short circuit around the swim. All you then need to do is to lower your bait onto the spot whilst the carp is elsewhere, confident of its likely return.

Of course, you can cast directly at a feeding carp, and a big bunch of maggots or a slowly sinking lobworm are very difficult for a carp to resist, but the direct approach will spook a carp more often than not. If the carp does melt away, I always leave the bait untouched for several minutes and I've hooked many fish that have returned and taken the offering confidently, once their initial unease has subsided.

If I can't see any signs of carp in a likely swim, I bait it lightly with a scattering of particles and creep away, returning an hour or two later to see if one has moved in on the feed. Sneaking between the baited pitches in rotation usually guarantees several chances during the course of an afternoon and it is rare not to hook at least one carp in the course of each session.

When you do hook a carp the excitement really begins. If you're used to playing fish hooked at range on a heavy lead, the explosive power of close quarter combat is shattering. It's a brutal game in which milliseconds count and you feel each powerful beat of the carp's tail like a physical blow. The secret of success is to outwit the carp as much as to overpower it. I apply rapid side strain, first one way then another; raising the rod and then plunging the tip below the surface, constantly changing the angles to throw the carp off-balance and confuse it. If the fish gets its head down it has the upper hand and the trick is to never give it constant pressure from a single direction that it can use as a reference point against which to pull. With a large dose of luck and a great deal of spray, you may slip the net under the carp before it has worked out what is happening.

One thing is certain, if you try stalking it will open up a perspective on your angling and the waters you fish that you will never experience from any other approach. By merging into your surroundings, all sorts of wildlife other than just the carp will accept you. I've had a tree creeper eating midges on my waders, a squirrel run across my shoulders and I once nearly sat on a badger. Even a blank session can be exhilarating but if you are fortunate enough to have an up close and personal encounter with the fish of your dreams, your nerves may never be the same again.

Just now I can hear a blackbird running crazily up and down the octaves, to welcome an afternoon of warm spring sunshine. The jazz beat is calling and I'm off to grab a rod and see where it leads me.....

Move Over Laurel and Hardy

I've mentioned before that one of the joys of angling is that it gives us a chance to escape back into childhood. Things can get out of hand though and when reason is swept away by single-minded obsession I sometimes find myself doing things so ridiculous that my own children think I've gone mad. I'm normally a pretty rational person but angling seems to upset the equilibrium and spark moments of complete lunacy.

The signs were there from an early age, going right back to the time that I stuck a gardening fork right through my foot whilst digging for worms in my parents' garden. I didn't tell mum and dad in case they stopped me going perch fishing and when I got back to the house after a day on the river, my boot and sock were welded to my foot with dried blood. I didn't care in the least, though, because I'd landed eight good perch, which seemed well worth the risk of blood poisoning. I still have the scar as a memento of the day.

I clearly remember my first night fishing trip, probably because I was lucky to survive it. One April when I must have been about thirteen, my friend Monty talked me into going night fishing on the River Parrett after trout. It didn't matter a jot to us that you weren't supposed to night fish the river or that the trout fishing was equally good during daylight. No, we had read in a carp book somewhere that night fishing was a good way of contacting the better specimens and we decided that this may apply to trout, equally as much as it did to carp. We were angling pioneers! We were going to slay them! We were off on an adventure and we were going catch the biggest trout in the river to boot!

All we had to do now was sneak out past our respective parents without being caught... We rendezvoused at the end of my drive, loaded down with every piece of fishing and camping gear we owned and armed with an umbrella for shelter and worms for bait. It took an hour to cycle to the river and when we got there it was well after dark. Monty had forgotten the torch (I still maintain that he said he would bring one!), and so tackling up proved challenging. It didn't help that Monty fell in an hour after we arrived or that I got soaked pulling him out again.

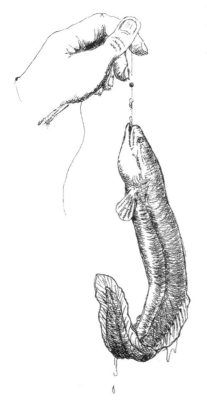

We didn't have any spare clothes of course. But did we care? No! There were huge trout to be caught... And for a second it looked as if the pioneering spirit would bear fruit, as Monty had a clonking bite on his very first cast. "I've hooked a monster!" he shouted, before swinging in a bootlace eel of about four inches long. Untangling the snig and wiping the slime off our kit took ages by match light (if only Monty had remembered the torch...).

By one in the morning we had caught more than sixty fish between us, all of them long, slimy and very un-trout like. It seemed that the Parrett eels liked worms quite a lot. We had run out of hooks, bait and patience but, worse still, the temperature had started to plummet. Under a clear sky, a hard frost had formed and our soaking clothes were turning rigid with ice. We couldn't find any dry wood for a fire and so we started to set alight anything we could find that looked as if it may burn. Our fishing line, plastic bags, the plastic bait tin, all went up in smoke until five in the morning found us huddled around the glowing embers of our last crisp packet, which we had lit with our last match. Hypothermia had set in and we were both almost comatose with cold. "I th... th... th... think wu... wu... wu... we shhhhh should g... g... g... go" Mont said.

How we managed to cycle home I will never know but I don't remember going night fishing with Monty ever again.

I'm not alone in my madness and some people seem to leave themselves open to more than their fair share of bad luck. Probably the most disaster-prone angler I know is my old friend Romper.

Several of us had been invited to fish a charity barbel match at Bisterne on the Hampshire Avon, to raise funds for a Trust that provides support for disadvantaged children. Thirty or more anglers were involved and we were all looking forward to an enjoyable day on the river, whilst supporting a worthwhile cause.

The "match" was a very relaxed affair but we did follow the proper protocol for such events. We even had a draw at the start of the match, in which each of us had to pull a number from a bag in a dramatic and expectant silence. No one quite understood what the draw was for though, as there were no numbered pegs and at the end of it we all simply ambled off across the fields in search of likely swims. There were no whistles or weigh-ins, no stewards or keepnets and no one even seemed to know when the match started or finished. The only instruction was that we should meet at the Bat and Ball at six in the evening to report our results.

That is not to say that a competitive edge to the proceedings was completely missing. Friends huddled in small groups before the "off" and whispers of tactics and "hot" swims clouded the cool autumn air. Four of us had hatched a cunning plan that involved a dash for the lower end of the fishery, where a punt was moored to ferry anglers across the river to the far-bank swims. The scheme was to take the punt across and then leave it tied up on "our" bank, so that we would have exclusive pickings of the rich pools to be found there. The other anglers would be stranded beyond casting range and we could feign deafness if any should call for a ferryman.

We laughed in excitement as we dashed across the fields to the ferry, pursued by another pair of competitors who clearly had similar plans. On arriving at the ferry, three of us piled into the punt. I was first on board and took the helm, after propping my rod and small creel against the gunwale. Next came Angelus with even less tackle carried in his shoulder bag and Alonso, who had gone a trifle overboard and brought a seat as well as his rod and creel.

We were about to launch when we realised that someone was missing! In the distance, Romper was blundering across the field towards us, like an action figure from some D-Day epic. Romper is renowned for carrying an excessive amount of tackle in his enormous rucksack and he is known affectionately as the "Bury Action Man", because in silhouette he looks just like a Marine Commando yomping across Mount Tumbledown for Queen and Country. The other competitors were gaining on him and it looked as if our plan might fail at the first hurdle.

Photo courtesy of David Miller

I may laugh at Romper's ridiculously large rucksack but I am also first in the queue for the endless supply of bacon butties that it produces. However, on this occasion the rucksack was a distinct disadvantage and we could see that his pursuers might succeed in catching him. He arrived at the punt in the nick of time and threw his gear on board. The punt immediately sank ten inches and took on an alarming list to port as his rod holdall, chair, bait buckets and brolly filled the deck. Then he clambered in himself, still wearing his rucksack. The punt was now too heavily grounded to move and Alonso and Angelus had to leap out and push, diving back on board just as our pursuers reached the riverbank.

We were off, with me pulling hand over hand along the wire cable that guided our craft across the stream. Alonso and Angelus were sitting comfortably on the deck, enjoying the gentle rocking of the river and looking towards our destination with anticipation. Romper on the other hand was standing in the middle of the punt, on the upstream side of the cable, with his massive pack still strapped to his back. He was peering over the side into the clear waters beneath our keel.

Suddenly, the inevitable happened. The current latched onto the punt and swung its tail downstream. The cable caught Romper cleanly amidships like a guillotine and with a cry he was swept from the punt and into the river. Somehow one of his legs caught on a rowlock and Angelus had a second in which to grab the webbing of the famous rucksack before Romper disappeared into a watery grave. Romper was left clinging to the upstream side of the punt with his pack submerged and the cold Avon current threatening to carry him away. Alonso reached for the buckle of his rucksack to undo it so that we could haul Romper to safety but Romper had other ideas.

"Don't undo that!" He yelled, "I'll lose all my gear".

By this time the punt was taking in water and we were in real danger of going down with all hands.

"Lose your gear?" Alonso shouted, "You've lost your mind!"

We were caught between blind panic and hysterical laughter at Romper's protest.

"If I go down," Romper shouted "I'm taking the rest of you with me!"

This threat spurred Angelus into action and with a burst of superhuman strength, he heaved Romper and his pack aboard, just as the water pouring into the punt reached a critical level. Somehow we reached the far shore safely and only Romper was soaked.

"Thanks lads," he gasped as we dragged him ashore "you saved my bacon".

An hour later, a familiar smell of sizzling rashers drifted down to us on the wind.

What of the match? We had set forth at the beginning of the day in high spirits and with high hopes of success but as time drifted past on a fishless current, the hope also ebbed away. However, the high spirits remained, bolstered by Romper who spent the day wandering around without any trousers on, showing

his bruises to anyone who made the mistake of showing an interest.

After the match, we gathered for a meal at the Bat and Ball, which was followed by the presentations and a raffle. As only one barbel had been caught, the presentations didn't take very long but the raffle provided a final twist in the day's events. It was a result of either poetic justice or a cunning sleight of hand that Romper won a can of waterproof spray........

Mention of Romper reminds me of an incident that centred on the building the Severn Oaks Syndicate hut on the river near Shrewsbury. Several of the members arrived for the chosen weekend of the "hut-raising", armed with wood, nails, tools and creosote and we all agreed not to give in to the distraction of fishing until the hut had been completed.

We decided to build the hut in a small copse, well away from the river. There were no plans as such and the hut grew organically from the foundations upwards as the "construction engineers" chipped in with bright ideas on how we could best use the available timber. The sun blazed throughout the weekend and the sawing, foundation digging and creosoting left all of us exhausted, thirsty and smelly. Worse still, the actual building process took much longer than anyone had expected and none of us had the time to try and catch a barbel.

It was late in the evening on Saturday when someone asked innocently where Romper was. We had all been so busy that no one had noticed that he disappeared. In fact, he hadn't been seen since we arrived and he had wandered off with his tackle to "take a quick look at the river". Of course he had been fishing all the time, having tucked himself away in a secluded swim a mile or more from the building site, where he thought he would not be found. Some sharp words were exchanged when the rest of us did find him. This was partly because we were tired and tempers were a little frayed but mainly because we all resented the fact that he had been fishing and we hadn't. The exchange ended with Romper skulking off back to his swim and the "workers" stomping off to the pub for a well-earned drink.

Romper wasn't seen again until the early hours of Sunday morning, when we were rudely awoken by the roar of tractors. Arable contractors had moved in to lime the fields by the river, ready for them to be ploughed and drilled with the following year's crop of winter wheat. Have you ever seen a field being limed? It is quite spectacular, with the tractors tearing up and down flinging the acrid white dust across the landscape. The lime covers everything, permeating every nook and cranny. From our safe vantage point in the copse, we watched as the fields vanished beneath a white pall of dust that clung to everything it touched like a skin. By the time the contractors departed, the whiteout was complete and it looked as if a blizzard had struck the Shropshire countryside.

Suddenly, we remembered Romper! Somewhere out there in no-man's land, the Bury Action Man had just suffered a major assault. Finally, in the distance we spied a spectral figure that left a trail of disturbed dust as it made its way towards us across the eerie landscape. It was Romper, caked from head to foot in congealed lime.

"Do you need a hand?" He asked, "I think I'll give up on the fishing........"

I also seem to find myself in crazy situations more often than I should and at times what started out as a simple day out can degenerate into pure farce.

When I set off from home in Somerset one lunchtime, to travel up to Llandudno for a business meeting, it seemed like a perfectly normal day. The meeting was early the following morning so I had arranged to stay overnight with Dave Preston in Shrewsbury. I've always travelled light, so I just wore a suit, which would cover all of my clothing needs for the quick overnight trip and took nothing else with me apart from my laptop and a toothbrush.

The traffic on the motorway was really heavy, presumably due to the start of the summer holiday season. I was in no particular rush to get to Shrewsbury, so I dived off the busy main road at Gloucester and headed northwards along the far less frantic and much more pleasant roads, which wend their way through the Marches, via Ledbury, Leominster and Ludlow. This route was one that I knew well, as it ran past the Kyre Estate, where my friend Keith and I leased the fishing rights on the historic Kyre Pool.

Chapter Twenty Three – Move Over Laurel and Hardy

In contrast to the motorway, the roads I followed were quiet and I made really good time, so naturally I called in at Kyre and followed the farm track down to where it crossed the dam of the syndicate lake. There was a lovely summer breeze blowing up the lake from the dam and under an azure blue sky the pool looked absolutely stunning. I knew that the carp would follow a breeze like this one up to the shallows at the head of the pool. There were bound to be some good fish up in the snags and the chance of spotting some of the monsters I believed the lake held seemed too good to miss.

Of course, I was dressed in my only suit and had just my city brogues for footwear but I decided that it didn't matter, because it was high summer and the fields were parched. Despite the ruby-red soil, the worst I could suffer would be a bit of dust to brush off when I got back to the car. I made my way slowly along the lakeside, pausing every so often to scan the water for signs of fish. Where the path petered out and gave way to a thicket of alder and willow carr at the head of the lake, I stumbled across an enormous carp that was feeding hard in the shallow water. The carp appeared and then vanished repeatedly as it meandered through the clouds of red silt, thrown up by its activity. Due to the silt and the shadow from the overhanging alder branches, I couldn't see the carp clearly and was unsure if it was a common or a mirror but I could see that the fish was far larger than anything I'd ever encountered at the lake before. It was a sight that got my adrenaline pumping.

Without so much as a second thought, I fought my way through some brambles at the foot of an alder and swung myself up into the branches with practiced ease. I cursed when a bramble snatched one of the buttons from my jacket but I found it easily enough and popped it into my pocket to sew back on later. Alders are like a step-ladder to climb, with branches neatly spaced like rungs that allow you to gain height quickly. The carp had moved out slightly towards the far bank and I had to shimmy out along a branch a little way until I was directly above my quarry and could get a perfect view of it when I looked down. I could see it was a dark mirror, broad across the shoulders and with large scales that glowed like golden rings in the sunlight. How big? Perhaps thirty pounds... Maybe more if it had a depth to match its length... If I just leaned out a little... CRACK!

Suddenly, the branch on which I had been standing gave way and I found myself in freefall. No, not quite freefall actually, because I bounced off every branch on the way down, like Pooh Bear falling from the Honey Tree. "I think...," I surmised, as I plunged head first into a branch and bounced off, "In fact I'm quite sure...," I thought, as my backside crunched into the branch below. "Yes, I'm horribly certain...," I said, as I bounced and buffeted my way through the last three branches, "that I'm going to get wet!" And I splashed down into eight feet of dirty, cold water and found myself buried up to my knees in the foul silt of the lakebed.

I'm half convinced that I saw the shocked carp staring back at me when I looked around but it was probably just a hallucination caused by the bang to my head that I'd suffered on the way down. I do remember looking up at the sunlit surface above me and watching mesmerised as a large bubble of air escaped from my mouth and wobbled upwards like an amoeba. I fought my way free of the silt and kicked upwards, eventually crawling out of the lake like a drowned rat. Not only was my suit completely drenched but I was also covered from head to foot in the ochrous red silt of the lakebed. At least my car keys were still in my pocket.

I squelched back to the car and assessed the disaster. I was soaked through, my clothes were ruined and I had nothing to change into, I was a few hundred miles from home and if I headed there I would probably end up being late for my early morning meeting in Llandudno. I decided that Dave would be able to lend me some clothes when I got to Shrewsbury, or at the very least I'd be able to run my suit through his washing machine.

I stripped off to my underwear and opened the boot of the car to put my sodden suit away. Here I found some relief for my embarrassment, in the shape of a tatty old Barbour coat and some wellies that I wear for walking the dogs. I'd forgotten they were in the car and I put them on quickly. The coat covered most of my naked upper body, although the zip was broken, and it hung to mid way down my thigh. The wellies were ripped but they came up to just below my knee. I looked like the archetypal flasher but at least it would be less embarrassing than driving around in just my soaking underpants. The hour long drive to Shrewsbury went quite smoothly, apart from a few strange looks from other travellers when I stopped at some traffic lights and had to buy fuel.

The final twist of fate came when I spotted a large Matalan clothing store on the outskirts of Shrewsbury. Braving embarrassment, I decided to run into the store and buy a complete set of new clothing. My appearance raised a few eyebrows as I roamed the shop like a tramp, dripping water and silt as I squelched around looking for the clothes I needed. The greatest embarrassment came at the checkout, where the close confines of the queue meant the other shoppers around me could not only see that I looked like a drunken old tramp but also smell the foetid odour of silt and slime that hung about me. The queue melted away miraculously and I found myself confronted by an attractive young blonde lady at the till.

She grimaced as she rang up my purchases but remained professionally silent until she had finished. "Card?" She enquired, and I proffered my credit card in payment. "No, I need your membership card" she said. "Membership card? What membership card?" I asked. It was at this point that the young lady explained that Matalan is like a cash and carry and that you had to be a signed up member to shop there. "You can complete an application form now" she said "and get immediate membership. Of course, approval will depend on your financial status". She added, clearly thinking that this would present a problem.

There was no way out and I let myself be escorted to the customer service desk to complete an application. The staff were very thorough about it all and they seemed particularly keen to establish beyond any doubt that I was using my own wallet, that I had a bank account, that I really did hold a senior job at the National Trust and that I did actually own a home a few hundred miles away in

Somerset. By the time they had signed me up and given me my Matalan membership card, a muddy puddle had formed under my seat and half the shop staff had gathered around to gawp at me.

I shuffled back to the till and finally paid for my clothes. "Is there anything else I can do for you today, sir?" the assistant asked, trying hard to keep a straight face. "Actually there is," I replied. "Can you show me to the changing rooms please? In fact, if you have any toilets in the store that would be even more useful."

A short while later I emerged from the toilets, washed and dried and wearing my new outfit. With my old Barbour over my arm and my wellies in hand, I strode boldly from the shop, pausing only to show my soggy receipt for the clothes to the security guard at the door, when he demanded to see it. I still keep my Matalan card in my wallet, just in case; you never know when it might come in useful again…

Simple Pleasures

I'm often asked what the attraction of fishing is, by people who don't understand the pastime. I gave up long ago trying to debunk the stereotype of fishing as boring and the angler as someone who sits under an umbrella in the rain for hours on end, waiting for a fish to bite. If any non-angler reads this book it is just possible that they may come away with enough of an understanding about the many and varied attractions of fishing to want to try it for themselves and that is the only way anyone can discover what it is about angling that is so compelling.

If a non-angler did want to explore the simple pleasures of fishing, then I know a place where I would take them that epitomises everything that makes fishing special. In fact, why don't you come fishing there with me just now and see what you think?

The river where we will fish is a famous one. In fact, it is probably the most famous river in the country because it is our capital river. Where we will go, however, it is little known, small and intimate. Newborn, it bears no resemblance to its adult nature downstream. In fact, if one was unable to trace a fluid link through the countryside, it would be impossible to believe that my little river and that which passes beneath Tower Bridge are one and the same. My river still has a gentle, country soul. It has yet to move into town, let alone suffer the hard-edged pressures of city life. It is pleasant company, easy to get to know and understand, easy to be with.

All we will need is a rod, reel and net, a pocket full of bits and pieces of tackle, a tin of worms and loaf of bread. The seed encrusted brown is definitely the best.

It is a mild afternoon and it rained last night, so the river will be running full and coloured. Conditions will be perfect for the chub and we may even tempt a barbel. We should start at the top of the club length and fish our way back downstream to the car. That way, we will cover more of the good water and you will get to see all of the pools. There are so many twists, turns, pools and glides that if we started fishing by the road bridge we would become engrossed and never make it beyond the first field.

There are no cars in the lay-by, so I think the river is ours alone. Nine times out of ten it is like this but I still derive a selfish pleasure, a sense of proprietary justice, when I have the river to myself. A quick glance over the bridge confirms that the river is well above summer levels and chocolate brown. Optimism grows into smugness and I am certain we will catch. During the spawning season, shoals of barbel can be seen on the gravel below the bridge. The large females cut a redd, just like a salmon, while three or four smaller males compete to fertilise the eggs. I have counted as many as forty fish here in an area smaller than a tennis court.

We will cut straight across the fields rather than following the river. It is overcast and the sky is a winter grey but the air is mild and still. By the time we have covered the brisk mile to the upper fishery limit we will have worked up a sweat. The top field is bordered on two sides by the river and floods frequently. This is a great spot for watching waders feasting on drowned worms. Large numbers of geese visit these water meadows to feed in the winter, as well as any number of other winter migrants. There! A sparrow hawk hunting the hedge lines has panicked a flock of plover, sending the birds shrieking into the sky in a jumbled tumble of wings.

The first cast is always a moment to savour and a chance to gauge the feel of the river and the day. Bait is crust on a size 6, which is tied directly onto our 5lbs line and loaded with a simple swan shot leger. The sensitive tip of the Wizard flickers and knocks as the bait trundles across the riverbed and I am immediately absorbed by and into my surroundings. The mechanical simplicity of centerpin and rod form a conductor between me and the nature around me. It is a connection across the void between the modern world and a more fundamental reality.

The conductor turns live suddenly and an instinctive strike connects with yet another world, unseen within the river. Thumping, boring, flashing chub! Big enough to take line and set my heart racing and big enough to eclipse the rest of my surroundings. Every sense is focused on the tension in the rod and the feel of the fish, until it is drawn over the net. Weighed quickly (Three and a bit) and returned, it adds a new glow to the day.

We work our way slowly downstream. On a noted barbel bend, our lobworm was greeted with what my friend Demus would call "a polite enquiry". It was enough to keep our attention for nearly an hour but the fish declined to become more firmly acquainted. We move on, catching a dace from the swift water below the bend and a chublet of a similar size from the next pool. Then the river straightens its course and follows a crow's flight across the next two fields.

In the summer this long straight is choked with bullrush and the channelled current of the river scours out numerous small pools and scoops in the gravel. Here the barbel and chub lie in wait for dinner to be delivered by the flow, safe within the tunnels of rushes. Sometimes the fish can be spotted directly using Polaroid's but often it is the shadow they cast on the riverbed that betrays their presence or, better still, the flash of a flank as they turn to intercept some morsel of food.

The straight is perfect for fishing fly or floating crust for chub in the late summer evenings. During my first summer here I was fishing into the dusk when a silver arrow of moonlight on the river pointed out the shadowy form of a fairly large animal, swimming against the flow. I didn't see it clearly (it dived before it drew level) but I think it was an otter, rather than a mink. I haven't seen it again since but I did find a large chub carcass during the close season that had its head twisted off and eggs stripped, which are classic signs of an otter kill.

In the present winter conditions the straight is suited ideally to trundling a bait through the decayed remains of the rush beds. In the poacher's pocket of my Barbour, there's a mouldy lump of luncheon meat, left over from a visit to the Severn a few weeks ago. The bait is freelined and allowed to pull about ten yards of line from the pin before we start to follow its tumbling progress downstream. The banks are clear of obstructions and we should be able to follow the bait for some distance before we need to cast again, easing it on its way with an occasional flick of the rod.

A flicker and jab of the tip indicates the attentions of a fish, then a sudden lunge and I'm attached to a living, pulsing resistance that holds fast to the river bed. Winding steadily, I work my way downstream, recovering line until I am directly above my adversary. Then I give the tackle all the pressure it can take, to get the fish moving and to gauge the size of the barbel I have hooked. There is a brief sensation of the fish lifting from the gravel and turning before a powerful, lightning-fast run with the current takes back the line gained. The barbel turned back against the flow and I can imagine it tucking itself beneath a fretwork of dead rushes to sulk. I repeat the process of working my way down to the fish but this time I continue beyond its lie before applying significant pressure. There is a worrying judder of stems as the fish is forced to run again, this time against the flow. Rod and river in unison tire it rapidly and with a final flurry at the net it is mine - a pristine barbel of perhaps five or six pounds.

This bend is a good spot to try. At first glance the encroaching hawthorn on the far bank and the fallen willow bough downstream look too daunting to risk a cast. However a worm, weighted with a single AA shot and lowered beneath the rod top, usually settles nicely under the willow branch. Past experience has shown that the river beneath the trees is free of snags and a hooked fish can usually be steered safely to the net, providing the rod tip is kept low.

I was fishing here once when the silence was shattered by a tremendous roar that frightened the living daylights out of me. At first, I thought a meteor had struck and that the world was at an end, but then the huge bulk of an aircraft appeared above the trees opposite, climbing and banking steeply, like a monstrous hornet. It was a B52, leaving nearby Fairford and en-route to Kosovo. The troubles of the world outside had disturbed even this quiet backwater. Today there are no planes to disturb the tranquillity but instead a kingfisher flashes past in a streak of red and electric blue as it twists and turns in its piping flight upstream.

The push of the extra water has carried the worm slightly further downstream than usual and I have to step up the weight to a swan shot before I'm sure that it has settled under the thickest cover of the willow. No need to watch the rod top here, a tremble of the line across my finger and the cane sprang round as a small chub hooked itself. One, two, three sharp thumps and the fish allowed itself to be lead gently upstream and straight into the net.

Here we are at last, back in the shadow of Hannington Bridge. The hours have flown past and we must hurry if we are to enjoy a leisurely pint at the Wild Duck Inn at the end of the day. So, have you enjoyed yourself? The fishing hasn't been spectacular but there has been plenty of action and the fish, as always, have been beautiful. The scenery isn't spectacular either is it? A few miles of intimate river, flowing through a gentle, pastoral landscape that is so typical of the English countryside and has a timeless quality that is enchanting.

Unless I was an angler, I would never have visited these meadows or walked this stream and I hope I have shown you some of the simple pleasures that fishing here can provide. There is so much more to fishing than the selfish escape of a day by the river, though. If it wasn't for the fishermen who care for this river and many others like it up and down the country, I believe it would be in a poor state compared to the oasis of wildlife we have just enjoyed together. Anglers are often the only people to notice pollution, over-abstraction and the other abuses that can threaten rivers such as this. Without anglers to keep watch, my river, my little haven of peace, could be lost forever, along with the voles, otters, kingfishers and waders that depend upon the diversity of habitat it offers. Spawning barbel would no longer flash on the clean gravel beneath the stone arch of Hannington Bridge and the world would be a poorer place.

P.P.S. R.W. said he was 'delighted' when he heard that the GSC was in possession of his ancient weapon. He also asked to be considered for an honorary President! The nerve of the man! Mind you... Shall we allow the old warrior into our esteemed midst? What do you think? The Russians, Aggies & BCSG would hate it! P'raps we better not tell Bistwhistle.

The Golden Scale Club

Casus Ubique Valet

Club H.Q.
Vale Cottage
Whitmore Vale
Hindhead
Surrey
Midsummer Day.

Dear Skeff,

Sorry to be so long. Communications within the club are, out of necessity, extremely long-winded & rambling, for we are traditionalists & that is the way traditionalists behave. Perhaps one could say we were boring.

Well, we had our AGM & we still couldn't decide on ~~four~~ two absolute favourites. We had, instead, four favourites & we couldn't reject any of them. So we have decided to be diluted as well as diplomatic & offer each of our favourites <u>associate</u> membership for a year. Full membership, the ultimate accolade, will be poured all over you if you are deemed worthy after that time — you could prove yourself either by some heroic deed, by catching a carp from the London Zoo aquarium, by insulting a member of parliament, by supplying a classic article for Waterlog or by catching a 20 lb wildie.

Naturally associate membership will still entitle you to free copies of Waterlog, access to our delectable club-pool (in Sussex — if you could arrange a trip, I'd be happy to be your guide & ghillie for a day!)

limitless supplies of club notepaper & the Divine Right to debunk all ultra-cultists & members of the BCSG. You will also be able to debunk the editor of the Angling Times.

What do you think? I shall fully understand if you turn this offer down with a curt note, but I think you should realise that in the last ten years only five new members have got past the application board & your place is almost guaranteed if you play your cards right, show the right environmental awareness, respect traditional values & behave like a raving Bolivian (or Lap).

I look forward to hearing from you — & I hope you do decide to play along with the chairmans idiotic plan. You could become our <u>fourteenth</u> member & take us nearer to that final number of 21, after which the membership will be closed for ever after, even if every member passes away into that carp-pool in the sky.

Serene sunrises,

Fenny Hough

P.S. The G.S.C. have just acquired the Excalibur of the carp-world, R. Walkers original '44' Mk IV. It had been reclining in a glass case for nearly 30 years, but will now do battle once more. One day, perhaps, the G.S.C. will fish Redmire & the '44' could slay the '88' (or thereabouts).

P.P.S. Hope your 16th was glorious. Trottingshaw was the first to catch a carp at our water — 4.0 a.m. I was second, casting from a tree at 8.0 a.m. The chairman made up for his success last year by blanking.

F.

The Leney Legacy

I have the stocking receipt books for the Surrey Trout Farm on loan from Chris Yates at the moment. I've always been fascinated by Donald Leney and the special carp he stocked into our lakes and rivers but until I saw the records for the first time I had no idea how great his contribution to carp fishing in the UK had really been. The records span the period from 1929 up to the closure of the farm in the early seventies and there isn't an area of the country that didn't receive Leney carp at some point during that time. The list of names and lakes within the records reads like a roll-call of the most influential carp anglers and important fisheries in the history of British carp fishing.

My personal interest in Leney is due to the fact that the first double figure carp I ever caught were Leney's from a series of little lakes near Haslemere called Waggoner's Wells. These lakes lie in a steep Surrey valley, just over the hill from where Chris Yates used to live. I used to travel up and stay with Chris for a few days each summer during the early eighties and he took me fishing to ponds and lakes throughout Surrey and Sussex, a couple of which were Golden Scale Club waters but many of which were club or day ticket pools.

As we flew through the narrow lanes in his white Renault van Chris would point to the left and right, saying, "There's a lake down there that Donald stocked in 1958 that has huge carp in it. I've got an invitation to fish but I still haven't been…." or "Across that field there's a lake where a friend of mine caught a 35lb mirror but it's very private and we've never been back…" To a fledgling sixteen year old carp addict it was intoxicating.

We fished Waggoner's in the evenings. Chris ran his Renault permanently on empty and we would set off from his cottage and crawl up the steep hill in low gear, never sure if we would reach the crest before running out of petrol. If we did, he would freewheel down the steep lane to the pool and we would set off to fish for a few hours before reversing the process and crawling back up from the valley on empty and freewheeling back to Vale Cottage. The process added a bit of excitement to the journey but I can't remember Chris ever actually running out of fuel on the way there or back.

It was not as if we needed any extra excitement, as the carp of the Wells liked to show themselves. Most evenings were spent stalking highly visible and profoundly frustrating fish that would investigate every item of possible food on the surface of the pool but very rarely make the mistake of taking a baited hook. On our first visit I finally tempted a good fish, that was cruising under a leaning tree, into taking a hookful of Purina cat biscuits. I fed it for half an hour at really close quarters until I could see that it had finally relaxed its guard and was slurping down the free offerings without inspecting each one to see if it had a line attached.

My ancient Allcocks Delmatic really wasn't designed for the task of playing a powerful carp but the MK IV compensated enough to cushion the early runs and eventually a wonderful mirror rolled into the net. The carp was my first Leney and at Fifteen pound exactly, my first ever double. A deep mulberry colour along its back gave way to a deep bronze on the flanks and a pale ivory belly, with each of the large mirror scales etched in gold. It was a truly beautiful old fish.

According to the stock books, Leney stocked 100 four-inch carp into Waggoner's Wells on 24th January 1956, meaning that if this carp was one of the survivors of that original stocking (and I'm pretty certain it must have been), it would have been nearly twice as old as I was. Over the course of a couple of years, I took several good fish to nearly eighteen pounds from the Wells and these lovely carp sealed my enthusiasm for carp angling in general and Leney's in particular.

Chris and I also used to fish for the Leney's in Frensham Little Pond, before the tragic fish kill. This was at the time that the likes of Chris Ball, Jan Wenczka and Andy Little were catching the most incredible Leney carp from this lake, to over thirty pounds in weight. Although I never came close to hooking a Frensham fish, I had the privilege of seeing some of them in the water. I remember one hot, sultry afternoon when Chris and I fished in the reeds following a tremendous thunderstorm. The carp went mad for about half an hour, rolling like porpoises under our rod tips and sending up enormous sheets of bubbles that fizzed as they broke through the surface. I've seldom felt such tension whilst fishing since, and if I close my eyes I can still see one great, blue-backed linear that launched itself from the margins of the pond and crashed back, soaking me with spray.

The National Trust owns both Waggoner's Wells and Frensham Little Pond and it feels a little like fate has taken a hand, in that I now work for the organisation charged with looking after these special places. Some of the original Frensham carp survived the fish kill in the late eighties and are still alive today. A few years ago I organised a stock assessment at Frensham and Dr Nick Giles netted the lake to get an idea of the health of the fish population. In the net they caught a fabulous double row linear that was a well known carp from the original Leney stocking. Sadly, that fish died of old age last year but I believe one or two of its contemporaries are still alive and I'm determined to have another go at catching one, before the last of their generation are lost through old age.

My favourite Leney fishery is also owned by the Trust, although it wasn't at the time that I used to fish there. Woodchester Park lies close to the Cotswold town of Nailsworth, where Donald Leney owned a second fish farm that he used to hold fish destined for transportation to the west of the country. Rumour has it that if any carp grew too large for these ponds, he would simply pop up to Woodchester with them

and release them into the four lakes there. This may be true, but the Surrey Trout Farm record books also hold a note of a formal order from The Nova Piscators Association in February 1962 for 100 seven-inch carp, purchased through the auspices of a local farmer, Eddie Price. This is the same Eddie Price who caught the largest mirror carp in the country at the time at Forty pounds Eight ounces from the Stile Pitch at Redmire, in September 1959. This fish grew on to become the Bishop, Chris Yates' Fifty One pound Eight ounce record.

When I first fished Woodchester, the old boathouse had a list of carp caught from the pools, their captors' names, the date and their weights, written on one of the walls in pencil. Sadly, when the

National Trust acquired the valley they restored the old boat house and white washed over this unique carp angling record, not realising its significance. Actually, to be fair, it was probably only of interest to a carp fishing anorak like me but it still seemed a shame.

I believe The Priory Angling Club has held the fishing rights at Woodchester ever since the Nova Piscators Association gave up the lakes. Under the stewardship of Brian Ponting and the other excellent members of the Priory AC committee, the lakes are in the safe hands of anglers who really care about their future. When I was a member of the club, long before the Trust acquired the property, the valley was a magical place to be. The valley was private and closed to the public and when I unlocked the gate and walked through into the ancient woodland, I felt as if I'd entered another, secret world of wild woods, spirits and adventures. It was rare to see another angler and I often had the entire valley to myself.

The Woodchester valley is known as one of the most haunted sites in Britain and after dark it was alive (or rather dead) with headless horsemen, highwaymen dangling from gibbets and moaning monks. It could be a creepy place and under the shelter of the oaks the nights were as black as pitch. I never saw a ghost but the badgers, deer and foxes were always around for company and the bats used to flicker over the water like a swarm of vampires.

The valley holds four lakes stocked with carp, which step steeply down the valley floor, separated only by their dams. Each lake is very different from the others, with its own character and atmosphere and each is lovely in its own unique way. I used to walk up one side of all four lakes and return back along the other, stalking the carp as I went. The walk might take anything between one and five hours, depending on how active the carp were and how many chances I had on my way around. I always travelled light, with just a single rod and net and with all of my bait and tackle carried in a light shoulder bag.

I often took my Golden Retriever, Cuilean, with me on these walks and he developed into a fantastic carp dog. Cuilean would trot along the path in front of me and drop to the ground quietly whenever he sensed the presence of a fish. His senses were far more acute than mine and his skill led to the capture of many a carp that I would have missed if I'd been on my own. When I hooked a fish, he would watch the fight with interest and then amble over and give the carp a gentle lick as I returned it, before trotting off to look for another one.

The three lakes at the lower end of the valley held the biggest carp, but my favourite water was always the imaginatively named "Lake 4" at the top of the chain. This lake was far more overgrown and mysterious than the others and because there were no pitches where you could really set up a bivvy, it was little fished. My favourite spot was up in the shallows, where an alder trunk swept out over a large bed of lilies. The alder was quite easy to climb and from a perch about twenty feet above the pads I could hook the carp on the surface and play them to a standstill before shinning back to the ground to use the net. Despite the acrobatics involved in fishing from the treetops, I only fell in once and I never lost a fish. After a couple of years of watching me catch carp in this way, Cuilean seemed to spend as much time scanning the treetops as he did the water because I think I'd convinced him that carp grew in trees...

Woodchester still holds some fantastic Leney's. Some of the commons I have caught at Woodchester are amongst the most superbly proportioned carp I've ever seen; deep bodied, elegant carp that are scale perfect and glow with life. I remember one common in particular that I hooked near the dam on the boathouse lake whilst float fishing. It was only a mid-double but it fought longer and harder than many fish that I've caught which were twice as big, and I had to jump into the margins to land it when it made the sanctuary of the reeds and snagged my line. Somewhere I have a photograph of the fish, looking like a moulded ingot in the evening sunshine as it lay on the damp mesh of my landing net (this was before the days of unhooking mats). That carp was probably the most flawless beauty that has graced my net.

I also remember the wonderful linear mirrors that Woodchester held. These were long, lean carp that never seemed to grow particularly big (I regarded a double as a specimen) but they more than made up for their lack of size with their stunning looks and the quality of the fight they gave when hooked. I fished Redmire this year and a friend of mine, Martin, caught a linear from there that looked just like one of the Woodchester mirrors, except that it had benefitted from Redmire's rich environment and grown far larger as a result.

I caught my biggest Leney from Woodchester during a short stalking session back in the summer of 1998. I popped in for an hour or two on my way home from work and because I didn't have much time available I made my way straight to an area on the boathouse lake where I had found signs of carp the day before. A young alder had come down in a gale and its trunk ran out into the lake, perpendicular to the bank and alongside one of the extensive lily beds. The day before I'd climbed out along the trunk and made a mental note of two spots just off the lilies where the carp had swept away the silt to reveal the golden clay beneath. Before I left I trickled just enough bait onto the nearest of these spots to hold the carp's attention until I could get back with a rod.

I tucked myself behind the roots of the fallen alder and flicked a float-fished tiger nut out before settling back to await events. I didn't see any carp but the float swayed and dipped a few times to indicate their presence. Time was marching on, however, and I knew I had to leave, so I stood slowly and peered over the grasses to see if there were any carp around. Nothing moved near the float but then a dark shadow appeared right under my feet and a big carp nosed down to feed, tight against the margin below me. Very, very slowly I drew my float back towards me and lowered the tiger nut slightly to the side of the rooting carp. I half expected the carp to bolt from such a blatant approach but instead it just paused, swivelled and sucked in the bait. I'm sure it thought a tasty morsel had just dropped into the lake from the branches of the fallen alder and I struck before it realised its mistake, and before the float had even cocked.

That carp fought like few others I've hooked and I never had time to think as the line first grated against the branches of the tree, then hissed through the open water and finally rubbed to a stop through the stems of the lilies, as the fish thrashed violently towards the sanctuary of the various snags. To end the spectacular fight I had to shin out over the pool along the trunk of the fallen alder, to free the carp from a dense clump of pads where it had finally gone to ground. All the time I could see the fish twisting and

turning in the deep, clear water of the margins and I was sure I would lose her, right up to the point when another angler stopped to watch the entertainment and helped me with the net. That lovely long, Leney mirror carp of Twenty Four pounds Eight ounces is still one of the finest carp I've ever had the pleasure of catching.

The great thing about falling in love with Leney carp is that seeking them out takes you to the most wonderful and historic carp waters. In the nineties I was lucky enough to fish Woldale a few times through a friend of mine who is a member of the syndicate. Woldale might be seen by many anglers today as a small and rather uninspiring carp lake but it was here that Maurice Ingham caught the carp that initiated his correspondence with Richard Walker, which was immortalised in the book "Drop Me a Line". Woldale was then at the very pinnacle of carp fisheries and its banks have been trodden by some of the most famous carp angling pioneers, including the members of the Carp Catchers Club, who saw Woldale as a pool with the potential to equal Redmire. It was at Woldale that Fred J Taylor landed his Sixteen pound Four ounce mirror carp that qualified him for his membership of the prestigious Carp Catchers Club in 1957 (the benchmark for membership was to land a double figure carp, which shows how much carp fishing has changed in the last fifty years).

Dick Walker, Maurice Ingham and Bernard Venables recorded a live BBC broadcast from Woldale on July 20th 1953 and as far as I'm aware that recording was the first ever live fishing programme. During the recording, Walker hooked and landed a Sixteen pound Four ounce carp, which was an absolute monster by the standards of the day and must have caused huge excitement amongst the stars of the programme. I've tried to find a copy of the recording in the BBC archives but to no avail.

Woldale held carp long before the Leney's were introduced and I believe the carp Maurice fished for there were stocked as fingerlings in 1925. The Leney stocking of Woldale was on 1st December 1956, when eighty king carp were stocked as a gift from Donald Leney, which was arranged by Dick Walker. At the time when Dick Walker, BB and Maurice Ingham fished together at Woldale, they thought the

lake might hold carp large enough to break the record, which at that time was held by Albert Buckley's Twenty Six pound Mapperley Reservoir fish. Despite their optimism, though, the biggest they landed was a Seventeen pound carp caught by Maurice Ingham.

The Woldale carp may never have attained the size of their counterparts in Redmire but they are still magnificent fish. These days, the pool holds one or two twenty pound carp but most are still double figure fish, including some of the original Leney's. The Leney carp that remain are long, lean, ancient looking carp that have an air of refinement and character you would hope for, coming from such an historic pool. They have grown to the natural limit of this small Lincolnshire water over the decades since they were introduced as fingerlings, and whilst they may be small by modern standards, they are a joy to catch.

Fishing Woldale is about so much more than the size of the carp, it is a journey back to the start of modern carp fishing. In fact one of my biggest Woldale carp is an ancient linear mirror that I caught from the shallows of the carp lake on a floater back in the early 1990's. I'm almost certain that this lovely old carp is one of a brace held by Richard Walker in an old black and white photograph I have of him, with a catch of three fish that he made at Woldale in 1952. The carp must have been about fifty years old at that time. Taking the punt out on the tench lake on a still summer evening and float fishing the reed line with an old quill, a cane rod and a centerpin is like falling backwards through a crack in time, to a more gentle age when carp were considered uncatchable and mysterious and their pursuit was the obsession of just a handful of pioneers.

The other historic Leney water I've been lucky enough to fish is the wonderful Bracken Lake in Sussex. Bracken has remained out of the spotlight in recent years despite its early prominence as a carp water. I don't want to say too much about it here out of respect for the privacy of the current syndicate who care for the lake, but I must mention it in passing or my account of my love affair with the Leney carp would be incomplete. Unlike Woldale, Bracken is still an exciting water to fish today in terms of the

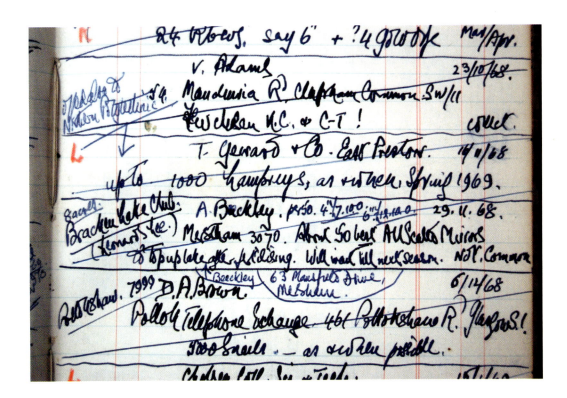

potential size of the carp that live there. It is a beautiful water that is the very epitome of the perfect carp pool, from its crumbling boathouse to the extensive lily beds and encroaching woodland. Bracken was first stocked with Leneys by Murray Rooker, who introduced one hundred six to eight inch fish on 7th April 1958. Then, a Mr A Buckley introduced a further fifty mirrors on 29th November 1968 (the records show a note that "Only the best all scaled mirrors and no commons" were required). Although it has been restocked since (partly with Leney offspring reared by my friend Vic Shilling) the water still has the same atmosphere that must have been enjoyed by the anglers fishing there at that time.

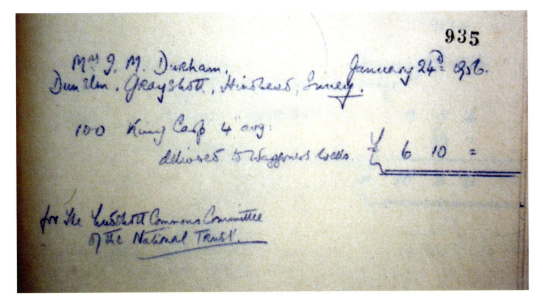

Before I leave Bracken I must tell you about one of the strangest experiences I've ever had when fishing. The east bank of Bracken was far less accessible than the rest of the lake and the bank had no open pitches suitable for the paraphernalia of the modern carp angler. As a result, it was fished far less than the other parts of the lake and I loved to tuck myself away amongst the trees there and fish the margins with the minimum of tackle. One night, I was sleeping on the bank when the Thump! Thump! Thump! of stamping feet on the path next to my head woke me. I sprang up expecting to remonstrate with another angler about their clumsiness, only to find a wallaby looking at me with a quizzical expression on its face. I wondered if I was hallucinating but the wallaby bounced off into the woods, where two of its friends joined it before they disappeared into the undergrowth. I later learned that there was a large colony of wallabies in the woods near the pool that had established themselves in the wild after escaping from a private collection. It was like fishing through the plot of an episode of Skippy.

"Tch, Tch, Tch!"

"What's that Skippy? The carp are feeding by the boathouse?"

"Tch Tch!"

"What? You reckon a floater would tempt one? Show me the way...."

The stocking records from The Surrey Trout Farm not only hold the details of some of my favourite old haunts, they also hold gems of information that are simply fascinating. It would take years to research the records properly and it is difficult to trace many of the stockings because, all the records hold are details of a name and address, a date, the number and size of each species of fish stocked and the price. Only rarely is the name of an angling club given and the name of the recipient lake is hardly ever mentioned. Every record has to be carefully researched before its secrets can be unlocked but the investigation is addictive and there is always the possibility that one of the records will lead to an unknown Redmire...

Within the pages of the books are recorded the stocking of carp into Savay, Frensham, Capesthorne, and Billing and, of course, the stocking of Redmire. The records also hold the names of the likes of Denys Watkins Pitchford (BB), Richard Walker, Fred J Taylor and Bill Keal. They are alive with the names of anglers and waters that shaped the history of carp angling in this country and flicking through the pages I can trace the progress from the experimental stockings of the 1920's through to the capture of Clarissa from Redmire and the subsequent burgeoning interest in stocking with carp.

Beyond the straightforward records held in the stock books, there are also decades of further movements to trace. For example, there is an entry for the stocking of Lymm Dam in Cheshire with Leney carp in December 1962. When I showed this record to Nick Elliott, a well known carp angler who has been involved in the northern carp fishing scene for a few years, he remembered an angler taking carp from Lymm Dam and moving them down to the Isle Pool, just north of Shrewsbury, on the back of a moped. In turn, I believe that carp from the Isle were taken down to the Shropshire mere that is now known as The Mangrove and managed by Tim Paisley, whose writing has made this water one of the most iconic of modern carp lakes. So the famous Mangrove carp may well owe their origins to the work of Donald Leney.

Other records are less obscure and more easily identified and traced. The records hold the details of BB's stocking of Wood Pool, a small water made famous by his book of the same name. According to the records, BB introduced one hundred three inch common and mirror carp into Wood Pool on 2nd November 1951, after picking them up from Kettering station (Leney used to regularly send his fish out by train, transporting them in large metal canisters). BB added a further fifty carp to augment the Wood Pool stock in November 1953. By 1957 the carp had grown into double figures and his best carp from the water was a Fourteen pound Ten ounce common carp caught in the June of that year. One of the pieces of writing that inspired and excited me most as a budding carp angler was BB's description of "The Island Battle" from Wood Pool, a tense description of a battle with "one of the very big ones" that ultimately ended with the loss of the hooked carp and a shattered rod.

As the name of Donald Leney's business suggests, the Surrey Trout Farm did not originally major in the stocking of carp and other coarse fish. The records of trout stockings from the farm are every bit as interesting as the carp records and they show that Leney had the same pioneering approach to developing trout fisheries as he did to stocking British lakes with carp.

There are several records detailing trout supplied to the Crown Agents and shipped all over the world to establish new fisheries. I have this great image of British diplomats being posted to the far flung corners of the globe with the promise that "It won't be for long, Caruthers, and you needn't despair, we'll set

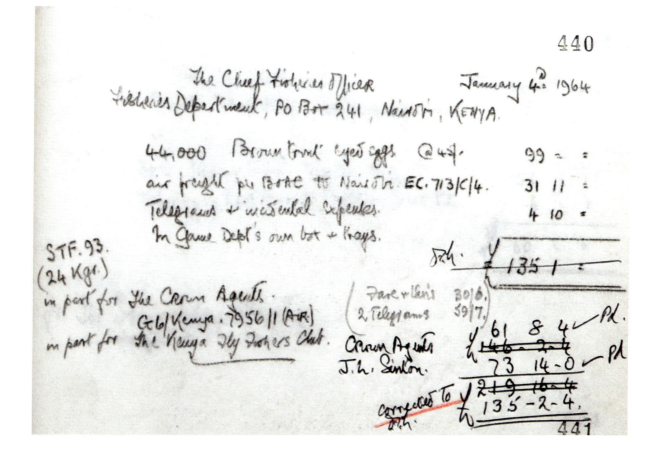

up a trout fishery out there for you to enjoy, old chap!" Leney was virtually enacting Paul Torday's wonderfully bizarre plot of "Salmon fishing in the Yemen" for real throughout the 1950's.

The trout records show the shipment of trout eggs to Nicosia in Cyprus, the British Embassy in Kathmandu in Nepal, Natal and Johannesburg in South Africa, Columbo in Ceylon, Nairobi in Kenya, India, Australia and the Falkland Islands. Not only did Leney export the trout eggs, he sometimes exported an entire ecosystem, from snails to caddis fly larvae and shrimps to accompany them. I don't know how successful these stockings were in developing self-perpetuating trout fisheries in the far flung corners of British influence, but I do believe that many of the stockings might have taken root and had a profound impact on the local ecology.

Ian Chilcott told me that he caught a brown trout on the slopes of Mount Kenya during his time in the forces and of course the Falkland's sea trout fishery is now famous, as are the large sea trout of Tierra Del Fuego. Could it be that these populations are also attributable to the vision of Donald Leney? I'd like to think so. One of my greatest angling dreams has always been to visit Patagonia in search of the enormous sea trout that live there. Since finding the Falklands records in the Leney stock books, that dream has grown even stronger, reinforced by the idea that I might be fishing for the offspring of Leney fish. That's quite a legacy!

Some of the records are closer to home and hold a more personal interest for me. I've found nine separate records detailing 2,615 carp purchased by a Mr Ray Perrett of Bridgewater, Somerset spanning a period from 1931 to 1964. I fished the Bridgewater Angling Association waters throughout my youth and I spent many days on their pools at Dunwear, Screech Owl and Combwich, as well as the drains, such as The Kings Sedgemoor, that criss-cross the Somerset Levels. Until I stumbled on that first stocking entry, I had no idea that Leney carp had such a pivotal place in this part of my angling life as well. I imagine few members of the Bridgewater AA have the faintest idea that Leney carp have graced their waters and may do so to this day.

One of the Ashmead members, Shaun Barrell, remembers Ray Perrett during committee meetings of the Bridgewater AA, sitting quietly at the back, smoking his pipe. Ray Perrett, one uncelebrated and unassuming visionary, who ensured that the carp anglers of Somerset could enjoy the bounty provided by another, the great Donald Leney.

Photo courtesy of Chris Yates, Carp courtesy of Donald Leney and Chris Ball

Chapter Twenty Five – The Leney Legacy

The Disposable Avocet

A good friend of mine called Jeremy has developed a slightly disconcerting interest in cavalry swords. He has started a collection not only of fine officers swords but also of military manuals on cavalry tactics, which go into gory detail about which stroke of the sword is most effective in killing your adversary in any given situation. The manuals have diagrams and are best avoided before meals.

Actually, the swords are magnificent. They were produced from "blued" steel (the colour of a new brass ferrule) and engraved intricately with military scenes and emblems. Gold dissolved in mercury was run into the engraving and the mercury boiled off, leaving a tracery of gold behind, so that the engraving glows against the blued blade. The military stopped the process in the late 19th century when they realised that all of their best sword smiths had died of mercury poisoning.

The whole sword collecting scenario makes my interest in fishing rods seem very safe and mundane but, despite that, I wanted to write about rods and not sabres. The cavalry sword connection is that Jeremy called me one morning to tell me that he had been searching the website of a local firm of auctioneers for details of their annual auction of militaria. He hadn't found the sale he wanted but he had found that there was a tackle auction on that day and had called to see if I was interested.

I checked the website and found that one of the listed items was a B. James Avocet. I'd been looking for a good Avocet with a whole cane butt for more than twenty years and the forty-mile drive to the auction seemed worthwhile. I couldn't get away until late morning due to work commitments and by the time I found the auction it was well underway.

The rods were stacked in racks in a side room, away from the main auction, and I soon tracked down the Avocet. It was a disappointment. The rod was tatty, had a set in the tip and the varnish was cracked and chipped. I have never been a cane "collector" as such and the aesthetic imperfections didn't trouble me because I'm not interested in amassing ranks of unblemished rods to gather dust in a rod-room display. No, I didn't like the Avocet because it had a built cane butt section, rather than the whole cane for which I had been hoping.

I believe that Avocet's constructed entirely of built cane are rarer and more valued by collectors but from my perspective they are cumbersome, ill balanced brutes of no interest. I only buy rods I want to use, although the craftsmanship of the maker and the history of the rod also influence my judgement. Anyway, the auctioneer knocked down the Avocet for nearly four hundred pounds, so that was that!

There were one or two other very nice rods at the sale. There was a very early B. James MKIV Avon with green whippings that would have made a lovely chub rod. I find Avon's floppy and I'm not usually a fan but this one had a bit of steel about it and it danced in my hand. An early, green-whipped MKIV Avon is even more of a collector's rod than the Avocet, though, and I didn't bother to bid as it spiralled away towards the sort of price that would have caused me a messy divorce ("Cancel that holiday with the kids, sweetheart, and come and look at this…").

B. James also made the other rod I really liked. It was a "Peter Tombleson", which was a design I'd never even heard of, let alone seen before. It was a bit like a lightweight Kennet, made of hollow-built cane with a fine tip section and a detachable butt. Given the name, I assume it was a match fishing design and it looked like a great roach rod but then, I'm not really a roach angler. I lost interest as the bidding for that rod sailed away downstream into the hundreds of pounds as well but I made a mental note to keep my eye out for one in the future.

Tucked away at the very end of the last rack, in the furthest corner of the dimly lit room, was a tatty old brown rod bag. I very nearly didn't look at it but something about the faded canvas drew my attention. As soon as I undid the bow and pulled back the top of the bag, I knew I had found something rather special and the hairs on the back of my neck bristled. I revealed the ends of three rod sections, with the butt and middle ferrules plugged with simple, stylish brass stoppers and a fine tip section topped with a clear agate eye.

As I withdrew the plain honey coloured cane I fell head over heels in love. The rod was like a cross between a Wizard and an Avocet; far more powerful than a Wizard but more crisp and alive than any Avocet I'd ever handled before. Every rod with a whole cane butt is unique and the action of each one is different because no two pieces of whole cane are the same. This was an early Avocet and the diameter of its whole cane butt must have been a tad thicker or have had slightly more steely fibres than any I'd held before because it had an unusually sharp and powerful action. The rod was in perfect condition, as straight as a well cast fly line and with several of the rings still encased in rod maker's varnish and glowing like flies trapped in amber. The plain black whippings and the absence of any intermediates imparted a slightly sombre yet refined simplicity, as if it had been made to fish with after a funeral. The only marking was a transfer on the butt section that read "Restored by B James and Son, London England".

Tense as a burglar, I slipped the rod back into its case and tried to bury it in the darkest corner I could find. I checked the catalogue, which listed the lot simply as a "Three piece cane float rod – estimate £50 - £70". I was pleased to see that the auctioneer who had prepared the catalogue had overlooked any sense of artistry, craftsmanship and magic completely. It was like describing Turner's 'Fighting Temorare' as "a picture of a boat, done in oil paint on canvas".

When the lot came up, the auctioneer sought an opening bid of fifty pounds but had to drop to twenty before anyone in the room showed interest. I held back and then put in a bid of twenty five pounds, just as the auctioneer was about to bring his gavel down. It was a masterclass in bidding and I played the part of doubtful and reluctant buyer to perfection. "Twenty-seven," countered the original bidder but we were the only two contestants and he shrugged his shoulders in resignation and dropped out of the race when I pushed the bid to thirty pounds. The rod was mine for the glorious sum of thirty-eight pounds and seventy-five pence, including tax. At that price I knew I could relax and enjoy using the Avocet. In fact at less than forty pounds it was virtually disposable!

As I queued to pay for the rod, the man who had started the bidding sidled up to me and whispered "I think you got a real bargain there!" We chatted for a bit and it turned out that he had recognised me from a picture in one of my articles in the fishing magazine Waterlog. He told me that he was a collector and that the rod was an early Avocet worth ten times what I had paid for it.

"Why did you stop bidding?" I asked.

"I saw you looking at the rod earlier and I could see you had fallen in love with it," he replied. "Anyway, I know you'll use it," he said, "and it's good to see it going to a good home."

For a collector to let a bargain slip through their fingers for purely philanthropic reasons is unheard of and I'll always be grateful.

I also suspect that the rod itself chose its new owner. It sounds crazy but I think the spirits of previous custodians continue to look after some special old rods and ensure they go to someone who will take them fishing regularly, rather than confine them as trophies in some stuffy collection. These rods are always "lucky" because I think the spirits also tag along when their old rods are used and guide the casts of the new angler.

That is certainly the case with my two favourite fly rods, although in their case the owner was still very much alive when I bought them. I'd called a local number after seeing an advertisement in the local paper for a "ten foot fibreglass trout rod £10, plus two others, old cane". The glass fibre rod was a horrible beast of a thing but the cane rods were a dream. One was an Allcock's Halcyon, a lovely little three weight that casts as gently as a brushstroke and the second, also by Allcock's, was a slightly more powerful Marvel. Both were in perfect condition, as fresh as the day Allcock's made them, and perfect for the sort of small stream fly fishing I love. Even when I told the old boy who was selling them what I thought they were worth, he still insisted on letting me have all three for ten pounds. We sat and talked all afternoon about the places he had fished with them and the wonderful trout they had caught together.

I stayed in touch until he died a few years later, giving him regular updates on how I was getting on with the rods and what I caught on them each season. I'd like to think he still keeps an eye on how I'm doing every time I take the rods out fishing, and I hope he is still happy with their new home.

The great thing about cane rods is that, unlike their modern carbon counterparts, each rod has a personality of its own, which owes something to the nature of the bamboo from which it is made, something to the craftsmanship of the maker and something to the use and abuse it has received in the hands of its owners.

I've always admired craftsmanship, and whenever anyone expresses astonishment at the price of a cane rod I gently point out that carbon rods are made on a factory production line and that even the most expensive blanks probably only cost the tackle manufacturer a few pounds each. Every one of my cane rods is made from cane that has been skilfully selected, split and tempered, hand planed, glued, whipped and finally varnished in a process that takes days to complete and a great deal of knowledge and experience to perfect. The comparison between the value of a cane rod and a carbon one is as meaningless as comparing a Bernard Leech pot with a vase from IKEA.

"Ah! But why would you hamper yourself with a cane rod when carbon is so much better?"

Well, the answer is that I don't believe that carbon is better than cane; it's just different. I agree that even modern cane rods aren't designed to throw a five ounce lead to the horizon in search of a gravel pit carp, but in any other fishing situation I genuinely believe that cane is the better material. For a start, cane is so much stronger than carbon and will put up with so much more abuse. How many carbon rods can you think of that will still be catching fish in fifty years time? Yet I have rods that are over a hundred years old that are still in perfect working order.

Hollow carbon can be crushed or may fracture with the least blow. Carbon is virtually useless for stalking carp from the branches of a tree or fishing a fly in a tight, bush-lined stream where each crack against a branch might spell disaster. Cane takes this sort of abuse in its stride. Granted it is heavier but even that can be an advantage. The weight of my small cane fly rods impart their own momentum to the cast and make them so much sweeter to use than their carbon counterparts, which weigh nothing and have no "feel" as a result.

At the other extreme, when it comes to fly rods I believe the most effective conservation measure that could be brought in to protect our diminishing salmon stocks would be to make the use of cane fly rods compulsory. I own a thirteen foot Hardy Wye that is a joy to play a salmon on, but I can only throw a decent line with it for an hour before every muscle in my body aches for a rest and my casting goes to pot. Making rods like this compulsory would halve the level of fishing effort overnight and do far more to help salmon stocks than any numerical catch limit.

I have my favourites in the rod rack and of these my Barder Wizard stands apart in a class of its own. I use this three piece rod for fishing for everything from the biggest barbel to the slightest dace and it

is versatile enough to be ideal for both. The butt holds astonishing power that I can call upon when a barbel dives under the weed, yet the tip is so fine that the fight of even a small dace can be enjoyed.

The Wizard is a work of art that Edward Barder made for Pete "Magpie" Rogers in 1992. Edward and Magpie are both members of the Golden Scale Club and the rod bears the Club Motto, "Casus Ubique Valet" (There is always a chance), written on the butt section in Indian ink. Edward whipped the rod in the Crabtree colours of bottle green and ruby red silk and the attention to detail is remarkable. Edward has whipped silk over the nodes on the whole cane of the butt section, so that there are blocks of green silk spaced along its otherwise plain length. To keep the pattern of these whippings, the butt ring has one leg whipped in green silk and the other whipped in a silk that has turned transparent under the varnish and is therefore invisible when the rod is held. All of the fittings and ferrules are of the finest nickel silver and the butt section is subtly flamed to give it a mottling of spots like a leopard. In making this Wizard, Edward crafted something of sheer beauty.

The only thing I don't like about the Barder Wizard is its value. I dread to think what Edward would charge me if I cracked the tip against a branch and more often than not these days I leave it in the rack and take a less valuable weapon with me when I head for the river. It's a shame in a way but the Barder still gets taken out on special occasions. In fact I've just realised that this year the rod will celebrate its twentieth birthday, so I'll have to try and catch something special with it to mark the event.

I probably have more cane carp rods than any other type and this of course reflects the balance of my fishing. My carp rods are also at home fishing for the big pike that have grabbed my attention in recent seasons, and I've used them for spinning for salmon as well. Their suitability as salmon spinning rods really isn't any surprise, as the original cane carp rods were all adapted from salmon patterns.

Of all the cane carp rods made, the most famous by far is the MKIV designed by Richard Walker. I have owned a few MKIV's over the years but these days I just have two left. One is made up on an old impregnated cane blank by Sharpes of Aberdeen and is nothing very special, although it's a good knock about rod for everyday use. The other rod is one I'm very attached to, however. It is a stepped up MKIV hand built by Gray's for Trevor Houseby, an angler better known for his sea fishing exploits but who was also an early carp fishing pioneer. I bought the rod from Trevor when Chris Yates and I met him beside the Royalty one winter. Chris bought a Fred J Taylor roach rod from him (too cumbersome for roach but a great barbel rod) and I bought the MKIV, which Trevor had brought along to use for pike fishing. The MKIV is whipped in bottle green and ivory and it is pleasing aesthetically as well as having a lovely action.

Both of my MKIVs are broken at the moment and have been sitting in a friend's house in Lincoln awaiting his attention. Actually, now I come to think of it, they've been with Barry awaiting his attention for about five years now but it doesn't do to rush these things! I imagine he is growing a new tip section for each of the rods in his back garden and I'm sure they'll turn up eventually, looking as good as new.

In the meantime, I'm using carp rods of my own design that are ideal for handling the big carp I'm pursuing at Ashmead and elsewhere. They're not designed for whacking a heavy lead to the horizon but that sort of fishing doesn't appeal to me in any case. The rods are eleven foot of tempered and impregnated cane, far more powerful through the butt section than the standard MKIV and with a lovely through action that cushions the lunges of even the biggest fish at close range beautifully. The rods have landed carp to over fifty pounds from Ashmead as well as all of my biggest pike. Barry Grantham, who made them for me, took a couple of goes before he got the tapers planed up to my specifications but he got them right in the end and I really don't think you could find a better cane carp rod.

I took the disposable Avocet out for its first testing to the Somerford Syndicate water on the Bristol Avon. The Avon is amongst my favourite barbel rivers and at Great Somerford the river is narrow, twisting and sinuous, sliding through the fields like an eel. The weirpools are the known barbel hotspots and these hold shoals of mid-sized fish. My greatest pleasure, though, is to search through the shallower, natural pools in the hope of finding one of the lone fish that are nomadic throughout the upper river and that are often the largest specimens.

The river can be waded in wellies in places and a lot of the time you are fishing for barbel you can see as they mouth your bait. It's tremendously exciting fishing.

My first cast with the Avocet was into a shallow, shaded run beneath a maybush, where a large boulder had scoured a short pool that often held a few barbel. I was delighted by the balance of the rod with my favourite centerpin attached and rejoiced at the crisp and lively feel of the cane as the freelined lump of meat bounced and rolled into the hotspot behind the rock. I watched intently and before long a golden flash on the gravel bed in the shade of the maybush signalled that at least one barbel was in residence. Even better, it looked like a big fish.

The rod quivered, rapped and then slammed over as a barbel took the bait and I had to bring the full and substantial power of the butt section into play immediately as the fish ran for the far bank and cut quickly upstream behind the boulder. I'm sure the barbel was trying its best to chafe the line on the rock but I jumped in below it and thrust the rod top under the surface to keep it clear. The rod was fully locked over now, yet the sweet cane still seemed to give just that little bit more when the barbel surged forward, allowing me to give a few inches of line from the pin, thus avoiding a snappy conclusion but keeping the pressure on the fish.

She turned then and ran fast and deep along the river bed, exploding onto the shallows and thrashing downstream towards the next bend and deeper water. I had the measure of both the rod and the fish by now, though, and she didn't make the sanctuary she sought, as I had the confidence in the Avocet's hidden strength to stop her short and bully her into the net.

The barbel was as elegant as the rod that had caught her and she had the same golden honey glow about her as the Avocet's cane. She weighed Ten pounds Four ounces and was my first double from the river.

Since then the Avocet has landed a number of really big barbel from the stretch, including my biggest ever, a fantastic, thickset fish of Twelve pounds Ten ounces. Thinking back, I can't remember losing a single barbel that I've hooked on the rod. Actually I can't even remember missing a bite! I'd love to know who owned the Avocet originally, what caused it to need restoration and what stories of battles with huge fish it could tell. I'll never know of course but it is enough that I can enjoy writing the next chapter in its life on the riverbank. When I, too, am gone to join its original owner, I'll make sure it goes to a good home, for a disposable sum, so that my spirit can accompany its new owner to the river.

Amber and Gold

I love Spring more than any other season. The arrival of spring transforms the atmosphere of Ashmead overnight, as the bleak harshness of winter, with its cold, grey skies, gives way to azure blue optimism. The weeping willows take on a mantle of fresh green and the reeds, grasses and rushes seem to grow taller with every passing day. It is now early May and soon they will be waist-high and full summer will be here.

I've really enjoyed the Ashmead spring this year. The peregrine falcon that hunts the lake throughout the winter months left with the arrival of the first warm weather but the sparrow hawks are still very active and Barney, our imaginatively named barn owl, has been hunting the pool on most evenings.

Nest building and the period when the adult songbirds are rearing their young must be a time of plenty for the sparrow hawks. I often see them perched on one of the many willows around the pool, marking the comings and goings of the songbirds as they dart in and out of the hedgerows. Any regular movement in a certain area will capture their attention. The hawk will drop suddenly from its vantage point, swooping low and fast along the hedge line like a Spitfire engaged in a dog-fight, weaving from side to side and suddenly twisting to catch its unfortunate prey in mid air, before swooping off with it clutched in its talons. Of course the sparrow hawks' own nesting period coincides with this easy availability of food to feed its young. I haven't found the sparrow hawk nest as yet but I hope to before the chicks fledge and leave it.

Last year the sparrow hawks fledged three chicks successfully, which is quite unusual. I saw them most evenings in the late summer, learning to fly in the dense hedge that lies along the southern boundary of the wetland. It was wonderful to see their flight develop and within days of taking wing the young were weaving in and out of the willow pollards with almost as much speed and agility as their parents. Then, one evening, I found the remains of one of the chicks dead beside the path. There was just a pathetic puff of mottled brown feathers and a few drops of blood but enough for me to identify the loss.

The next day I found a second fledgling dead outside the fence. This time the body was intact but the breast was stained scarlet and an open wound still seeped blood into the hawk's feathers, showing that the bird had only been killed recently. I didn't for one moment think that anyone would have shot or otherwise intentionally harmed the sparrow hawks but clearly something was very much amiss.

I saw the remaining youngster and the adults regularly over the next few days and I visited the lake more often than usual to keep an eye on them. The next weekend I spent a day working on the lake, pottering about and doing some simple maintenance, as well as taking some photographs for a magazine article. The hawks were out and I watched them flying throughout the morning. I watched as the surviving youngster launched itself from the branch of a willow and swooped along the hedgerow and then, just as it turned and beat its wings to gain height, a bolt of blue-grey stooped down from the clear blue sky at an impossible speed and hit the hawk, which seemed to disintegrate in a cloud of feathers.

It took me a moment to realise that it was the peregrine and that this dominant raptor had sealed the fate of all three of the young sparrow hawks.

The dawn chorus has grown in recent weeks, as if a full orchestra is tuning up in readiness for a symphony, with each new arrival adding its melody to the flow and beat of the music. The trees and hedges have been alive with nesting tits and finches and the ducks, coots, moorhens and geese have been squabbling over reeds and sedges with which to weave their own nests amongst the reedmace. Despite their excellent camouflage, the mallard's nests have almost all been raided by stoats and there are eggshells everywhere. One duck kept her nest intact, though, sitting on twelve eggs which hatched this week.

Throughout the year, Ashmead is a haven for wildlife but it is the spring and early summer months when the surroundings of the lake become fully alive.

Ever since I started fishing as a small boy, I've always loved the excitement of exploring overgrown and neglected pools. I dislike fisheries with neatly levelled, "regulation" pitches covered in bark, and I loathe numbered swims, although I can see the need for such "improvements" on popular day-ticket fisheries. Most of all, I hate fisheries that have banks which look like a manicured lawn. Grass mown to the same lifeless uniformity as a bowling green comes from having someone around with too much time on their hands, access to a mower and no imagination.

The members of Ashmead need to be able to get around the lake with their tackle and we do have to keep the jungle under some sort of control. It's just that I prefer to find a more environmentally friendly and conservation savvy way of managing the bankside vegetation, so that the lake looks wild and unkempt, even though it can still be fished in relative comfort. As a result, a progression of wild flowers brightens the banks of Ashmead throughout the year and a wide range of plant species flourish there, supporting an equally diverse range of insects and birds.

In an ideal world we would let the wild grazing animals maintain the lake but sadly the fencing that is essential to protect the Ashmead carp from otters also excludes the local deer and other animals. We do find the odd roe that has leapt the six foot mesh wandering through the fishery but we knew we had to invest in buying our own livestock to manage the banks. The plan is to move them between the fishery and the field next to our cottage as needed.

Through my work with the National Trust I have a good understanding of how grazing can be used to enhance the wildlife value of grassland and produce a sward rich with the sort of species we want to encourage around the lake. Using livestock in this way is far more environmentally friendly than burning fuel in a mower, and there is the added benefit of producing some high quality lamb and beef.

The only question was what sort of animals to invest in? We needed stock that can happily spend the entire year outside, require minimum handling and that can cope with everything from soft grasses through to the toughest of rushes and thistles.

We now have five ewes that are ideal for grazing the softer grasses and will keep the freezer stocked with lamb. I was busy lambing them last spring and it was quite a strain on the nerves because it must be more than twenty years since I had last worked a lambing season. The only disaster was when we lost one of a pair of twins to a big old dog fox that lives somewhere along the disused railway that runs along the boundary of our field.

We also wanted some cattle to deal with the heavy duty grazing but we were struggling to think of a breed that was hardy enough to meet our needs, and distinctive enough to appeal. The answer came to us on our annual trip to northwest Scotland last year. We had climbed Ben Hope with the kids (the most northerly of Scotland's 3,000 foot Munro's) and were weaving our way back to our croft along a winding, single-track road when the most majestic beast you could imagine confronted us. With my wife Shona being a fiercely patriotic Scottish lass, something just clicked and we knew we had found the answer, or rather it had found us.

Careful research led to the purchase of a couple of two year old Highland heifers called Annie and Georgina, so we now have our own fold of Highland cattle! Amongst many things I've learned about the breed in the last few months is that the collective noun for Highland cattle is a "fold" rather than a "herd" and that only Highland's have this distinction. Despite their impressive horns, they are the most gentle, easy-going and chilled out cattle I've ever handled (not that I've handled many) and they will happily let the children feed and brush them. They are hardy and can live on the toughest vegetation and thrive outside through the harshest of winters. Not only are they beautiful but their bull calves will produce fine quality beef and any heifer calves will sell easily at a premium price and help to support the fishery finances.

I told some of the anglers that we were getting these beasts, just to gauge their reaction to the prospect of having a couple of tons of beef armed with huge horns wandering around the lake. Most were intrigued rather than worried, but Stuart simply refused to believe I was serious and he still thinks the whole thing is just a joke. I think the fact that I told him the girls were due to arrive on 1st April might have something to do with his scepticism... I'm not going to mention the girls to Stuart again; I just hope I'm there to hear the scream when their hot breath wakes him up one morning and he finds Georgie's head blocking his view of the lake!

Another, rather more short-term addition to the livestock joined us last year in the form of two Saddleback piglets. They were only with us for six months to be fattened for slaughter and I was determined that we wouldn't give them names, to remove any chance of upsetting the children. As it was, the kids had named the smallest of the pair Wilbur within minutes of their arrival. Also within minutes, the other weaner had found a gap in the fencing I'd erected painstakingly around the paddock and she was off across the field with my friend Neil and me in hot pursuit. Neil rugby tackled her eventually and we got her back into the newly reinforced paddock, only for her to find another gap almost immediately. This game went on all day and by the end of an exhausting, mud splattered afternoon Houdini had earned herself a name as well. I'm reminded of the old adage "Never pick a fight with a pig; everyone gets dirty but the pig likes it".

Of course, once we had given them names, we all became very much attached to these two characters and it was a big wrench when the time came to take them to the abattoir. They had enjoyed a good life with us (even though it was a short one) but it was still quite difficult when November arrived and I loaded them up with our three anonymous lambs for their final journey. I watched the slaughter procedure to see that it was humane (it was) and we had the carcasses delivered to our local butcher. Ian Gould and his

family have been butchers in Martock for decades and the quality of their meat should ensure that they have a thriving business for many more years to come. The family have also been volunteer firemen for generations and they are very much part of the community fabric of the village. Ian spent an afternoon showing Shona and me how to butcher the lamb and pork and prepare the various cuts for the kitchen. I'm proud to say that the meat was outstanding and Ian raved about one lamb carcass, saying that it was the best he had seen in over thirty years in the trade. I took this as a sign that our very extensive grazing regime had paid off, although he probably says the same to every smallholder that uses his services!

The livestock management is good fun but I never forget that the animals are a practical management tool and are there for a purpose. It's not just about producing wholesome meat for the table and teaching the children about where their food comes from either. The well managed grazing on the banks of Ashmead is really starting to pay off and show its future potential for wildlife. The number and diversity of insects around the lake are increasing every year, along with the wildflowers that support them. These insects in turn provide food for the large number of small mammals and birds that use the Ashmead wetland, and the banks of the fishery are teaming with life.

I relish every wildlife encounter but one stands out as the most beautiful sight I think I have ever enjoyed. The early summer sun was dipping towards the horizon, settling amongst the silhouettes of the willows on Ashmead's west bank as if it was snuggling under a duvet to sleep. The light it cast had that lovely golden quality that lasts for just a few minutes before it takes on the orange and reds of a full sunset.

I was walking back along the north bank of Goat Willow Pool after an afternoon spent clearing some swims of weed, when suddenly the most incredible sight confronted me. The rushes beside the small stock pond started to glow with dozens of spots of vivid amber, where the sunlight caught on something clinging to the thin stems. A slight breeze ruffled through the rushes, making them sway, so that the amber highlights danced before me. Other spots of amber hovered in the air and sped off as I approached, like the most dazzling display of fireworks. It was as if someone had set a ladle of liquid honey on fire and cast it over the grasses and the effect was quite beautiful.

I took my camera and crept forward until I could see that the amber jewels were in fact dozens of dragonflies that were clinging to the grasses or darting amongst them. You must have seen primeval insects trapped in amber, formed when the sap of some ancient tree caught and then fossilised them? Well, these dragonflies looked as if someone had carved them from the amber itself and then set them free. The sunlight didn't just hit their translucent bodies; the thorax of each insect absorbed and then reflected the rays, so that it glowed as if lit with an inner fire. The effect was quite the most amazing thing I'd seen in years.

I only had my 400mm lens with me and depth of field was a bit tricky to handle but I got some passable shots from the dozens that I took, before racing home to identify the source of such beauty.

I soon found the dragonfly on the British Dragonflies website, which described it dismissively as "Libellula quadrimaculata - Four-spotted Chaser. A plain brown dragonfly common throughout the British Isles." That was it! No poetry, no excitement, no soul. I had witnessed the most staggeringly beautiful natural display and the website dedicated to its cause might as well have said "Brown and common as muck. Not even worth a second glance. Don't waste your time....!" And we wonder why our children are losing interest in natural history!

I've been inspired by the Four-spotted Chasers to spend some time trying to photograph the Ashmead dragonflies this year. I've managed some passable shots of various species at rest on the reeds but the challenge I've set myself is to get some good photographs of the dragonflies in flight. This is far from easy, as

their swift and erratic flight patterns make tracking and focusing difficult, particularly with my 400mm lens which pulls focus quite slowly and has a narrow depth of field at the full zoom necessary to get a close-up of the insects. I eventually worked out a technique that involved focusing on a reed a set distance away and then holding that focus. By tracking the dragonflies flight in the same way that a wildfowler would track a duck with a shotgun, I could then shoot off a rapid succession of shots on a high speed ISO setting, as the dragonflies flight coincided with that pre-set focal distance. It's as tricky as shooting snipe in poor light and a high wind.

I'm quietly pleased with some of the results and in one or two photographs the flight is frozen in quite sharp focus. Whilst I like the clear shots, I prefer some of the more blurred images, which convey the feeling of movement and have an impressionist quality that I like very much. I'm sure I'll spend a few more days this summer trying to capture the Ashmead dragonflies in flight and I might just get the perfect photograph of an airborne chaser before the autumn ends their flight.

The other tricky shot I've been trying to get all spring is a good photograph of a Willow Warbler. These warblers look fairly non-descript when seen as a brown blur amongst the Goat Willow thickets but in close-up they are attractive, dainty birds. Just like the dragonflies, they are hard to capture with a camera, though, or I found them so until I realised that after a heavy rain shower they would happily sit still for a portrait on the shelter of a low lying willow branch, rather than flee and get their feathers wet. While I was taking the photos of this common bird it struck me just how much beauty we anglers have around us that we take completely for granted. Even the commonest wildlife, such as the mallards and herons with which we share our waters are stunning and fascinating to observe, yet how many people have really had the chance to see them at close quarters? And how many of us would have seen them if we weren't fishermen?

Those moments with the Amber Chasers (as I now prefer to call them), the other dragonflies, Willow Warblers, sparrow hawks, owls and the other wildlife that I encounter when fishing, give a depth of pleasure that makes all of the hard work involved in managing Ashmead worthwhile.

Of course, it's not only at Ashmead that my fishing lets me experience nature at close quarters.

I've fished Woldale in Lincolnshire many times, a pool that is famous in the annals of carp angling because it is one of the places where Walker and Ingham first proved that carp were fallible and could be caught by design. The fishing is unspectacular these days but I loved my annual pilgrimage there, partly because of the history of the water but mainly because of the surroundings and the nocturnal company. One of my favourite pieces of writing from the "Walker era" describes a carp angler at the pool waking up to the sound of the ram pump and finding a badger snuffling for bait in his rucksack. Whilst the carp have declined and the old ram pump silted up, the badger setts are thriving and I've spent far more of my snatched hours there watching these wonderful animals than fishing.

The first time I saw the badgers, I was at the lake with Bill Reeves. I went for a wander up to the sett at dusk and settled behind a tree, up-wind of an active entrance. Within half an hour, a striped muzzle appeared and a young badger emerged. It truffled about at the sett mouth for a while, busy about the business of the evening and unaware that I was watching, before romping off into the bracken.

I went to get Bill, who was fishing at the head of the pool. It was difficult to drag him away from his swim because a decent common was feeding on his bait but eventually I persuaded him to come with me. We saw the first badger almost immediately, or rather we smelled it. Badger musk is very distinctive and it marks the runways used by the fern bears on their nightly excursions as clearly as a signpost. In this instance, the smell was caused by a young cub, rooting amongst the bracken stems at the edge of the path. We watched for a while but couldn't get a clear view because of the dense undergrowth, so we went on towards the main sett.

The sett was in a classic position in a steep, oak clad bank of sandy soil. At the top of the bank was a heath like area of open bracken, criss-crossed with grassy paths. Bill and I were walking along one such path in the gloom when we picked up that musk again, drifting down to us on the wind. We stopped and before long the musk was followed by a large boar badger, which came bumbling along the path with a rolling gait. Badgers have an acute sense of smell, but their eyesight is appalling. This one trotted right up to us before he realised we were there and when he finally spotted us he was no more than a rod length away. He stood stock still, tilting his striped head from side to side in puzzlement. "Funny, I'm sure those weren't there when I set off this evening." I think he must have caught a whiff of Bill's aftershave just then, because he suddenly spun in a whirl of dust and fur and vanished into a nearby hole. He poked his head out once more, just to see if he had imagined us, and was gone.

"That," said Bill, "was amazing." He was shaking with excitement and although he has never mentioned the common carp again, we now talk about badgers every time we meet.

As an angler, of course, it is the fish themselves that entrance me most. Whether it's a salmon leaping a fall, a shadow of chub lying beneath the trailing willow fronds, a quicksilver of dace darting across the gravel or a regal majesty of carp basking amongst the weedbeds, the presence of any fish sends a tingle down my spine.

Often the fish themselves are invisible but the slightest hint of their presence can be just as alluring because of the mystery and expectation generated by the smallest of signs. That small ripple on the water might have been made by a shoal of tiny rudd, but it might have been caused by the largest carp in the lake. That dimpled rise might be a mere fingerling or it could reveal a huge brown trout, smutting on the swarms of tiny midge. That splash! Well that splash must have been caused by the salmon of your dreams, rather than an over-excited grilse... A fertile imagination can conjure dreams from the most mundane piece of water and the glory of going fishing is that, just once in a while, you can make those dreams real and even get to hold them.

There are two natural events in the angling calendar that I love to see and they both revolve around sex.

The first is the incredible sight of a run of salmon leaping a substantial fall on their migration upstream to the spawning redds. The three best falls I know are at Stainforth on the Ribble, the Falls of Feugh on Deeside and the spectacular Falls of Rogie on the Blackwater to the west of Inverness.

I worked on a project at Stainforth Fosse when I was with the National Rivers Authority and charged with fisheries research in the Ribble catchment. The fall there consists of three steps over which the Ribble tumbles and foams, presenting a formidable barrier to the migrating salmon and sea trout. Water cascading over the upper step has carved out a small but deep pot in the limestone, from which the river then plunges over a second, larger fall into another small pool. The river then drops vertically by about five feet into the lower pool, which is large, deep and quite menacing. A shear limestone cliff cradles the dark circle of water below this lowest fall, giving the pool an atmosphere of bottomless despair. In a million years there will be a dry pothole here and the Ribble will have carved itself into a subterranean memory.

It is in this lower pool that the fish collect to test the flow and gather their strength for the ascent. The second fall used to be too ferocious for

many salmon to pass and the river above the falls was almost devoid of redds as a result. By the simple expedient of bolting and concreting some large boulders to the river bed when the river was low in the summer, we created a series of shorter steps that helped the salmon conquer this second fall with ease. This was a simple but effective method of extending the spawning range of the fish and boosting the capacity of the river to produce young salmon.

We spent some time monitoring the salmon jumping the falls, to gauge how easily they could now surmount the obstacle. One afternoon I was sitting by the middle pool counting fish when a large grilse mistimed its leap and jumped clean out of the river to land neatly in my lap. It slapped me twice around the face with its tail before dropping back into the flow. So much for being appreciated by nature when you try to help out!

The second orgy I love to watch is the annual spawning of the Ashmead carp. The process starts with the fish pairing up and swimming rapidly through the shallows in a graceful ballet that suddenly turns into a thrashing break dance when the females release their eggs and the males compete to fertilise them. It is astonishing to see the larger females erupting through the surface of the shallows, as they are pushed upwards by the combined strength of four or five smaller males. This is the one time when the carp are oblivious to my presence and I can wade out amongst them without disturbing them or diverting them from the compulsion to spawn. I've been knocked off my feet more than once by a surge of sex-crazed fish.

By the end of spawning, impossible numbers of small white eggs cover the weedbeds, all stuck to the leaves of the Elodia and Hornwort with mucus. When you see the mass of carp eggs and contrast this with the relatively small number of young that survive, it is impossible to comprehend the scale of the carnage that takes place each year. Shoals of perch, eels, beetles, various aquatic larvae and even the adult carp themselves are already feasting on a hundred thousand eggs or more before the spawning has even finished. It is a symphony of procreation and death on a scale as dramatic as anything in nature

If I wasn't an angler I would never have experienced these wildlife wonders. For me, it's those moments when I experience the force and beauty of nature, and still feel that I'm part of the natural world, that make life worthwhile.

Redmire

I always had a strong desire to visit Redmire, to see where so many of the greatest tales from carp angling folklore had been set and so much of carp angling's history forged. At the same time though, I'd always feared that a visit to the pool would be a profound disappointment, so clear were the images I had of how Redmire must have been during its heyday; from the time of Walker and the Carp Catcher's Club through to Chris Yates' capture of the Bishop, his record carp. For many years, the photographs taken by Chris of Redmire and the Bishop fired my dreams and my copy of the old Angling magazine, which first broke the news of the new record to the angling world, was a much thumbed treasure. In fact I still have my copy of that magazine twenty years later and I still get a thrill whenever I read it.

Recently, the spate of deaths of some of our best known carp made me think again about fishing Redmire. The death of the wonderful double row linear from Frensham, one of a diminishing number of large, original Leney's that remain in this country, made me realise that the Redmire era was waning and that if I was ever going to fish the pool and experience some of the old magic for myself, I would have to do it soon.

Then Rob Major had a quiet word with me at the Ashmead opening night social, to say that he had booked Redmire for a week at the end of September. "Martin and Ryan are going to join me and I wondered if you fancied coming along?" he asked. Here was a chance to fish Redmire at the prime time of the year, with three anglers who shared the same respect as I did for Redmire's heritage.

I spent the summer like an excited schoolboy, reading all of the books I had about Redmire from the Len Arbery and Kevin Clifford history of the water, to Chris Yates' Four Seasons (his evocative diary of his time on the syndicate). I even sorted through my carp tackle, cleaned my rods and put some new line on my old Mitchell reels in readiness for our visit.

The last thing I did, as our week drew near, was to telephone Chris to hear firsthand about what a visit to Redmire in September might have in store for us. I could hear the excitement in Chris' voice as he described the way the carp would visit the shallows during the sunny autumn afternoons, dropping back into the deeper water in the evening chill. He recounted the amazing tale of one of his most memorable autumn captures, a long common carp of Twenty Four and a half pounds that looked like a wildie and

fought for nearly two hours before Rod finally scooped it into the landing net. It was during this session that Rod saw the King (the great uncaught common carp that only a handful of the syndicate members ever saw) and Chris remembered thinking that it was the King that he was playing throughout the epic battle.

For the first time in the thirty years we have been fiends, Chris spoke about the King itself and how he saw it just once, passing through the margins beneath the willows of the '35' pitch in July 1979. His voice was electric as he relived the moment. "It was just so impossibly big, it was enormous" he said. "Was it bigger than the Bishop?" I asked. "Oh yes," he replied, "much bigger; so much bigger that it looked unreal."

Chris also spoke to me for the first time about the capture of the Bishop. I'd never really asked him about the record because I'd read his account so often. Now that I was going to fish Redmire myself though, I wanted to hear the tale afresh. Chris described his fifth cast into the shallows, the way a gust of wind just blew the corn hookbait beyond the leaves of the old pollarded willow and how the great carp drifted forward and took the bait on the drop. I've fished for wildies with the Walker-built MKIV Avon with which Chris landed The Bishop and to this day I've never quite understood how he landed such an enormous carp on such an underpowered rod. If it hadn't been for Barry Mills climbing into the branches of an overhanging willow I'm sure he would have lost the fish and I could still hear the relief in Chris' voice as he relived the moment when Barry calmly chased the record out from the snag.

These days, fifty pound carp are not uncommon but in 1980 Chris' Fifty One and a half pound record was simply staggering, in the same way that Walker's '44' had been in 1952. Whilst there are so many huge carp around these days, Redmire is still one of the most astonishing carp lakes in the country. Three different record carp have been caught from its banks and for such a small lake to hold this incredible track record only emphasises the productivity of Redmire and the astonishing quality of the original Leney carp.

I wrote in my diary, *"I called Chris today to tell him I'm going to fish Redmire. Even though Camilla had just arrived home from London and he hadn't seen her for ages, he still wanted to talk at length about my visit. Any lingering doubts I have about going to Redmire have now been dispelled by the tangible excitement in his voice."*

Chris even had some specific advice on where and how I should fish. "You must keep your eye on the right hand corner of the dam, where it shelves up. Right under the dam wall is the spot," he said, "whenever the wind pushes into that end of the pool at this time of year, the carp follow it. If the wind isn't pushing towards the dam, you should concentrate on Bramble Island or the old pollards opposite, where the shallows start."

Just before he went, Chris insisted I should ring him from the lake at the end of the week to let him know how we had fared and whether the old Redmire magic still remained. "Catch one of the old commons!" He said, "I know you will…"

On Sunday 26th September, I picked Martin up from home and we set off to drive to Redmire, meeting Rob and Ryan for a pub lunch on the way. Redmire lies in a small fold of the Herefordshire countryside, just far enough from the main road to mean that the traffic noise doesn't carry to the pool. I've driven that main road many times but never with so much anticipation. Eventually, I arrived at the entrance of Bernithan Court, following the driveway past the old tithe barn and the well proportioned Georgian house, which stands on a rise amongst well grazed pasture. I liked the approach to the pool, past the farm cottages and down to the wooden five bar gate which leads to the pool itself. Until you pass through the gate and catch the first glimpse of the water through the trees, you would never know the lake was there and it isn't until you leave the car and walk past the old overspill and onto the dam that the full extent of Redmire reveals itself.

When you arrive at Redmire these days, you park in the Oaks swim next to the lake. Now, as I said earlier, I had prepared myself to be disappointed by my visit because I couldn't believe that the Redmire of today could be anything more than a shadow of its past glories. Even so, I really thought I had made a big mistake in coming to fish when I climbed out of the car to be confronted by the anglers scrap that littered the car park area. There was an old barbeque rusting away under a bin bag next to a couple of cut down plastic pub chairs and the banks of the adjacent swims were boarded and wood chipped; my first impression was that the place looked more like a municipal park lake than the cradle of modern carp angling.

I remember Mohammed Ali being interviewed by Michael Parkinson late on in his career, in the days when the punches had taken their toll, and how desperately sad it was to see the shadow of the great sportsman that remained. I had feared I would experience the same painful sense of decline on seeing Redmire and it seemed that my fears had been realised.

Then we saw the carp. There were three of them milling about in the gin clear water near the overspill (just where Chris had predicted they would be!), circling slowly before dipping down to feed. The sighting led us from the Oaks pitch onto the dam and in just those few short steps, the atmosphere changed completely and my fears were swept away. The dam was green with fresh grass and the view along it seemed unchanged since Dick Walker, Pat Russell and my friend Maurice Ingham had their photograph taken leaning on the dam rail in 1952.

The four of us gathered on the middle of the dam, just as they must have done, and gazed up the lake. The view was timeless and quite beautiful. Like so many anglers before me must have been, I was immediately taken aback by the small size of Redmire and the close intimacy of the lake. The first signs of autumn had painted the oak trees and their reflections in the glass calm surface created the feeling of a pointillist painting with splashes and dots of colour, each meaningless in their own right, combining to create the image of the perfect carp pool.

Then a very big fish appeared in the crystal clear water before us and stole the moment. The carp swam nonchalantly towards us, maybe four feet below the surface and ten yards out. "That's a good fish," said Ryan but we didn't realise how big until it turned tail (I'm certain it saw us) and drifted back up the pool, showing the width across its shoulders. "It must be over thirty," said Martin. "A common," added Rob. "That would do nicely!"

The fish transformed the moment. Any thought of the care worn appearance that greeted us in the Oaks faded away with the shadow of that common. Suddenly, I could relate to the first Redmire anglers and how they must have felt to see such carp gliding through the lake's clear waters. For a brief moment I felt some small frisson of the excitement they must have shared, seeing such unimaginable monsters for the first time.

We set off along the east bank, pausing in each swim, but I quickly left the others and walked on ahead, wanting my first impressions to be personal ones. At Bramble Island I paused and climbed the alder to watch a group of about ten carp that were feeding on the back of a bed of weed. They sent up great plumes of red mud as they rooted on the lakebed and before long I could no longer pick out the individual carp in water turned to the colour and consistency of tomato soup.

The others joined me and we carried on to the shallows at the head of the pool. I liked it here; inevitably there were signs of anglers but this area felt wilder and less trammelled than the pitches nearer the dam. The tangle of fallen willows and the thick silt seemed to have deterred some of the angling pressure.

We drew lots for our swims, although I don't know why we bothered because we all fancied slightly different areas. Robbie and Ryan both fancied the West bank, setting up in the Stile and Kefford's, whilst Martin and I both liked the idea of watching the sunset and opted for the East bank. Martin set up in the Stumps and I settled in the Open Swim.

I liked the fact that the Open Swim was a bit too tight for a bivvy and felt rather neglected as a result. I liked the look of the thick weed in front of the swim even more and I had a feeling that the carp might take shelter here once they realised we were fishing for them. Most of all, I liked the look of a tight, clear patch in the weed to the right of the swim and a quick cast with a light lead showed that the bottom here was smooth, clean silt with just a light covering of silkweed.

These days Redmire is under almost constant angling pressure and every week must see another group of anglers walking the banks, introducing bait into the popular pitches and casting out three or four rods for the duration of their stay. I planned to keep my lines out of the water for long periods each day and to just fish the swim from dusk until dawn. I hoped that leaving the carp undisturbed during the day would encourage them to settle in the area and gain enough confidence to feed. I baited the clearing in the weed lightly and climbed an alder to watch the lake.

A large pod of carp was basking in the centre of the pool, between my pitch and Ryan's on the opposite bank. After an hour, a good mirror peeled away from this group and entered the weed beneath me. It was fascinating to see the way the carp entered the swim, first circling repeatedly before settling deeper into the water as the concentric circles grew tighter. It looked as if she was being drawn down slowly into an enormous plug hole and whilst it's easy to make anthropomorphic assumptions when you see this sort of behaviour, I'm convinced the carp was checking for lines.

I started fishing on the Sunday evening. I adopted my usual approach for fishing in weed, which consists of using small PVA bags of bait and short hooklengths, to ensure a good presentation when casting into small gaps in the weedbed. I had a couple of line bites during the night but no takes despite constant fish activity in the area, with fish head and shouldering throughout the night. A band of rain swept through and when it passed at dawn, carp started to bubble furiously all over the lake and every ten minutes or so a fish crashed out, setting the reflections dancing.

I had to go to work on the Monday but the day flew by and I was soon back in the alder, looking for signs. The best chance of a carp during my absence had fallen to Ryan, who had enjoyed a nerve-tingling encounter with a big mirror that nearly took his floater.

The second night was very warm and clear, with a brilliant starscape above us. Owls were active all around the pool but the carp were dormant and I didn't hear a fish all night. Martin and I spent a long time chatting over a bottle of wine about the modern carp scene and the value of places such as Ashmead as a counterpoint to the commercialism and competitiveness of it all. "You either get it, or you don't," said Martin. We discussed Redmire itself of course, and whether the open access to the pool was part of that commercial trend. I felt Redmire had somehow retained its soul despite the angling pressure.

I wrote in my diary the following morning, *"There is a deeper magic here that survives behind the cracked facade and I'm able to sense it now. It has taken time for the pool to speak to me but I can hear its small, clear voice, talking softly, like a mewling buzzard through the mist. I wish I could be here alone, so that I could hear it more clearly still. If I could tune in to its gentle whisper for a while, without interruption from human voices and disturbance, I might really start to get to know Redmire. I might even catch a carp."*

One of the Redmire mysteries that intrigued me was the haunted Evening Pitch and the apparitions and ghostly happenings experienced by anglers fishing that part of the pool. Martin was closest to the haunted spot and he did experience "something strange" during our stay. On two, still nights he saw a strange ball of light float slowly through his swim at about waist height before disappearing. Martin is not one for mysticism and magic but he was clearly bemused by the experience. We decided it was a Will-o'-the-Wisp of marsh gas, which had caused the phenomena but perhaps it was something more spectral...

By mid-morning on Tuesday the September sunshine had started to warm the shallows and the carp drifted up the pool like shadows through the water. I watched Ryan stalking from Bramble Island, fascinated at the way that a large group of carp basked and sunned themselves just out of range, aware of his presence yet completely at ease. I took a stalking rod and some maggots right up to the head of the shallows, near to where Chris had hooked The Bishop over thirty years ago. I crawled out onto a willow branch, which hung out over the shallow water and waited. Before long a group of five carp

drifted into view, keeping to the centre of the pool and passing some ten feet beyond my precarious perch. They ignored my float-fished offering completely and then spooked and surged back towards the dam when I quietly dropped in a handful of free grubs to try and attract them down to feed. Another lesson learned; the carp were used to anglers being around and they were skittish and nervous when looking for a meal.

I learned another valuable lesson later in the day, watching some fish grazing over the silt near the inlet stream. The carp moved incredibly slowly, sucking and blowing all the time. When one came across my corn, it hovered to a stop almost a foot above the lakebed, its mouth working as it hoovered up the free grains and left my hookbait behind, tethered to the swanshot leger by the short hooklink. I wondered if this explained the lack of chances on Monday night, despite the carp activity.

Before I cast on Tuesday evening I rearranged my terminal tackle to reflect my observations. I lengthened the hooklinks by over a foot and weighted them with smears of tungsten putty. I also spaced blobs of putty up the line behind the lead, to pin the mainline down into the weed and onto the lakebed.

The night was quiet and Wednesday dawned bright and clear. The sun caught the trees opposite, enhancing the green, red and gold of their reflections. Out of the blue, I had a fast run on the rod cast into the weed. Kettle flying, I grabbed the rod and lifted into the carp, only to have the tip dragged back down, as the fish first surged away from me and then exploded through the surface, crashing over and shedding the hook. The whole fight lasted for about ten seconds but in that brief, explosive encounter I had time to see the mirror scaling of a carp that looked to be well over Twenty pounds, before a painful stillness returned to the scene. I threw the rod down and stood staring at the spot where the subsiding ripples marked my failure. I glanced over to see Martin watching me and he had the grace to turn away without a word; no words would have been adequate.

Why had I held so hard, when everything I'd read about the Redmire carp stressed how soft their mouths are? Why hadn't I slackened off and dropped the rod tip when the carp hit the surface, when I'd have done so instinctively if it had been a leaping trout or salmon? Why? Why? Why?... Then a buzzard appeared above the alders and wheeled past in the still dawn light. It was truly beautiful and suddenly the lost carp no longer mattered; I was tuning into the water and I knew I would have another chance.

"Contrasts: Martin, perched as still as a hawk in the alders above the shallows, silent and inconspicuous; Rob and Ryan, standing talking quietly as they shared a cup of tea in Ingham's, their voices the only discordant note in the morning symphony of birds and water. Lessons learned: even the quietest conversation carries here and even the slightest movement stands out."

The carp came back to bask again in the weed between Kefford's and the islands. Ryan had moved to fish the Willow Pitch for the night and it was interesting to see how close to Kefford's the carp were now cruising in his absence. I had felt sorry for the carp, thinking they must live in a state of permanent paranoia and tension. Now I realised that they treated the presence of anglers as no more than just another facet of their daily lives. They had drifted away from the occupied swim, yet they soon returned when Ryan had gone and now seemed perfectly relaxed as they cruised through the margins.

After losing the carp I felt the need to move because of the disturbance. I liked the look of Quinlan's and moved up there, hiding my brolly behind the cracked trunk of a pollarded willow. I had settled into a pattern of angling and I baited my swim lightly before leaving it, to go for a walk through the fields and to spend some time stalking in the shallows. I had a good chance on a floater, when a common came up and slurped in the free pellets on either side of my hookbait. Even though I had cast the line over a willow twig, the fish didn't like the way the hookbait behaved and it flared its fins and surged away without taking the bait into its mouth. So close...

In the evening, I lowered a bait under the willow branches and then flicked a second out towards the slightly deeper water, off the end of some weed. All was quiet until dawn when a carp rolled right over this second rod before diving back to the lakebed and sending up a stream of bubbles. "Any moment now…" I thought. Then Martin appeared behind me in the half-light. "Got one!" he said before disappearing back along the path. I reeled in and went to see the lovely mirror carp that had picked up his bait. He had been watching the way the carp moved through his swim and had dropped his bait over the top of the weed on a very light rig, so that it rested well up off the lakebed and the take had come at first light. He had been lucky to land the carp because he had hooked it lightly just inside the lip and the hook dropped out with just a light touch of finger pressure. The Twenty Two pound linear gleamed in the early morning light and Martin smiled as I tried to capture the excitement of the moment with my camera.

I thought my chance had gone for the morning but just as I got back to my pitch behind the willow a carp rolled off the weed in the same spot as before. I climbed up into the branches and watched as a dark common rose up through the disturbed silt and cruised off. I climbed back down and cast quickly using a light, flat lead to minimise the disturbance. The common appeared again, just off the willow, and swam purposefully back to the baited area. Thick red clouds of mud billowed up as she fed for a while before reappearing and swimming off along the same route as before.

The tension became almost unbearable until a single beep from the buzzer was followed by the drawn out note of a take. I was on the rod in seconds but my Mitchell was churning and I hardly dared lift into the carp as it ran steadily and powerfully for the far bank. I played the carp incredibly gently, with

thoughts of my previous loss and of Martin's frail hook hold running through my mind. I let the fish move out beyond the weed before slowing its run, using gentle side-strain to turn it away from a fallen branch that was floating amongst the weed. The carp turned but then accelerated and cut back in towards Quinlan's willow. I couldn't reel fast enough to keep in touch and the bend went out of the rod as the carp headed for the sanctuary of the sunken branches. I ran left, splashing through the margins

and reeling frantically until I was back in touch, and managed to heave the rod over just in time to steer the fish away from the reaching willow.

The carp paused and then swam straight out again towards the far bank, a slow wave and the weed flags on the line tracing its route towards Bramble Island. I let it go on a light line, praying the hook hold was still good after bullying the carp away from the tree. The fish was now close to the floating branch again and I had to bend into it once more as it cut left towards this snag. I stopped it short of its goal and suddenly it seemed to give up, wallowing and rolling as I eased it back towards the bank and into the net. "Yes!"

I just stood in the margins, laughing like a schoolboy at the glorious long dark carp that was cradled in the mesh.

"Well done…" It was Martin and I realised he had been standing behind me for much of the fight. "Nice one Skeff!" Rob shouted from the far bank, where he too had been watching events unfold. Anyone would have thought I'd never caught a carp before; I was shaking with adrenaline, unable to think clearly about scales and slings and mats and rods and … It was all too complicated! Martin was on hand though and we soon had the carp unhooked, weighed (Twenty Two pound Fourteen ounces) and ready for a portrait.

I held the carp for a long time as I slipped her back, trying to remember every little detail, but eventually she had waited long enough and kicked back into the deeper water with a strong thrust of her tail. The others left me, standing in the margins, still smiling as I drank in the beauty of the pool. Redmire still has the magic of dreams swimming beneath her calm surface.

The morning's excitement wasn't over just yet though and Martin landed a fresh looking common of just over Sixteen pounds about an hour later, to complete his brace.

That evening we all gathered on the dam to enjoy our last sunset on the lake and to reflect on the week we had enjoyed. I retrieved a bottle of Champagne from the cooling water of the overspill and popped the cork on the centre of the dam, so we could toast Redmire. Autumn had arrived during our stay and the trees that had been green when we arrived were now cloaked in gold leaf. The whole scene glowed in the evening sunshine and Redmire itself lay like a rich jewel, mounted within the golden setting.

It was almost sixty years to the day since Redmire gave up the first of her record carp to Bob Richards on 3rd October 1951. The quality of the lake and its carp today is testament to the quality of the anglers who have fished there and to the current management of Les Bamford. I thought back to my initial disappointment at the beginning of the week, when I saw the state of the Oaks swim, and smiled. I was left in a state of wonder at the atmosphere of Redmire, the intriguing fishing and the beauty of her carp. I telephoned Chris to tell him that the Redmire magic is still strong.

The Quest for Fugglestone Red

I'm going to take you carp fishing. I've been wondering about whether or not to take you to my favourite pool because it's such a secret place, but it has had such a deep influence over my fishing that this book would seem hollow and unfinished without a visit there. I can't tell you where it is, of course, and I'm going to have to be careful on the journey, to make sure you can't find it later for yourself. I'm sorry about that.

If we leave our cottage and turn right towards the sunset, we can slip back through nearly three decades as we pass Gawbridge Mill at the end of our village. If we keep going back for a few more years and then turn left when we reach 1982, we'll find ourselves on the narrow, steeply banked lane that twists its way back for another thirty years, as it runs down the hill to the farm. The high banks on each side of us will be buzzing with bees and aflutter with butterflies visiting the foxgloves and cowslips, because it is high summer. It is always summer here and the neat hedges frame a ribbon of weak sapphire blue above us. The lane is the final tunnel back through Time and it brings us at last to a tumbled farmyard where cattle low gently in the barn and the air is rich with their warm, bovine breath.

We must stop at the farm or we might go too far and end up back in Celtic times because this is an ancient place. The meadows here are dotted with standing stones and cromlechs, arranged in a complex pattern to serve some ancient religious rite known only to our Celtic forefathers and lost now in the mists of time. Man has shaped this piece of landscape over thousands of years, yet today it is a wild and romantic place where nature holds sway. I'm certain that the ancient, natural power that drew our Celtic ancestors to this area has protected it and kept it safe.

As we climb out of the car there is no sign of the lake, but a hint of its presence hangs in the still summer air. Above the heavy, heady odours of the farmyard float the gentle, more subtle perfumes of watermint and wild cress, mingled with the rich smells of silt and still water and of carp. The smells lead us past the wooden farmhouse and onto a promontory cloaked with huge oaks and great beech trees. The ground falls away steeply and a hundred feet below us we can just make out the shimmer of summer sunshine on the water of the pool that nestles hidden in this natural bowl in the landscape. Our path leads through a rickety old gate and down the slope to the water. As we shut the gate behind us it creaks on rusted hinges and as we slip the catch into place we lock the real world outside and Time slows to a stop. We have passed through the looking glass and entered a different, better reality, here on the banks of this ancient pool. Time doesn't run away with you here but settles softly around the water like dew, so that we can savour every moment. As the gate shuts, the meaningless pressures of the modern world drift away, your heartbeat slows and Nature reaches out to touch your soul.

Prof brought me here. This is Prof's place, far more than it will ever be mine, but over the thirty years we have fished here together I have grown to know and love this carp lake more than any other. Pitt

came close but Pitt is now dead. Ashmead may steal my heart in time but if I had to make a difficult choice right now, I would rather spend my days here, fishing some deep and shadowy corner of this lake, although I would miss Ashmead enormously. This is a lake that has never been troubled by the pressures of the modern carp scene, a lake where quill floats and cane rods are still perfectly at home and where buzzers and bivvies would be completely out of place.

The first time I came here, we left Prof's house at dawn and followed a full moon over to the lake in the car. On the way, Prof fired my anticipation with tales of his past successes and failures, of monsters hooked and lost and of great carp basking amongst the snags.

We spent the morning exploring the pool together. There were no open pitches, in fact there wasn't even a proper path around the lake and we had to follow the badger tracks through the oak and beech woodland surrounding the pool. These tracks skirted the banks, sometimes clinging precariously to the oak roots twenty feet or more above the water and then leading away from the lake into the trees, before circling back and reappearing on a short length of fishable bank. The lake revealed itself in a series of snapshot images, sudden vistas that enticed us onwards to explore further. It took nearly two hours to complete our circuit, even though the lake was only five acres in extent. The day was cold and the sky had clouded over and we didn't see a sign of a carp.

We baited a couple of pitches and then retired to the nearest pub for a ploughman's lunch. When we got back to the pool the feeling of the day had changed completely. A strong westerly wind had broken the ceiling of clouds apart and allowed the sunlight to kiss the water. Down in the sheltered bowl of the lake the air was still and the wind just rattled the very top leaves of the surrounding trees. The water surface was like a mirror and it was warm here, where breaks in the canopy of leaves allowed the sun to touch the thick humus of the woodland floor.

We walked the same trails around the lake as we had that morning, only now with far more hope that we might see a fish. We reached the far end of the pool without seeing any signs but then, creeping around the corner of a dense rhododendron, Prof gasped and pointed. There, lying amongst the skeletal branches of a fallen oak lay about a dozen huge carp. They were all commons and I'm sure that not one of them could have been smaller than twenty pounds. The carp lay amongst the branches, clearly enjoying the feeling of the warm sun on their scales. Every now and then one would sink from sight and a short while later a frothing patch of bubbles appeared as the fish rooted through the silt below for food. At one point, the surface of the lake bulged upwards and a carp rose out through the surface as far as its pelvic fins before crashing back in a shower of golden scales.

Prof chose to fish a tight swim at the back of a nearby snag that looked like a great serpent; a thick oak branch that snaked through the water forming an arch above the surface and ending in a twist of timber that looked just like the head of a great snake. I fished a more open swim because I didn't think my tackle was strong enough to stop a carp of the size we had seen close to the snags. I felt less likely to get a take in the open pitch where I chose to fish but at least I stood a chance of landing a carp if I did hook one.

From my pitch I could see Prof crouching behind his two rods, watching the line where it entered the water for signs of a take. Suddenly, he reached forward and struck and I clearly saw the line cutting upwards through the surface film as he bent into the fish. The carp accelerated towards the snag and pulled Prof literally off his feet with the power of its run. Prof steadied himself and then clamped his centerpin tightly to stop the fish reaching the safety of the serpent. I saw his MKIV bend over and

lock way beyond its normal curve and for a moment the whole world was frozen in tableau, before the carp thumped the rod top over even further and with a crack like a rifle shot the line snapped. A big bow wave swept away through the snag and spread out towards the centre of the lake. Prof fell over backwards when the line went and he sat for a moment, looking stunned before he reached calmly for his tackle bag and started to look for a new hook.

I watched Prof hook five fish that evening and five times witnessed the same cracking, shattering end to the battle. The power of those carp was just impossible. It wasn't that the carp broke Prof off in the snags, they never got that far; no they broke him on a straight pull against fifteen pound line and a powerful carp rod. I'd never seen anything like it.

I didn't have a touch all afternoon but the drama in Prof's swim still made it the most exciting day's fishing I'd ever enjoyed. Just as the day came to an end, I spotted a shadow moving through a tangle of branches along the margin to my right and my carefully presented floater was taken quickly by a fish. This wasn't a leviathan like the carp that had overpowered Prof but a lightning-fast wildie that zipped this way and that through the water before I finally bundled it into the net. The wildie looked as old as the Celts themselves and it reflected the sepia tones of the setting sun as I held it.

The lake (I nearly gave its name away then!) is a strange place and has a unique and powerful atmosphere, like no other place I know. In Celtic times the area was a mine and Peter Wheat, who knows about Celtic mythology, is sure this means it would have been a place of human sacrifice. Apparently, the Celts believed there were three important gods; one that ruled the air, one that ruled everything that lived upon the earth and the third and most powerful that ruled everything below the earth's surface. Mining was like an act of violence against the earth god and to appease this deity the Celtic miners would dig a narrow vertical shaft, into which the hapless sacrifice was lowered head first on a rope lashed around their ankles. The victim would continue to dig downwards until the end of the rope was reached at which point it was released and the hole backfilled, burying the sacrifice in the arms of the earth god. I'm not sure where Wheaty gets this grisly detail from but I can believe that it is true and that this intense and gruesome history has left its mark upon the atmosphere of the pool.

There are times when the lake shuts you out with a physical force, like a cold and hard door slamming shut. The lake takes on a dark and lifeless appearance, the air is sucked out of the woodland and even the birds and animals are stilled. At these times the place has an almost evil, threatening atmosphere and it is best to leave it to brood in peace. At other times, though, it is a warm and welcoming place to be and the woods are alive with birdsong and the rustlings of the wood folk as they root through the leaf mould for their supper.

The carp sense the atmosphere just like all of the other wildlife around the water. The second time I remember fishing the water was on a day that felt unusually intense and menacing. There was no breeze, no birdsong, no rustling from the dense mat of leaves on the woodland floor, not even the buzz of an insect. The tension built until it was almost unbearable and I remember the hairs bristling on the back of my neck as a feeling of outright hostility seemed to emanate from the pool. Then, a zephyr of wind rustled the leaves of the tallest oaks. Suddenly, almost as if someone had thrown a switch, the insects started to hum and a blackbird began to burrow in the leaves behind me. The squawk of a jay from across the pool made me jump and I felt the tension that had built over several hours vanish in an instant, as the world let out the breath it had been holding and relaxed.

A bow wave started opposite my pitch and tracked more than a hundred yards across the surface, to the very spot where my bait lay. The wave flattened out and a huge froth of bubbles appeared, before the line began to peel from the reel. I struck and the carp turned deeply beneath the surface and thrust through an unseen snag. I was using a light MKIV Avon and my reel was only loaded with eight pound line and I was sure I would lose the fish, but miraculously it swam free and after a short fight I landed a good mirror. My line was so frayed and weakened that it parted like cotton as I scooped the carp into my net. It was a lovely deep mirror that had clearly been aware of my single

hookbait for some time but had only decided to come and take it when the hostile atmosphere had evaporated. I learned from the experience and stepped my tackle up in strength before my next visit. I also decided never to stay at the waterside again when the atmosphere of the lake turned hostile towards me.

I went back the next summer and Prof and I got the carp taking floaters just off the scum line at the windward end of the lake. We could see half a dozen big shadows hanging deep off the edge of the ripple, where a large bed of detritus had collected in the surface film. I fed some mixers in, well upwind of the carp, and then took my tackle around to the windward margin to await events.

A big swirl on the surface announced the arrival of the bait in front of me and the interest of the carp. Another swirl followed and then a third, followed by two more takes in quick succession in different parts of the scum. I could see the carp now, moving quickly and purposefully back and forth as they searched out the food. I waited until they were competing actively for the free bait and then cast a single mixer out into the scum on a simple freeline. I lost sight of the bait and my heart raced with each of the vortices that marked the spot where another biscuit had been taken. Finally, a swirl was followed by the line slicing through the scum as a big common took my bait. I wound down and struck hard, turning the carp's head as I did, so that its first run came straight towards me. I wound frantically to take up the slack line but the carp just accelerated when it felt the pressure from the rod and in a blind panic it swam straight into the bank at my feet with a mighty thump that stunned it.

I could see the carp clearly as it wallowed on the surface below me, a big, golden common of perhaps thirty pounds. Sure the fish was mine, I turned and reached for the landing net but just as I slipped the mesh under the stunned carp it shook itself, dived and sped off along the margin at an incredible speed and with unstoppable power. Ten, fifteen, twenty yards of line spun off the reel in the blink of an eye and then I felt a horrible grating sensation as the carp reached a fallen tree. The rod shuddered once and then the line parted and the carp, the biggest I'd ever hooked at that time, vanished forever into the depths of my dreams, where its loss still haunts me today.

That carp was the first of many big fish that I hooked and lost at the water over the following years. By now, a small group of Golden Scale Club friends had taken to fishing the water on the traditional opening week. We arrived on the 14th June each year and spent a couple of days settling in, before enjoying a meal on the evening of the 15th June and then starting the season off with a rocket and cast on the stroke of midnight. This year will be my 30th Opening Night at the lake and in all that time I've only ever missed one Glorious 16th there. This special group of friends are the best company I've ever enjoyed through fishing and my time with them beside this lake are the source of nearly all of my most precious fishing memories. The Glorious 16th is a time of laughter, of comradeship and of quiet enjoyment in equal measure, fired by the chance of a big carp at the most beautiful pool in the country.

I only fished the pool once or twice a year for a few days at a time, so it was very difficult to build up any picture of the movements and habits of its carp. Even so, over the course of ten years I learned enough to hook one or two of the elusive big carp each season. It was hard to get the big fish feeding and even harder to fish selectively for them because of the large number of smaller carp in the pool. A stalking approach worked to a degree but I could only get the big carp to pick a bait up close to the imposing snags and every time I hooked one the end result was the same snappy parting of the ways.

The first real breakthrough came when I realised that there were one or two areas that were further away from the snags where the big carp fed confidently. These were areas in which it was impossible to present a bait when fishing conventionally from the bank. The best place was up on the shallows, where the thick, glutinous silt and encroaching trees prevented an angler from getting close to the water. I tried to build a temporary pontoon out across the mire using branches and a pallet but even this was unable to bear my weight for long and soon sank. It was dangerous fishing and when I pushed a pole into the silt I couldn't find any solid ground, even though the pole was fourteen feet long. If I'd gone in, I wouldn't have come out again!

The answer was the Swamp Ring. The inflated inner tube from a tractor tyre with a length of stout rope tied across it gave me all the support I needed. Wearing chest waders, I could push my way out through the silt to the water's edge in relative safety and with a minimum of disturbance. On the very first launch of the Swamp Ring I managed to hook and lose a big mirror that I hooked right under the rod top, just off the edge of the ring itself. I also landed a double figure common, so the approach clearly had potential.

The next piece of the jigsaw came together in 1985, when I called in at a tackle shop on the way down to the pool and bought a gallon of maggots. The carp were wary of picking up a big bait and I'd decided to give a particle approach a go. Having watched the big fish feeding on the bloodworm beds on several occasions, I thought a bed of wriggling red and white grubs might just catch their attention.

The big carp I'd seen feeding in the silt showed a fascinating pattern of behaviour. They would dive along the bottom in a straight line with powerful thrusts of their tails, ploughing through the silt and kicking great clouds of it up into suspension. Then they would turn and pause before swimming slowly back along the same line, feeding as they went. I realised that the heavier, inert detritus would sink quickly back to the bed of the lake and that on their return route they were swimming through a cloud of suspended bloodworm and other food, which they sifted from the water column like a baleen whale filtering plankton.

Dawn on June 16th found me bobbing around in the Swamp Ring, with my float riding amongst the swamp snot in front of me above four or five pints of paprika flavoured maggots that I'd catapulted into the margins. The first carp appeared as shadows in the water and before long, great sheets of bubbles rose up and sparkled like diamonds in the dawn sunlight, as the fish ploughed into the silt after the breakfast I'd laid out for them. I slipped a small piece of cork onto the hook and used super glue to attach a handful of maggots to it, creating a writhing ball of food. I watched as a trail of mud marked the passage of a carp through the silt and then cast the float out gently into the disturbed cloud, so that the maggots popped up about a foot off the bed of the lake. I pictured the carp cruising slowly back through the silt, feeding as it went and suddenly the float just turned and dived from sight.

I struck and the margins exploded in a great vortex of water and mud that seemed to suck the rod tip downwards as a big carp surged away from me on the end of the singing line. Wallop! The carp's tail broke the surface and spray and silt flew everywhere. The carp turned back into the margins and then accelerated, diving under the goat willows and driving hard for deeper water and the safety of an oak tree that lay in the lake about fifty yards away. I plunged the rod under water to keep the line clear of the willow branches but I could still feel it grating horribly as five, ten, fifteen yards were stripped from the reel in as many seconds. The carp had its head down now and it was pulling unstoppably against the force of my rod. Thirty yards, forty, with the eighteen pound line singing at breaking point and the rod locked under full pressure. Then, unbelievably, I saw the bow wave accelerate into the oak and the branches of the snag shook before the line gave out and peace returned to the silt soaked scene.

One particular carp I used to see quite often was a big, ruddy mirror that I'd nicknamed "Big Red". How big? Well Demus saw it once at close range and described it as being "like a submarine." "When it turned end on," he said, "it looked like it had ballast tanks strapped to its sides!" I hooked this fish for the first time when I was fishing the shallows with maggots. I'd stepped up the strength of my tackle and was now using a Dennis Pye pike rod, made by Chapman's of Ware, which was strong enough to stop a charging bull.

The maggots had induced the usual frenzied feeding response from the carp and my swim in the shallows was a sea of bubbles. A patch of large bubbles appeared and a cast into their midst soon resulted in a firm bite and a hooked fish. The carp paused to gather its thoughts and then set off directly away from me, up the centre of the lake. I locked up hard to turn it but it had no effect and in the end I had to give line grudgingly, as the carp plodded determinedly towards the far end of the pool. The rod was doubled over, the eighteen pound line sounded tinny in the rings and my old Aerial ticked like a slow, ponderous metronome as it counted out the yards to the fish. The carp didn't deviate left or right from its path for over fifty yards, no matter how much side strain I applied. I felt like a spectator as it plodded past Bill, who was watching the battle from his swim some thirty yards to my left. I'd seen a deep orange glow when I hooked the carp, so I was sure I was attached to Big Red. We weren't attached for long, though, because after taking another twenty yards of line, the carp turned and kited into the bank beyond the same oak tree in which I'd lost the other monster and with the same final result.

We went to drown my sorrows in the pub at lunchtime and they were serving a beer called Fuggles, which nearly did the trick but couldn't quite fill the hollow feeling inside left by the loss of such a big fish. A few months later, Angelus and I were driving through the

outskirts of Salisbury on the way to a Golden Scale meeting when we came across a road junction called the Fugglestone Red roundabout. "Fugglestone Red!" we exclaimed in unison and so the name of the carp stuck. I've been chasing Fugglestone Red now for twenty six years and no other carp has ever dominated my dreams in the same way. I even have an extra strong stalking rod that was made with the pursuit of Fugglestone in mind and that has "Specially built for the Quest of Fugglestone" inscribed on the butt in Indian ink.

I'm not alone in my obsession with Fugglestone and all of the Glorious 16th anglers share it. Demus and Bill were fishing the far bank one day when Demus saw a huge red carp swim past through the margins under his feet. "Bill! Bill!" he shouted "I've just seen Fugglestone swim past!" "I know," came Bill's strained reply from the next swim, "he's on the end of my line!" At that moment there was an almighty CRACK! as Fuggles snapped Bill's line and notched up another smashed angler.

Prof hooked Fugglestone once as well and the fish completely smashed the new, extra-strong reinforced ferrule he'd just had made for his carp rod. On another occasion Prof had just cast and put his rod down to take a piece of cake from his creel, when he heard a splash and turned back to find that his rod had vanished completely. The rod was never seen again and to this day Prof swears that Fugglestone was the culprit.

One day I lost another huge carp that may have been Fugglestone, when I allowed a hooked fish to tow me out into the middle of the lake in the Swamp Ring. The idea had been to let the carp tow me beyond the big oak snag and then to paddle back in to the bank to play the fish from a more open position. The plan worked well until it came to the paddling part but then I found that the carp was a more powerful swimmer than I was. In the end I played the fish for over an hour as it towed me up and down the middle of the lake but then it got bored and swam into another snag and smashed me.

By now (after about ten years of trying) it had become clear that a direct pull from ground level against such powerful carp hooked close to the large snags was an ineffective recipe for disaster. There were snags everywhere and once a carp got its head down and built up steam, the sharp crack of the line against a drowned branch was the certain outcome. Not only were there several complete trees rotting away peacefully in the deep waters of the pool, the silt of the margins was littered with hundreds of lesser boughs. Many of these were embedded so firmly in the silt that the least twig was likely to provide a solid enough obstruction for a bolting fish to snap the line. I needed a completely new approach.

The answer came to me when I was perched aloft in the branches of an oak tree, overlooking one of the big snags. There were three large mirrors cruising through the snag and I had them taking floaters confidently. "I bet I could hook one from up here," I thought...

Although it seemed mad, the idea wouldn't leave me and before long I was back in the tree with a rod. Below me the three big mirrors had been joined by a large common carp and all four fish were now cruising confidently through the snag and slurping down every floating bait they came across. I was perched on an oak bough some fifteen feet above the calm surface of the lake and my bait lay in the surface film below, with the line rising vertically to my rod. Only three things were in focus; the bait, the carp and the adrenaline buzz in my veins.

Suddenly, a dark shape loomed up through the sapphire water like a thunderhead in a cloudless sky and the world drew in a deep breath and held it. Beneath me, the water seemed to unfurl like a flag as the carp turned away at the last moment, the sweep of its tail leaving my floating bait bobbing about on the surface in an oily swirl of disturbed water. I breathed out in a long, low whistle of frustration, although my heart still pounded with the tension and excitement of the encounter.

Three times now the carp had inspected the floater and three times rejected it. I was shaking and this was transmitted through the line to the bait, making the floater dance about on the water. Tightly spaced concentric rings emanated from the floater and spread out across the surface of the pool, telegraphing danger to any fish in the vicinity. "Breathe slowly. Relax," I whispered aloud to myself, as I tried for a third time to calm my frayed nerves. I passed the line over a twig to keep it still and a mirror calm returned to the water below.

The presentation of the bait looked perfect but the fact that the carp was so wary proved that all was not quite as it should be. From my perch I had a grandstand view of the carp below. The common looked to be well over twenty-five pounds and one of the others was a very deep mirror that looked enormous.

A small common carp that I hadn't seen previously appeared and made a beeline for the bait. It looked completely bemused as I lifted the hook gently from the surface and away from its opening mouth. It hung motionless below the surface for a second and I thought for a moment that it was going to launch itself from the water to grab the dangling bait, so I lifted it quickly out of the way.

The huge mirror drifted into view and I lowered the floater back into the water. Her dark form ghosted beneath the scum and passed on without interest. The big common followed in her path but, unlike the mirror, it stopped suddenly and tilted upwards. The rod bucked briefly as the carp took in the bait and then sprang straight as it flicked back through the surface before I could strike the hook home. My heart stopped and I cursed silently. Then suddenly, that shadow was back again and rather than spooking at its companions' dive for safety, the huge mirror had returned to see what the commotion was about. I lowered the bait quickly onto the water and, despite the way it shook from my trembling grasp on the rod, the mirror engulfed it immediately and this time my strike connected.

I knew I couldn't give an inch of line because of the proximity of the viscous snags, so I tucked the butt of the rod into my stomach and held fast. The line sang but the hook held and the powerful rod cushioned the lunges of the carp. Just as it seemed as if the line might reach breaking point, the cane beneath the corks gave just enough to avert disaster. From ground level and pulling directly against the carp I would have lost her in the snag for certain but with all the strain coming directly from above, the carp could not get her head down. The straining rod knocked the carp off balance, dragging it up to the surface and rolling it off course.

The fish thrashed the surface of the pool into foam but with her mouth hauled repeatedly above the surface she tired rapidly until finally she just gave up and lay on the surface below, bewildered and exhausted. I was able to work my way back along the branch, whistling and shouting for help. Darren appeared and grabbed the net and when he saw the size of the fish, he just waded into the margins and scooped the great mirror into the mesh at the first attempt.

The carp was carved like a Maori warrior. Deep black gouges along its body bore testament to a lifetime spent fighting amongst the snags. The fish's back was the colour of an over-ripe plum and its flanks

were a Mediterranean palate of blues and browns, merging into the ochre, orange and ivory of its belly. A sparse scattering of large scales gleamed on its back and shoulders like a gilded wreath, mirroring the yellow flag iris in front of which we photographed her.

I'd cracked it. During every opening week at the lake since that first success I have landed big carp from precarious swims in the branches of trees. My most extreme pitch is in a big old oak tree near the shallows, where I fish from a branch that is at least thirty feet above the lake. I've got this arboreal carping down to a fine art and I have found that I can land the fish quite safely without help, from each of my perches. I don't even have to jump in and get wet very often! Sometimes a carp will reach the snags and break free but it is a very rare occurrence and I land at least nine out of every ten carp that I hook, which is far better than I would ever achieve through a more conventional approach.

From on high, I can observe the fish and select the biggest from a basking shoal. Sometimes I'll spend seven or eight uncomfortable hours watching the fish and lifting my bait away from lesser carp before a chance to hook the one I'm after presents itself. When the hook is set, all hell breaks loose and the fights are short, explosive dramas that invariably leave me shaken and stunned. I've even had a Mitchell 300 explode under the pressure from a hooked common on one occasion, but I still managed to land the fish through a bit of frantic hand-lining and sheer dumb luck. It is the most exciting and intense fishing I've ever enjoyed.

The fishing is helped when the omens are good. One year, Prof had found BB's old hot water bottle at an auction in the village where he used to stay when he was on holiday. It is a lovely old stoneware pot with 'BB' inscribed on the stopper. Prof bought it for just a couple of pounds and he took it down to the lake for luck. That same year Demus arrived with a bottle of "Skeffington" port that he had found (Skeffington is my Golden Scale Club name). That was a particularly fine opening week and I landed an amazing old mirror from the Chestnut tree snag, which we photographed next to the lake with both of these lucky charms.

I have hooked Fugglestone from up in the trees, of course, but I still haven't landed him. The first time he just made it to the snags before I could turn him. Then, a few years later, I hooked him again and managed to bully him out into open water after rolling him right over, just short of the branches of a sunken Chestnut tree. As he sailed off into the middle of the lake and away from the snag I relaxed for just one fatal second to draw breath, at which point the hook just dropped out. Perhaps I will never land Fugglestone Red but the annual quest continues. I reckon I've got about ten more years left before I get too old and sensible to fish like a monkey. At that point the time will have come to hang up my special rod and acknowledge defeat by the finest carp I've ever met.

A New Swim

Today, I found an acorn that was lying partially buried in the wet clay of the path beside my favourite carp pool.

It seemed an unlikely place for an acorn to take root and even less likely that it could ever grow successfully into a mighty oak. The path is little trodden but the danger of a careless heel destroying the acorn or sapling, before it could mature into a tree capable of bearing my weight, seemed too great. Failure, it seemed, would be the inevitable outcome.

So I picked the acorn up and carried it to an area of the lakeside that is far away from any pathways and crushing feet. The bank of the pool here is devoid of large trees and in need of an overhanging branch, from which an angler aloft could watch the wary carp without risk of detection. Here, I dug a shallow scrape in the deep, damp humus and planted my acorn at just the right depth, in the natural womb of the woodland floor. Here, in a pool of warming sunlight, I planted a new swim.

When I'm two hundred and eighty seven years old, I will return and fish it.

During the last twelve months, since writing the opening chapters of this book, Pitt Pond's recent history as a carp water sadly ended. The pond still hides away in the same beautiful fold in the Somerset landscape but its carp are no more. These days, the stately monkey puzzle trees cast a perfect, undisturbed reflection in a pool devoid of fish.

Last summer the fishing suddenly became far more difficult than it would normally have been. The fish were hard to find and even on a hot day, when numbers of carp should have been basking beneath the lily pads, it was difficult to spot any fish. Those I did see appeared agitated, darting from one bed of pads to another; they looked disturbed, fractious and on edge. It was in September that I found some scales from what looked to be a good common on the bank near the inlet and realised that an otter had been hunting on the pool.

Over the next few weeks I found more and more patches of scales around the pool, each one a sad memorial to a lost carp. One morning I found the distinctive large lateral scales of one of the three twenty pound Leney linear mirrors Pitt held, lying on the dam wall. On another evening I found a set of individually large common scales that must have been from a very big fish indeed, perhaps the common Alan hooked and lost last year whilst tench fishing, which he estimated to be well over thirty pounds.

One by one the otter took the carp and there was nothing we could do to stop it. Pitt is impossible to defend with an otter-proof fence and so remote that nothing could be done to protect the carp. By the end of the winter the otter had taken them all.

Pitt held a special place at the heart of my early carp fishing and it was where my son, Iain caught his first big golden common when he was eight. I wrote about Iain's carp in a Carpworld magazine article some time ago...

"All of our children have caught carp and by some strange coincidence, the largest carp each of them had landed was a common of a weight that matched their age. Katrina's best was a Seven-pounder,

Alistair "Bear" had caught one of Four pounds and the previous year Iain had landed one of just over Eight pounds. They are all interested in going fishing but Iain is now old enough to have really caught the bug and I had promised to take him out fishing at Pitt Pond on his own this summer.

We parked in the field at the top of the steep little valley and took a moment to savour the best view in Somerset, before gambolling down the slope towards the pool. Iain was running ahead in his excitement, shouting advice on where we should fish and how we would have to be quiet and move slowly if we wanted to catch a carp. It was like I was looking through a magical mirror and I saw myself, at his age, lost in a world of adventures made real through the thrill of fishing.

It isn't until you reach the gate to the pond that you get even the slightest hint of its existence from the musty, damp smell of silt and watermint that lingers in the hollow where the pond lies. In fact, you can't see more than a glimpse of water until you pass through the gate and enter the timeless world that is Pitt. The gateway took me through the magical mirror and I suddenly realised I was as excited as Iain. I felt a childlike buzz of anticipation as I entered that secret and special place, with the prospect of a carp to charge the calm beauty of the pond with an electric tension.

Even Iain had stopped running and shouting and he crept forward along the bank, scanning the water with an angler's eye for signs of a fish. I planned to fish up at the dam, where there was plenty of space and few trees for a novice angler to tangle with but Iain had his own ideas. "I'm going to fish here," he announced in a whisper, pointing to a small swim, dangerously close to a large bed of lilies, "and I'm going to catch a double-figure carp."

I offered to set up his tackle and help to bait up and cast as usual but he insisted on doing everything himself, threading the six pound line through the rings and picking out his favourite float (he did let me tie on the hook!). Eventually, he lost patience with my attempts to help. "Look Dad," he said, "you go and fish somewhere else and I'll shout if I need you." Actually, I was secretly pleased with the permission to go and find my own fish to cast for and I was also really proud as I paused to take a shot of him, staring intently at the orange tip of his float. Just as I left, I saw a dark shadow move under the canopy of the pads and one of the leaves shuddered as something substantial moved past.

I hadn't even made it to the dam before I heard his yell. It was sharp and demanding and I thought immediately that he had fallen in or stumbled upon a wasp nest. I sprinted back, only to find him standing on the small landing stage, his float rod doubled over and struggling to hold his feet as something huge ploughed up and down on the end of his line. As I reached him the carp turned and shot up the narrow

channel between the lily bed and the bank, running five, ten, fifteen yards before Iain brought it to a stop. I offered encouragement and advice; on how to let the rod take the pressure; how to let the carp run; how to apply side strain; how to stay calm and not panic. "You're the one panicking Dad!" he said calmly, over his shoulder… I resisted the temptation to take the rod from him; this was his moment and it would end in a triumph or disaster of his own making that would live with him forever.

Somehow he managed to lead the carp back through the narrow gap and into open water and I saw a glow of gold as a good common thrust past us, deep down in the clear water. Slowly it tired and after two clumsy and botched attempts that had Iain shouting in frustration, his Dad finally managed to get the net under the carp and hoist it onto the bank.

I carried it up to the mat and showed Iain how to remove the hook gently. He was completely overwhelmed and I suddenly realised that he was nearly in tears. "I can't believe I've just caught a carp as big as that," he breathed, "I just can't believe it!" We weighed it carefully (Fourteen and a half pounds) and a friend, Paul, who had been fishing on the other side of the pond, came around and helped Iain hold the carp for a portrait. Then we carried it back to the waterside in the weigh-sling and Iain cradled it in the margins for ages, before finally letting it go.

I took a photograph of him, leaning on the end of the landing stage, his faced filled with mixed emotions of wonder, excitement and pure joy. In that moment, Iain became a carp angler and I believe he will always be one. We owe him and other children like him that privilege.

Pitt fired my own love of angling and my passion for nature conservation, and it would not stretch the point too far to say that all of the conservation work I have done personally during my lifetime owes a debt of gratitude to the fishery that caught a young boy's imagination. Now it is a fishery no longer and never again will a child fish there and be inspired by the dip of a float as a carp makes off with their bait. Although Pitt will always be a lovely little lake, it is diminished by the loss of its carp, rather like a gilded picture frame with its canvass removed.

I have mixed emotions that are difficult to put into words. As a lifelong conservationist, I love the fact that otter populations have made such a good recovery and that this iconic mammal is thriving in our countryside once more. Yet, at the same time, I'm heartbroken to have seen such a special fishery, where so many of my angling dreams were shaped and fulfilled, destroyed by the ravages of this most effective predator.

I've always lived by the belief that the interests of angling and the environment are intertwined inextricably, like strands of ivy growing on the same bough. The recovery of otter populations over the past few decades and the challenge the otter now presents to anglers and fishery managers threatens to pull those strands apart. I find it deeply depressing that anglers and conservationists are being drawn inexorably into conflict over the threat that otters pose to the future of many of our fisheries.

At the heart of the problem is the fact that angling and fisheries have changed dramatically in the years in which otters were virtually absent from our countryside. Fishing, as both a recreation and business, has increased tremendously and the number of lakes developed as carp fisheries in particular has grown beyond recognition. People's livelihoods and investment are tied up in fisheries as never before and the resurgent otter population is confronted with a very changed environment.

I believe that conservationists must recognise that anglers have been a major partner in their success, not just with the recovery of otters but also with water-based conservation more generally. Not only do anglers support conservation work directly through the licence fee, anglers and fishery managers have also done an enormous amount of practical work to bring our rivers back to life and to create and protect our stillwater habitats. The restoration of the otter population is only a job half done if the presence of otters cannot be managed in balance with the future interests of fisheries and the businesses that depend upon them. It is not enough for conservationists to simply pat themselves on the back and then dust their hands of the consequences of their work.

In the same way, anglers must work with the conservation experts to find the solutions that will allow them to manage and develop their fisheries peaceably in the presence of the otter, which is a wonderful part of our indigenous wildlife and much loved by the wider public.

As for me, I mourn the loss of Pitt and yet, at the same time, I celebrate the fact that otters are once again haunting the rivers around me. Somehow we must find the balance that would have allowed them to co-exist.

Ashmead Dreams

We only really have one rule that governs the fishing at Ashmead and that is that the members must respect the environment, the fish and their fellow anglers. This ethos underpins our management of the fishery and reflects the three elements that make Ashmead so special.

Ashmead's environment is almost unique and is certainly very unusual in this part of Somerset. Much of the land of the Somerset levels where the lake lies is made up of thick acidic peat. This peat is formed from plant material from the ancient marshes that has decayed slowly over the centuries under wet, acidic and anaerobic conditions. These conditions retarded the process of decay and estimates suggest that the peat accumulated at a rate of just one or two millimetres a year. When you realise that peat deposits on the Somerset Moors are typically between one and four metres thick and in places are as deep as eight metres, it shows the staggering timescales over which the landscape of the Levels has formed.

The peat deposits represent many thousands of years of accumulation and man has exploited this useful and valuable resource for centuries. The Romans certainly extracted peat from the Somerset Moors, but there is evidence that Neolithic people exploited the reedy swamps for their natural resources long before Roman times. These Neolithic inhabitants of the moors constructed wooden track ways to cross the marshes and the remains of the world's oldest known timber track way, called the Sweet Track, runs across the Levels near Shapwick and dates back to about 3800 years BC. One theory suggests that the county of Somerset's name is derived from the name Sumorsaete, meaning land of the summer people, because winter flooding restricted human use of the Levels to the summer months.

Fisheries on peat soils are normally acidic and unproductive environments, but whilst there is a thick layer of peat underlying the moor around Ashmead, the surface geology of the wetland is made up of thick clay, cut through with thick deposits of chalk. This local geology not only buffers the water in Ashmead from the acidic effect of the peat, it also provides the calcium essential for invertebrates to build their shells. Ashmead is rain fed and so its water is very pure, and the presence of this layer of chalky clay allows swan mussels, freshwater shrimps and snails to thrive. Combined with the shallow nature of the wetland and the abundant weed growth, the perfect conditions exist to produce the unique and incredibly productive ecology of the lake.

The carp have benefited from their rich environment and also from the relatively low number of fish present in the lake. All of the scientific research on carp growth shows that there are critical points when food availability influences the ultimate size of the fish. The genetic make-up of the Ashmead carp clearly gives them the potential to grow very large indeed and the rich environment into which the original stock were introduced as fingerlings in 1971, and in which subsequent generations have been spawned, hasn't limited their growth at any time.

I do believe that the stock had reached the maximum size that the three acres of Goat Willow could sustain but the restoration work that has opened up the wider seventeen acre wetland to the carp has effectively cut the stocking density to a quarter of that held in Goat Willow, and this has given the carp a new lease of life and growth. The philosophy of concentrating on managing the natural environment, so that it maintains a vibrant and rich ecosystem, seems to be paying off and the Ashmead carp are definitely benefiting from our empathetic management approach.

I believe the other great advantage of focusing our management on the natural ecology of the lake is that the rich and diverse ecology that Ashmead supports gives the water resilience against environmental stress, such as drought or prolonged icy winters. The natural balance in the lake, and the wide range of plants and invertebrates present, regulate and maintain a healthy environment for the fish, even when conditions are far from ideal.

I've just read James Lovelock's fascinating book "Homage to Gaia" about his remarkable life and his development of the Gaia Theory, which sets out a similar hypothesis on a planetary scale. In a nutshell, Gaia Theory proposes that all living things on Earth interact with their surroundings to form a self-regulating system that maintains the right conditions for life on the planet to survive. Gaia suggests that you could almost think of the planet as a single, living organism. Lovelock's work led directly to the founding of the Green Movement and changed the way we now think about the earth and issues such as global warming, that show how man's influence can have a profound effect on the health of the planet.

I wouldn't expect for one moment that my empathetic approach to the development of the Ashmead fishery, by working with the grain of nature rather than trying to cut across it, will spawn a global movement. I do, however, hope to demonstrate that the approach can produce a fantastic fishery that benefits the environment in which we have developed it, rather than damaging the ecology like many modern intensive carp fisheries. If I can demonstrate that the approach can succeed and get other fishery owners and anglers to think more broadly about the ecology of their waters, and persuade some to adopt a more natural, self-sustaining form of management, then I will be happy.

So what of the carp themselves? Well, carp angling is fascinating because the long life expectancy of our quarry, and the fact that individual carp are easily recognised means that, unlike most other branches of angling, carp fishing has become focused on the pursuit of individual fish. It is commonplace now to give fish names and to follow their capture and growth in the same way that you might follow the career of a prize-fighter or athlete. Thousands of anglers know these "personalities" of the carp world and each carp has developed a character of its own. There are even anglers who study the behaviour of individual large fish and target them as if they are collecting a set of stamps, moving from lake to lake as each trophy fish falls to their rods.

I've never been someone who chases "target" fish; I'm much more interested in the environment and atmosphere of the lakes I fish than the size of the carp they hold. I like to develop a long-term relationship with a water, rather than just chalk up another monster and move on. Running around chasing targets is a young man's game and takes up far more time and effort than I have available to devote to my own angling. I was about to say my fishing is limited to one or two overnight sessions each month but that puts too negative a slant on things. Fishing for me is simply balanced with other passions, including my family, my work with the National Trust, looking after our small holding and managing Ashmead.

I'm more interested in forging a lasting connection with the waters I fish through the seasons and over the years. For me, it's rather like the contrast between a happy marriage and a series of one night stands; running from one encounter to the next might be very exciting for a while but ultimately such shallow, passing acquaintances are far less satisfying than a long-term relationship with the love of your life. That isn't to say that I'm not impressed by the skill and dedication of anglers such as Terry Hearn who have the drive and ability to chase the individual carp of their dreams. I'm in awe of the determination of such anglers, but I don't envy them or dream of emulating their feats. I find a different and more satisfying pleasure in my own fishing and especially in the management of Ashmead and my conservation work.

Having said that, of course I look on each of the Ashmead carp as an old and much loved friend. Ashmead stayed off the carp angling radar for many years and even now, relatively few anglers know much about the lake and its fish. At a push, some anglers would recognise Single Scale, the largest carp in the lake. One or two might also recognise Moonscale, our second biggest mirror but beyond that, the individual Ashmead carp could swim into most tackle shops and remain incognito without much effort.

Steve Maynard took Single Scale from the wider Ashmead wetland and stocked her into the newly created Goat Willow Pool in 1995, when she weighed ten pounds. At that time there wasn't anything remarkable about the carp at all and certainly nothing that would make an angler think that within twenty years she would have grown on to become one of the largest carp in the country. In fact, when Steve put her into Goat Willow, she wasn't even the biggest carp in the pool.

I suspect that she was amongst the youngest carp in the original Goat Willow stocking, though, and it was this that helped her realise her potential. If you draw a graph of Single Scale's weight at each known capture over the years and extrapolate the growth curve back to the year of her birth, I believe that she is no more than twenty years old. If I'm correct in my calculations, Single Scale was spawned in Ashmead in about the 1988 or 1989 and was not one of the original fingerlings. Steve transferred her into Goat Willow Pool as a young carp when she was at the peak of her growth curve. It was like setting a teenager free in the Harrods Food Hall and she soon outstripped the other, larger and older carp in size to become the queen of the lake.

By the time I formally joined the Ashmead Syndicate under Steve's ownership, Single Scale had established herself as the biggest of Goat Willow's mirror carp. She wasn't always the biggest carp caught from the lake though and I caught the lake record in 2002 with a fantastic Thirty Three and a half Pound common carp. I'll come back to this particular carp in a moment, as it is one of the current mysteries of Ashmead.

At the time that I fished the syndicate under Steve's ownership, Single Scale was pretty elusive. Although she was restricted to the three acre confines of Goat Willow along with the rest of the stock, she was only caught once or twice a season and sometimes went for up to two years without being landed. In 1999 she topped twenty pounds for the first time and a good friend of mine, John Marshall, caught her at just over Twenty Six pounds in the November of the millennium. In 2002 she passed the thirty pound barrier for the first time, when she set a new lake record of Thirty Two pound Four ounces.

Like all of the Ashmead carp, Single Scale has followed a predictable growth pattern with surges in size, during which she has grown by up to six pounds in a single season, interspersed with one or two years in which she hasn't grown at all. By April 2004 Single Scale had grown to over thirty seven pounds and then just four months later, in August of that same year, my friend Martin Head landed her at Forty One pound Six ounces. The wonderful thing was that even at over forty pounds, Single Scale didn't look in the least bit fat and in the misty dawn photo I have of Heady holding her she looks dark, vibrant and perfectly proportioned.

The first time I saw Single Scale was when I landed her at just over fifty pounds in 2006, as recounted elsewhere in this book. I had never imagined in my wildest dreams that I would catch such a huge carp one day, and it took me quite a few years to readjust the balance in my carp fishing afterwards. Throughout my life, there had always been a new horizon in terms of the size of carp I aspired to catch. Whether it was a double, an almost unbelievable twenty, an unimaginable thirty or even a forty pound fish, there had always been an inspiring goal to chase. I was never bothered if I caught the carp of my dreams or not and I have always been thrilled to land any fish, irrespective of its size, but I had always had that new horizon ahead of me. After catching Single Scale, I knew that I would never again have the same challenge in my carp fishing. Then we bought Ashmead and the much more satisfying goal of creating one of the best carp fisheries in the country, and of caring for this wonderful Somerset wetland and the vibrant wildlife it supports, has replaced those rather meaningless goals of catching a carp of a particular weight. My pleasure these days comes from seeing others enjoy and appreciate what we have created at Ashmead, far more than from my own fishing.

There are new fishing goals, though, and one of these is to catch Single Scale again because she has continued to grow to a truly astonishing size. When we carried out the restoration work at Ashmead, the removal of the silt from the wider wetland left just bare clay on the bed of the restored area. When we reconnected this area to Goat Willow we effectively quadrupled the area in which the carp could roam and initially most of the larger lake had a bed of unproductive clay. Whilst I knew the carp would benefit from the restoration in time, I fully expected them to lose weight in the first year or so because

the amount of natural food in the wider lake would be minimal and the carp would have to hunt harder to find it. As it transpired, the carp held their previous weights for the first year, rather than losing weight and one or two even gained a pound or two. Single Scale was amongst the carp that continued to grow.

In the year following the restoration I noticed that the carp were far easier to catch than they had been when they had just been confined to Goat Willow Pool. I think this was partly due to the lack of natural food available in the restored areas (giving the carp little choice other than to feed on angler's bait) and partly because the carp were disorientated in the unfamiliar surroundings of the wider wetland and had yet to learn the areas in which they needed to be wary of anglers.

Ian Chilcott was a member of Ashmead at the time and that winter he was just about the only member fishing the lake. Chilly soon worked out where the carp had settled for their winter rest and he landed a couple of lovely fish, including the fully scaled mirror called Patch at just over twenty nine pounds before he discovered where Single Scale was hiding. At nearly midnight one night I received a text just as I was going to bed that read "53.12! I don't know what to say…"

"I take it you're off to the lake?" Shona asked and of course I was, having called Alan and arranged to meet him down there. I found Chilly fishing on Wilson's Island and after shaking his hand and congratulating him, we sat and chatted about the amazing carp he had just landed and the future of Ashmead. Alan joined us and it was great to share a very special moment with the person who has done more than anyone to support our development and management of the fishery. The capture of Single

Scale at a new lake record weight seemed to confirm finally that the restoration of Ashmead had been a success. We sat drinking tea and talked about carp and carp fishing, about Ashmead and Single Scale and in between our conversation we shared a companionable silence, until one of us would suddenly exclaim "Fifty three twelve!" and set us off talking and laughing again.

After careful consideration we decided to sack the carp and I returned at dawn with my camera to take some photographs of Chilly with his biggest ever carp. I think that I was even more excited and pleased than Chilly, though, because Single Scale just glowed in the dawn light and looked magnificent, setting a golden seal on Ashmead's future.

Single Scale was caught six times that year, which was unheard of compared to previous seasons when she normally slipped up just once or at most twice in a season. Several other carp also visited the bank more often than was normal, but by the following year the environment of the restored areas had become as rich with natural food as Goat Willow had been and the carp became as elusive as ever. In fact, they are far harder to catch now than they ever were because they have four times as much water in which to hide and graze on the abundant natural food supply.

As I expected, the Ashmead carp have benefited from the reduced stocking density, increased space and the bountiful food availability in the restored lake. Single Scale set a new lake record when Larrie Clarke landed her in April 2010 at an astonishing weight of Fifty Four pound Twelve ounces and when Spike Slater landed her the following season at Fifty Five pounds. Single Scale seems to have fallen back into her old habits and she appears to be vulnerable to anglers bait only in the early spring, when she awakens from her winter torpor and prepares herself for spawning, and in the autumn, when the natural food supply starts to diminish but she still needs to eat in preparation for winter. During the summer months she seems to switch off bait altogether and to feast on natural food. I saw her regularly last year in the swim called The Throne, basking in the weed and hoovering up the clouds of rudd fry that swam past her cavernous mouth, unaware that they risked becoming a cyprinid bouillabaisse.

Single Scale's latest capture fell to Keith Jones last October. Keith had enjoyed forty nights fishing on Ashmead without a carp and inevitably the lack of success was beginning to undermine his confidence. Keith is an excellent angler; quiet, patient, technically skilled and (fortunately!) very resilient. He found signs of carp in Tom's Pond and set up as unobtrusively as he could. The take came at about midnight, on a bait fished in the margins under his rod top. Single Scale normally fights incredibly hard and it is common for an angler to play her for half an hour or more before she can be landed. On this occasion, though, she just made one or two runs through the weed and then plodded around beneath Keith's rod tip for a few minutes before rolling over his net cord. That wasn't the end of the excitement, though, because the sheer weight of the carp pulled Keith's landing net head off the pole and he had to drop everything and run for his second net before he could land her. Fortunately he managed to scoop up Single Scale and the head of his first net successfully and bring his forty-night blank to an end.

As always, everyone at the fishery that night gathered to see Single Scale on the bank and they weighed her at Fifty Six pound Fifteen ounces. I find it remarkable that this carp is likely to top sixty pounds if she is landed this spring, and looks set to grow on still further. Coming from a carp angling backwater like Somerset, where large carp are very rare, and having started my carp fishing at a time when a twenty pound carp was regarded as an enormous fish, it seems unbelievable that a carp as big as Single Scale is living in our lake. I'm very proud that her growth is a natural reflection of the quality of her environment and our management of Ashmead and the fish it supports.

Many of the character fish that swim in Ashmead have a tale to tell but perhaps none is more remarkable than that of Moonscale, the second largest mirror carp in the water. Moonscale was stocked into Goat Willow Pool in 1995, as part of the original stocking of carp from the wider Ashmead wetland. She grew well and when I first caught her in 2002 at a weight of Thirty One pound Ten ounces, she was the biggest carp I'd landed at that time.

Unlike most of the Ashmead carp, which are in pristine condition, Moonscale showed evidence of some well-healed mouth damage that I thought had probably been caused by a careless angler when she was young. Last year, however, Jon Marshall sent me a set of photographs of his Ashmead carp for my records and these included two shots of Moonscale that told a very different story. The first photograph shows Jon holding Moonscale at a weight of Twenty pound Fourteen ounces in 1999 and she shows clear signs of an otter attack. Her tail is shredded and her mouth damaged in a way that is characteristic of an attack by an otter, which will pull a carp from the water by its mouth as this provides the most secure hold. The second photograph shows Moonscale later that same year, when she had clearly recovered from her ordeal and the otter damage had almost completely healed. When you know what to look for, the marks of that otter damage are still evident on Moonscale today and the two photographs tell the tale of the remarkable escape of one of the largest carp in Somerset.

Moonscale is another Ashmead carp that is thriving. Stuart Flamsteed was the last angler to land her at Forty Eight pound Eight ounces and she looks likely to top the magical fifty pound barrier this year. Moonscale likes her bait and because she tends to get caught three or four times a season she has put a huge smile on the faces of quite a few Ashmead members over the years. I hope she continues to do so for many years to come.

The Ashmead stock has much more to offer than these two colossal mirrors. The Grey Mirror and a near leather know as Opal are both growing steadily towards forty pounds and there may be as many as five forty pound commons swimming in Ashmead's labyrinthine channels. The largest common in the lake has always been a carp known as JC but this year another spectacular fish named The Long Common took JC's crown when she was landed at Thirty Nine pound Fifteen ounces in June. JC had been caught by long-standing Ashmead member Jody Trayte at Thirty Nine pound Eight ounces in February

and looked likely to be the first forty pound common from the fishery, but now the race is on, as neither carp has been caught since. There are other carp that may steal that honour as well, with a beautifully proportioned carp called Heart Tail falling to Roy Williams at Thirty Eight pound Eight ounces this winter and another common called Psst also topping thirty eight pounds. All of these commons are young and growing carp, so it is an exciting time to be fishing the lake.

As well as all these known fish, there are other carp that are far more elusive and mysterious. From a fishery owner's perspective, and as a compulsive angler, I find these carp even more interesting and exciting than the "names". Just when I think I know every large carp swimming Ashmead's waters someone catches a fish that I've never seen before. A great example of this is a mirror called "Who?" for obvious reasons, which Simon Fisher landed in 2008 at Twenty Six pound. I don't think this lovely mirror carp, with a pattern of tiny gold dust scales, had ever been landed before and it hasn't been seen again since.

Other carp also seem to be far more elusive than their companions. There is a mirror called Curly Tail that has only been landed three times to the best of my knowledge and I believe I'm the only angler to have landed her. Each time I caught her on a floating bait during the first spell of hot weather of the year in the same area of Goat Willow Pool. The first time I caught this distinctive and beautifully scaled carp was in 2007 and at the time the carp weighed Twenty pound Ten ounces. I caught it again in 2010 when it weighed exactly Twenty Five pound and then a third time in the spring of 2011 at a weight of Twenty Seven pound Eight ounces.

It's a remarkable succession of coincidences. Of course it may just be coincidence but I'm convinced that she is only vulnerable in the spring when she moves into the weed in Goat Willow to feast on the newly hatched rudd fry. Where she goes for the rest of the season is a mystery but I can only assume that she has so much natural food available that she has no incentive to pick up a bait. In any case, I'll be back again with a floater this spring, to try and catch her again because she may weigh over thirty pounds.

Not all of the more elusive Ashmead carp are growing. There is one exception that proves the rule and that is a truly beautiful zip linear we called The Woodcarving, in homage to the stunning Horton carp of the same name. As far as I'm aware The Woodcarving has only ever been landed twice. I caught it at exactly Ten pounds in 2007 and the carp then evaded capture for four years until Martin Turpin landed it in June 2011 at exactly the same weight. Where it has been hiding and what it has been feeding on in all that time is a complete mystery.

The biggest mystery in Ashmead (quite literally) is a big common we call Enigma. It seems that every carp water contains a huge common carp that is seen by the anglers, discussed in hushed and excited tones but never caught, and Ashmead is no exception. When Chilly was fishing the lake he spent an

afternoon watching a group of carp that included Single Scale, Moonscale and a common that he swears was as big as Moonscale. I saw an enormous common myself two years ago when Stuart and I watched Heart Tail cruising in Tom's Pond with another deep, golden common that was far larger. We knew that Heart Tail weighed over thirty seven pounds at that time and we judged his companion to be mid-forties by comparison. Certainly the Ashmead commons are harder to catch than most of the mirrors and there are commons such as Barbs (a mid-thirty that wasn't caught for over three years) and Petals (last caught at Thirty Six pound two years ago) that avoid capture for years at a time.

Last year, Larrie asked me what had happened to the big common I mentioned earlier in this chapter that I'd caught at Thirty Three pound Eight ounces in September 2002. I thought the carp was Heart Tail but Larrie was adamant that it was a different fish, and close inspection of the photographs confirmed that he was right. At the time I caught it, this common was the biggest common ever caught from Ashmead and I'm not aware that anyone has caught this carp since. I don't believe a carp of that size could die in Ashmead without being found so perhaps this carp, now called Enigma, is the mystery giant? I hope to find out one day.

So what does the future hold? Well if we can continue to keep the Ashmead carp safe from disease and the ever present threat of otters, the future looks full of potential. There are many wonderful looking carp growing in the lake that will eventually take over from the current Ashmead royalty as they age and die. I love the heavily scaled mirrors that are creeping ever closer to thirty pounds and some of the young commons of a similar weight are also stunning. The future rests with carp like the linear mirror that put on eight pounds in the year after the restoration work. I expect this fish to show another surge in growth at some point over the next few seasons and I'm certain that one day it will be very big indeed. This linear is one of the best looking carp in Ashmead and it is typical of the young fish that will fire the dreams of the next generation of anglers in the same way that our dreams are filled with images of the matriarchs cruising through the weedbeds of Ashmead today.

Ebb Tide

Forty years! I don't know why it has only just struck me that I have been fishing for forty years this year. In those forty years an awful lot of water has flowed under Creedy Bridge on the River Parrett, where I first cast a line with a fishing rod. Angling has been one of the most important influences on my life and my love of fishing has flowed through those years like a gently meandering river, shaping the landscape within which I have lived.

Anglers have always been obsessed with milestones, targets and records. There is something in human nature that compels us to try and rein in the unfathomable complexity of nature and angling by constraining our pastime with artificial goals. Anglers have always measured success through catching the largest weight in a fishing match; landing a twenty, thirty or forty pound carp or pike; taking a limit bag of trout; or (for the less imaginative anglers) being able to cast further than anyone else. The truth of course is that success in fishing cannot be gauged by such simple statistics.

It strikes me that forty years spent as an angler is a significant milestone but it is really as meaningless as any other measure and I hope that I have another forty years of fishing and conservation ahead of me. Of course, as an angler, I'm not immune to the compulsion to have targets and even after all this time, I still have a number of fishing milestones of my own that I would love to meet.

I've never done much fishing overseas but right at the top of my list of angling ambitions is to catch one of the huge sea trout of Tierra del Fuego and the Falkland Islands. In this country a double figure sea trout is regarded as a monster and I do harbour an ambition to land a ten pounder from the Towy (I used to work with a fisheries bailiff who landed a brace of fifteen pounders in an evening). In Patagonia, such fish would hardly merit a note in the fishing log however, and a thirty pound, fresh-run silver sea trout is a possibility and twenty pounders are caught frequently. My interest in these fish is deeper than just their size and the beautiful landscape within which they are pursued; Donald Leney exported eyed brown trout eggs to the Falkland Islands from the Surrey Trout Farm and it is likely that these southern sea trout populations owe their origins to his vision. A double figure Leney sea trout: imagine that!

I'd also love to catch a big Nile perch. My parents use to live in Mwanza on the southern shore of Lake Victoria and in their garden was the stone that marked the spot where John Hanning Speke declared the lake to be the source of the River Nile. Apparently, whilst on that 1854 expedition, Speke became temporarily deaf after a beetle crawled into his ear and he tried to remove it with a knife, and he also went temporarily blind, so it's remarkable that he made it to my parent's garden at all, let alone recognised Victoria as the source of the Nile when he got there! I've only seen some old black and white Super 8 cine film of my parents' time in Africa and it would be fantastic to visit the spot to see where they lived. To catch a huge Nile Perch from the lake would be wonderful...

I'd also love to catch a Golden Mahseer, a Blue Marlin and a one pound dace, and if I last another forty years I hope to achieve all of these fishing dreams.

I joked with one of the Ashmead regulars that I'd like to close this book on a high note by catching Ashmead's first forty pound common carp. As an angler inspired by Richard Walker, the capture of a forty pound common is a target that resonates with me. Of all the meaningless fishing goals I have, I'd like to land a forty pound common the most. In fact, more than that, I'd like to land a Walker-weight common of forty four pounds, to equal the size of Walker's Redmire record common carp Clarissa. To catch such a carp from Ashmead would not only fulfil an angling dream but it would somehow complete the story of Ashmead's restoration and be nature's final endorsement of our management of the fishery.

Once it had dawned on me that I've been fishing for forty years this year, I began to see a pattern and inevitability revolving around the number forty. Like one of our ancestors reading the runes, I started to believe that the synergy of catching my first forty pound common in my fortieth year as an angler was a fate foretold by the gods... In my mind I had already written the final chapter of this book, certain that it would recount the epic tale of the hooking and landing of my Walker-weight common and close with a turn of the final page to reveal a stunning photograph of the carp itself.

Fuelled with the certainty of the omens, I began to search Ashmead for signs of fish as the first snowdrops heralded the arrival of spring. A number of the members had seen large carp in Tom's Pond and then a month ago Micky Gray called me down to the lake to look at a pod of huge fish he had found basking beneath the trailing fronds of the weeping willows, in the first warm sunshine of the year. Micky was certain that one of these carp was Single Scale, the matriarch of Ashmead, but by the time I'd arrived with my camera she had disappeared. Of the five carp that remained however, one was a huge common that dwarfed the other four. It was Heart Tail; one of five commons that I am sure will weigh well over forty pounds when they are next brought to the net.

I saw Heart Tail again in Tom's Pond the following week and when I finally went down to the lake to fish a fortnight ago I found him cruising through one of the small bays with another common that looked to be well over twenty pounds. Heart Tail was following a clearly defined course through the bay, entering by a narrow gap between the small island and the bank and then circling the bay before leaving along the far, reed-lined margin and cruising off along one of the narrow channels. It took half an hour for him to complete each circuit and I sat in the branches of a goat willow tree and watched as he followed the same route again and again, dipping down every now and then to feed.

Just before dark I crept around to the reedy margin with two rods and the minimum of gear; no shelter or other clutter, just the rods, a bedchair and a small bag of bait. I lowered one hookbait into the narrow gap by which the common had been entering the bay and the second under the rod tip on the carp's exit route. I scattered a few baits around each spot and then settled back to wait. The atmosphere was electric and I was buzzing with adrenaline and anticipation. I had found the carp I wanted, I knew where it had been feeding and the converging omens were so strong that success seemed inevitable.

At two in the morning I had a run on the rod placed in the narrow gap and I pulled into a heavy fish that ran powerfully and ponderously away from me into the bay beyond the island, where it buried itself in the dense weed. I held the carp on a tight line for maybe ten minutes, sometimes gaining a yard or two before the fish surged deeper into the weedbeds, taking back the line I'd recovered. Eventually I realised that I had no choice but to run and get the boat, which I knew was right at the far end of the fishery. I put the rod in the rests, set the clutch so that it would just give line if the carp kicked itself free of the

weed and ran along the long bank to the boat in the dark, stumbling like a blind man and falling over several times on the way.

By the time I'd paddled the boat back to the swim another twenty minutes had passed and it was a relief when I retrieved the rod to find that the carp hadn't moved and was still hooked firmly. I pulled myself towards the carp, using the rod and reel to tow myself out into the darkness in the boat. As I got above the fish I felt it lift from the lakebed and it surged away, towing me around the bay and then off up the narrow channel until I managed to turn it and it plodded back towards the spot where I had first made contact. I climbed out of the boat and continued to play the carp from the bank, as it bored around beneath the rod top, creating a succession of dramatic vortices on the moonlit surface of the water as it twisted and turned in the margin.

Eventually, I felt the carp's strength begin to ebb and for the first time I found I could exert some control over the fish. The fish was fighting near the surface now and I readied the landing net as the carp struggled for freedom beneath the rod top. I flicked on my head torch as I drew the carp over the net for the first time and saw a huge, pale shape in the torchlight before it thrust away from the mesh at the last moment and sounded to the lakebed once more. The carp circled once and then I brought it

back to the net for a second time. It was exhausted now and as I drew it over the net cord and began to lift I could see the enormous frame of a common carp, its scales smeared in clay, filling the landing net frame; I was sure it was Heart Tail. Just as I began to lift, the carp kicked again and I let it go, confident that it was beaten now and not wanting to risk a mistake at the net.

"One last run and I'll net you next time" I thought, as the carp swam weakly away from me. I readied the net again before stopping and turning the carp with ease and guiding it slowly and surely back towards the waiting mesh. Again the vision of the last chapter of this book sprang into my mind and I knew with complete certainty that the capture of this magnificent carp had been pre-ordained. In my imagination I turned the last page to look at the photograph of me cradling Ashmead's first forty pound common…

Then suddenly the rod sprang straight and the carp was gone.

It couldn't be! Yet although I reeled in frantically in sheer disbelief, thinking that the carp must have suddenly swum towards me, the line remained lifeless and limp. After forty five minutes and despite being drawn over my net twice, Ashmead's first forty pound common had slipped the hook at the moment of victory and defied all of the omens. A pit of despair opened and swallowed me whole.

One of the most compelling things about fishing is that it is so wonderfully unpredictable. The perfect ending to this book may have slipped the hook at the last moment but long after I've recovered from the loss, the tantalising image of that carp will continue to swim through my dreams and it will draw me back again and again to the banks of Ashmead, in the hope that next time the hook will hold firm.

Of course, if ever my dream is fulfilled and a carp to match the image of that lost monster does eventually grace my landing net, the feeling of elation will be incredible. Yet even if I never land my forty pound common, I will still rejoice in the wildlife I will meet in pursuit of that goal and the experience will enrich my soul. The truth is that going fishing is not really about catching fish at all; it is about chasing dreams and discovering that we are still part of the natural world into which this simple pastime leads us.

The management of Ashmead is also about so much more than the size of the carp that swim through its waters. Owning and managing Ashmead is about caring for one of the diminishing wild places in this busy country of ours and protecting a natural haven where not only our children, but those of future generations will be able to chase their dreams and enrich their own lives by touching nature through the simple expedience of casting a fishing rod.

This morning, at 5 am on the 14th April 2012, Shaun Barrell landed the Heart Tail common from Ashmead at an astonishing weight of Forty Four pounds Four ounces. Shaun is a gifted angler and a great friend who has a depth of integrity that is rare these days, coupled to a soft and slightly anarchic sense of humour. He is also Somerset born and very proud of the fact, so it is highly appropriate that Somerset's largest common should fall to his rods.

Ashmead's first forty pound common was a perfect, dark and beautiful Walker-weight fish that epitomised the quality of this remarkable fishery and the potential the future holds for those of us privileged to enjoy our time there.

What meant more to me than anything was the way that the capture confirmed my belief that empathetic environmental management can still deliver a fishery capable of meeting the dreams of any angler. Heart Tail is living proof that the futures of nature conservation and angling can still be entwined as they always were, and that if we only have the patience to develop our fisheries with this in mind, angling can still deliver something for all of us that is so much more important than the weight of any fish.

A new chapter at Ashmead has begun, just as this chapter and this book must draw to an end.

A Carp Pool

If ever there were time and place
To rest a while and contemplate,
The path I've known and if it leads to peace within some higher Grace,
Beside this pool, its hallowed calm reflecting greater pasts than mine
Unfettered thought cannot foresee the future, mortal or divine
But may yet come to understand the beauty mirrored in her face,
Let Nature take you by the hand
Now is the time, this is the place…

To fish here is an act of faith
Nature held with hook and line
It is not merely fish I seek but some far more elusive wraith
Is there some truth that I may find beyond the shallow cares of man?
Am I, and all around me, now small part of some far greater plan?
A burnished bar of living gold is all that I may hope to catch
Yet in that beauty to behold
Such art no work of man may match.

To sculptured beeches carved by Time
With elemental artists hand
My presence here is little more than shadow of a fleeting rhyme
Cathedral spans draw life from light; it is through them I draw my breath
Yet do they mark this life of mine? They would not weep to mourn my death
When Time cuts down the sweeping bough, will any then remember me?
My soul will rest beside this pool
At peace, by this immortal tree.